the Unofficial Guide™ to Acing the Interview

Michelle Tullier

Macmillan • USA

Macmillan General Reference
A Simon & Schuster Macmillan Company
1633 Broadway
New York, New York 10019-6785

ISBN: 0-02-862924-8

Manufactured in the United States of America

10 9 8 7 6 5 4 3 2 1

First edition

*To Alexandra, for sharing the first six months
of your life with this "other" baby.*

Acknowledgments

The things I've learned about interviewing during my years as a career counselor enabled me to write a decent book on the subject. The input of clients, colleagues, and new Internet friends as I developed the manuscript made this a better-than-decent book. And, the support I received from family and friends made this a book I was able to finish. I give heartfelt thanks to: Tim Haft, for his resourceful, creative, and reliable research assistance, and for his friendship that is also all those things; Clara Bouillon, for keeping the Little One happy and healthy, for humoring me as I gave her the daily chapter progress report, for research assistance during the naps, and for packing boxes when that sure wasn't part of the job description; my parents—Ronald and Patricia Gann, and Scott Tullier—for helping me move house and home throughout all this; Marci Taub, for her amazing ability to conceptualize the innards of a book she wasn't even writing and for getting me unstuck in Chapters 2 and 4 (and for caring enough to do so); Lubna Touban for being baby-sitter extraordinaire and single-handedly enabling me to complete this book.

Nancy Gratton, for skillfully and thoughtfully doing the hardest job an editor has—keeping the author motivated; Amy Zavatto, for her long-standing support and for bringing me into the fold; Jennifer Farthing, for getting me off on the right track at Macmillan; and Jennifer Perillo, for chasing down that person with the abacus and quill pen—and for keeping her promises.

The kind folks on the HRNet newsgroup for sharing the inside scoop and offering many valuable, quotable comments, and my friends and colleagues whose names appear throughout this book next to their quotes for sharing their time and insight.

And, as always, and most importantly, special gratitude to Michael for sharing one more summer with A-Book-I've-Gotta-Write.

Contents

The *Unofficial Guide* Reader's Bill of Rights

We Give You More Than the Official Line

Welcome to the *Unofficial Guide* series of Lifestyles titles—books that deliver critical, unbiased information that other books can't or won't reveal—*the inside scoop*. Our goal is to provide you with the *most accessible, useful* information and advice possible. The recommendations we offer in these pages are not influenced by the corporate line of any organization or industry; we give you the hard facts, whether those institutions like them or not. If something is ill-advised or will cause a loss of time and/or money, we'll give you ample warning. And if it is a worthwhile option, we'll let you know that, too.

Armed and Ready

Our hand-picked authors confidently and critically report on a wide range of topics that matter to smart readers like you. Our authors are passionate about their subjects, but have distanced themselves enough from them to help you be armed and protected, and help you make educated decisions as you go through your process. It is our intent that, from having read this book, you will avoid the pit-falls everyone else falls into and get it right the first time.

Don't be fooled by cheap imitations; this is the genuine article *Unofficial Guide* series from Macmillan Publishing. You may be familiar with our proven track record of the travel *Unofficial Guides*, which have more than two million copies in print. Each year thousands of travelers—new and old—are armed with a brand new, fully updated edition of the flagship *Unofficial Guide to Walt Disney World*, by Bob Sehlinger. It is our intention here to provide you with the same level of objective authority that Mr. Sehlinger does in his brainchild.

The Unofficial Panel of Experts

Every work in the Lifestyle *Unofficial Guides* is inten-sively inspected by a team of three top professionals in their fields. These experts review the manuscript for factual accuracy, comprehensiveness, and an insider's determination as to whether the manu-script fulfills the credo in this Reader's Bill of Rights. In other words, our Panel ensures that you are, in fact, getting "the inside scoop."

Our Pledge

The authors, the editorial staff, and the Unofficial Panel of Experts assembled for *Unofficial Guides* are determined to lay out the most valuable alternatives available for our readers. This dictum means that our writers must be explicit, prescriptive, and above all, direct. We strive to be thorough and complete, but our goal is not necessarily to have the "most" or "all" of the information on a topic; this is not, after all, an encyclopedia. Our objective is to help you narrow down your options to the best of what is available, unbiased by affiliation with any industry or organization.

In each *Unofficial Guide* we give you:

- Comprehensive coverage of necessary and vital information

- Authoritative, rigidly fact-checked data

- The most up-to-date insights into trends

- Savvy, sophisticated writing that's also readable

- Sensible, applicable facts and secrets that only an insider knows

Special Features

Every book in our series offers the following six special sidebars in the margins that were devised to help you get things done cheaply, efficiently, and smartly.

1. "Timesaver"—tips and shortcuts that save you time.

2. "Moneysaver"—tips and shortcuts that save you money.

3. "Watch Out!"—more serious cautions and warnings.

4. "Bright Idea"—general tips and shortcuts to help you find an easier or smarter way to do something.

5. "Quote"—statements from real people that are intended to be prescriptive and valuable to you.

6. "Unofficially..."—an insider's fact or anecdote.

We also recognize your need to have quick information at your fingertips, and have thus provided the following comprehensive sections at the back of the book:

1. **Glossary:** Definitions of complicated terminology and jargon.

2. **Resource Guide:** Lists of relevant agencies, associations, institutions, web sites, etc.

3. **Recommended Reading List:** Suggested titles that can help you get more in-depth information on related topics.

4. **Important Documents:** "Official" pieces of information you need to refer to, such as government forms.

5. **Important Statistics:** Facts and numbers presented at-a-glance for easy reference.

6. **Index.**

Letters, Comments, and Questions from Readers

We strive to continually improve the Unofficial series, and input from our readers is a valuable way for us to do that.

Many of those who have used the *Unofficial Guide* travel books write to the authors to ask questions, make comments, or share their own discoveries and lessons. For lifestyle *Unofficial Guides*, we would also appreciate all such correspondence, both positive and critical, and we will make best efforts to incorporate appropriate readers' feedback and comments in revised editions of this work.

How to write to us:

    Unofficial Guides
    Macmillan Lifestyle Guides
    Macmillan Publishing
    1633 Broadway
    New York, NY 10019

Attention: Reader's Comments

The *Unofficial Guide* Panel of Experts

The *Unofficial* editorial team recognizes that you've purchased this book with the expectation of getting the most authoritative, carefully inspected information currently available. Toward that end, on each and every title in this series, we have selected a minimum of three "official" experts comprising the "Unofficial Panel" who painstakingly review the manuscripts to ensure: factual accuracy of all data; inclusion of the most up-to-date and relevant information; and that, from an insider's perspective, the authors have armed you with all the necessary facts you need—but the institutions don't want you to know.

For *The Unofficial Guide to Acing the Interview,* we are proud to introduce the following Panel of Experts:

Hilary J. Bland is a Senior Human Resources Representative at Macmillan Publishing USA in New York, NY. Prior to joining Macmillan she was an executive recruiter and a training and development consultant in the financial services industry. Hilary is a graduate of Mount

Holyoke College and holds an M.A. in Organizational Psychology from Columbia University.

Since 1988, **Tim Haft** has assisted more than 7,000 job seekers of all ages and walks of life in finding meaningful and satisfying work. Mr. Haft launched his own job search consulting practice in 1995 after serving as Director of Career Development at New York University's Tisch School of the Arts. Today, Mr. Haft continues to dispense job search advice, but is also active as a freelance writer and editor. His books on the subject of career development and job hunting include *Trashproof Resumes, Job Notes: Resumes* and *Crane's Guide to Writing an Effective Resume.* He co-authored *Job Smart,* and was a collaborator in the creation of a CD-ROM and website called Career Toolbox (www.careertoolbox.com). Haft holds a B.A. in history from the University of Virginia and an M.A. in sociology from New York University.

Marci Taub is a career counselor in private practice based in New Jersey. She specializes in career counseling and testing, job search coaching, and graduate study advising services. Marci co-authored *Work Smart: What You Need to Know to Get the Job You Want.* She has been an adjunct faculty member of New York University's School of Continuing Education, teaching courses through the Center for Career, Education, and Life Planning. Her professional affiliations include memberships the American Counseling Association and the National Career Development Association. Marci holds an M.A. in Counseling from Montclair State University, a

Certificate in Adult Career Planning and Development from New York University and a B.A. from Oberlin College. Prior to entering private practice, Marci consulted and was employed in human resources with major financial institutions. She also held positions in colleges in New York and New Jersey, advising students on career planning and job search issues.

Introduction

This book is based on a paradox: The employment market is more favorable to the job-seeker than it has been in years, but competition for jobs is tougher than ever. How is that possible?

Though many employers are scrambling to find strong candidates—even going so far as to declare a labor shortage—they nevertheless have access to candidates like never before due to the emergence of online recruiting, the globalization of the workplace, and the use of contingency workers and outsourcing as major forces in the hiring game.

Just when it seemed that we'd never hear the end of massive lay-offs and economic recession throughout the 1990s, the tides turned dramatically to herald the arrival of abundant jobs and a booming economy. Newspaper headlines, magazine cover stories, and Website home pages have been welcoming job-seekers with the good news (and frightening employers with bad news):

> "Job Market Hottest in Years"—CNNfn—http://CNNfn.com—September 2, 1998

> "New Grads Enjoy Record Job Market"—*The Wall Street Journal* Interactive Edition—September 20, 1998

"Surviving the Coming Labor Shortage by Asking Employees What They Want"—*Kansas City infoZine*—September 1998

"Labor Shortage Hits New High: Worker crisis may threaten growth"—*Cincinnati Business Courier*—August 11, 1997

"Labor Shortage Alarms Local Economists"—*Boston Business Journal*—June 16, 1997

"Labor Shortage Spurs High-Tech Wage Hikes"—*The Portland Business Journal*—June 24, 1996

"The Y2K Labor Shortage"—Year 2000 International www.y2ktimebomb.com— September 8, 1997

"'98 Job Market Very Strong, 2 National Surveys Report"—*Daily Northwestern* (Northwestern University)—January 7, 1998

With such glowing reports of a labor market that favors the job-seeker, you might assume that you can waltz into any position you desire with little effort. Unfortunately, you can't. For one thing, nationwide statistics and media headlines do not always apply to each individual. The concept of abundant jobs and an employment world that favors the job-seeker may be irrelevant to the person who has been out of work for months or even years despite adequate—or more than adequate—qualifications. Individual differences and geographic or occupational variations always offset labor market trends. Nonetheless, most data and anecdotal information point to an improved job market, so much advice in this book is based on this premise. Still, if you are a job-seeker not benefiting from such circumstances, I encourage you to seek additional guidance from a professional career or employment consultant.

And remember that there is a paradox at work here. Despite the good news about jobs, there is also increased competition. Employers are more strategic these days in their recruiting and hiring methods. Many carefully plot the qualifications needed in a new employee, use formal assessment tools (tests and other measures, as discussed in Chapter 11, "Passing Muster: Tests, Observation, and Other Ways You'll be Assessed"), and learn the art and science of interviewing. They are simply more careful about how they hire. Their strategy results from four primary factors:

1. **Organizational belt-tightening.** Hiring in a methodical, cautious manner is a byproduct of the workplace upheaval—that is, the downsizing, mergers, acquisitions, and reorganizations—of the 1990s. No doubt you've heard the term "leaner and meaner" used to describe organizations at the cusp of the 21st century. Profound changes in the business world of the 1990s have meant that companies and not-for-profit organizations now must ensure that every person on the payroll is a human resource, not human surplus. As a result, you are likely to be screened more carefully and rigorously than in the past.

2. **Vision.** Pick up any book on the keys to success in business today, and you'll likely come across the word "vision" on many pages. The idea of long-range planning is not a new one, but it is, in a sense, a renewed one as organizations try to shed 20th century ideals and tackle 21st century missions. Employers these days are much more interested in bringing on board people who can help them meet their long-term goals

than in hiring people who can only fill immediate needs and manage the tasks in a specific position.

When re-organization became the norm throughout the tumultuous 1990s, the concept of "a job" died. Employees must now be versatile, flexible, adaptable, and able to take on any responsibility that a changing workplace demands. So, when it comes to interviewing, you are not just being hired to do a particular job but are being hired for your ability to contribute to an organization's long-range vision. (Chapter 3, "Research: The Root of All Strategy," tells you how to conduct research to find out what those long-range needs are.) Clearly, there is much more at stake these days when interviewing.

3. **The global workplace.** The much touted globalization of the workplace is more than a buzzword: It is a reality affecting your ability to get the job you want. This is happening for a number of reasons. First, the fact that even the mom-and-pop shop down the street is facing competition from all corners of the globe means that organizations need to hire people who can make and keep them competitive in a much larger arena than ever. Secondly, that globalization also means that there are many more applicants for any given position than there were before the Internet enabled employers to post their openings and prospective employees to network in such a large-scale way. While quantity doesn't always mean quality when it comes to a large pool of applicants, the bottom line is that, anyway you cut it, you are

going to be dealing with more competition. A long-distance job search no longer means hanging out at the newsstand that carries out-of-town papers; instead it means a few clicks of a mouse from the comfort of your home.

4. **The growing contingency workforce.** The final reason you are facing stiff competition despite the fact that the demand for good workers exceeds the supply is that there is a growing pool of contingency workers who offer top-notch qualifications and are expendable—in other words, cost-effective—for the employer. This workforce consists of the temporary employees, freelancers, and consultants who can meet an organization's needs at any given point in time, then be off on their merry way when the organization's needs change rather than hanging around as dead weight on the payroll. Trend analysts predict that 60 million people, which is almost half of all working people in this country, will be part of the contingency workforce at the brink of the 21st century. So, when interviewing, you are not only up against fellow job-seekers looking for a long-term commitment from an employer, but you're also up against these "disposable" employees.

In addition to these four reasons why you can't be blasé in your job search, there is the issue of why you shouldn't *want* to be blasé. Forget about the problem of keeping up with the competition for a moment, and let's look at what's in your best interest. It is to your advantage to see a potential dark cloud over this idea of abundant jobs. Why? Because you shouldn't take just any old job. You owe it to yourself to find the job that's really right for you.

You want—and deserve—the one that will make you the most satisfied, whether that's one with the most money, best location, most interesting responsibilities, most family-friendly company, or whatever. You don't have to take the first job that comes along. (Exceptions to this rule come in cases where you are job hunting in an extremely competitive field or when you don't have sufficient experience or skills and simply need a foot-in-the-door job.)

So, even though the favorable job market is good news, it does not mean that you can be complacent in how you interview. You must outshine the competition and must make sure that the prospective employer outshines its competition, making it worthy of employing you. To do that, you need strategies for acing the interview as offered throughout this book.

The Unofficial Approach to Interviewing

You'll find that the advice in *The Unofficial Guide to Acing the Interview* is based on the premise that an interview is a meeting of the minds. It is a conversation between two or more people who get together to try to make the best match. These are not adversaries but potential colleagues. As the job-seeker, your goal is not to outsmart, convince, or put on an act. Interviewing is not a game or a theatrical performance. This is a business meeting.

As with any business meeting, you go in with objectives you hope to achieve and an agenda to get you there. You enter the encounter with a strategy that will help you reach your goals. Most importantly, you go in seeing yourself on equal footing with the interviewer. You are not the lowly job-seeker desperate to be hired, but instead you're a potentially valuable asset to an organization with needs and wants.

How Employers Think

As part of the research I conducted for this book, I read many of the books and articles written by and for employers on techniques for recruiting and hiring the best employees. (I wanted to give you the inside scoop from the other side of the desk.) I then added the insights gained from this research to the knowledge I had already acquired about the employment process as a career counselor who has coached thousands of job-seekers and interacted with hundreds of headhunters and human resource professionals in the process.

Out of all of this, the most striking fact is a simple but powerful one: Employers want to ace the interview, too.

Books with titles such as *Getting Employees to Fall in Love with Your Company* (see Appendix C for complete reference) illustrate this fact beautifully. Employers have needs and wants just like job-seekers. When you see them as "employee-seekers," you're more likely to feel that you, the job-seeker, are on equal footing with them. Of all the "unofficial" advice, tips, and insights offered throughout this book, this one may be the most important. If you feel powerful, you will be powerful, and you will ace the interview.

The first two chapters provide more inside scoop on how employers think and how they make hiring decisions. The rest of the book suggests tried-and-true tactics which factor the employer's perspective into the equation.

How Job-Seekers Think

During the first week I was writing this book, a former client of mine called to ask if I would work with her husband, who was attempting to make a career change. (I'll call them Adrienne and Tom.) Adrienne was concerned that Tom was not taking the interviewing process seriously. He had several interviews coming up but was doing very little preparation for them. He considered himself a good conversationalist who was comfortable in most any situation. Adrienne, who had made a successful career change herself the previous year, knew firsthand how much effort it takes to get the right job. She had tried to counsel her husband, having learned a great deal about job-hunting techniques when she went through her own search, but like many things in life, an objective third party seemed to be necessary.

I agreed to meet with Tom and immediately saw why Adrienne had had trouble advising him herself. They were like night and day when it came to approaching the task of changing careers and finding a job. Tom was an affable, gregarious, fly-by-the-seat-of-his-pants kind of guy, while Adrienne was more reserved, methodical, and detail-oriented. She had conducted hours of research before her interviews and had carefully crafted a script to guide her in answering just about any interview question that might come her way—she had even rehearsed in mock interviews. Tom told me that he thought research was overrated and that he much preferred to wing it in the interview rather than prepare what he was going to say. He was by no means less responsible or conscientious than his wife; he simply had a different approach.

It was quite fortuitous that Tom and Adrienne came into my world when I was getting started with this book. They reminded me that each of us has a personality style and a preferred way of tackling projects that predispose us to success or failure when it comes to interviewing. While it may seem that Tom was headed for disaster and Adrienne was headed for an ace, the fact is that neither had the right approach. Just being a friendly guy is not enough, but being overly scripted and rehearsed is too much.

As a psychologist, I know better than to encourage clients to be someone they're not. (I'm sure that plenty of you who don't have a degree in psychology know that that's a losing battle!) I couldn't get Tom to be like his wife—something she had been trying to do inadvertently—but I could offer strategies that would work *with* his personality, not against it. Throughout this book, I have attempted to take into account the issue of individual differences and to offer advice that is not heavily skewed toward any one style. The best approach is a balanced one. Chapters 3; 4, "Making Yourself the Top Candidate"; 5, "Developing the Right Attitude"; 6, "Presenting the Right Image"; and 7, "Strategic Communication for Interviews" address the psychology of interviewing and how to present yourself through effective verbal and nonverbal communication—with strategies you can adapt to fit your own preferred way of doing things.

Making the Most of This Guide

Before you venture any further into this book, I'd like you to be aware of some decisions I made while writing it that may affect you, the reader.

First, let's address the issue of scope. *The Unofficial Guide to Acing the Interview* encompasses all topics directed related to interviewing, from understanding how hiring decisions are made, to preparing for an interview, to navigating the interview process itself, as well as handling the follow-up that leads to an offer. I chose not to include advice on job hunting in general or on choosing a career direction, as those are issues that warrant more extensive treatment than the handful of pages I might tack onto a book on interviewing.

If you find, however, that you are not quite ready to employ the interviewing strategies suggested on these pages—perhaps because you need to identify your career goals and target job, or because you need to figure out how to uncover job leads—then I recommend that you consult the books listed in Appendix C under the "Career Planning" and "Job Search" sections. They can help you get a focus, write your resume and cover letters, and craft a job-search strategy. You will also find several organizations in Appendix B that can lead you to a career counselor or job search coach, should you need more individualized assistance than those books can provide.

Secondly, the advice in this book is applicable to most all types of interviews, regardless of the setting, nature of the available position, or your career level. Too many books on interviewing focus exclusively on the recruitment process in the corporate world, overlooking the vast amount of opportunities in small businesses, not-for-profit organizations, and government. Job-seekers who don navy blue suits to meet with executives in high-rise office buildings may be the norm, but there are plenty of exceptions to that rule.

I realize that I might have a reader who finds herself in a desert of the American Southwest being interviewed by a paleontologist over a cache of fossils. Another reader might visit a writer in his converted-garage office to discuss work as a research assistant. Still another might be a preschool teacher who finds himself sitting cross-legged on the floor of a classroom being interviewed by a teacher trying to rein in a handful of toddlers.

With the business world such a dominant force in the employment market, occupational variations such as these are often overlooked when it comes to interviewing advice. As a result, I have alternated the use of the terms "company" and "organization" throughout the book to reflect the diversity of settings in which job-seekers interview. And, wherever possible, I have tried to use examples and contextual references that represent this variety. (By the way, the case study examples in this book are based on experiences of actual clients from my private practice, with all names and identifying information changed to protect their confidentiality.)

A final reminder of perhaps the single most important piece of advice I can give you: Be yourself. That is, find among the tips and strategies offered the ones that best suit your own personal style, strengths, and circumstances. A strong interview is one in which the real you, the natural you shines through. That said, it's time to get started...and good luck!

What You Need to Know About Getting Hired

PART I

GET THE SCOOP ON...
Three important hiring criteria ▪ The importance
of skills and personality ▪ Key qualities employers seek ▪ That elusive quality of "fit" ▪ How
employers make hiring decisions

How Hiring Decisions
are Made

A cing the interview is a lot like acing a serve in tennis. If you've ever watched a world-class tennis player send the ball careening past an opponent, then you know it takes more than sheer physical strength and an expensive racket to do so. It takes strategy and mental concentration to position the ball in just the right spot on the court and to know what kind of serve will be difficult for the opponent to return. Getting hired is not that much different. Having the basic skills required of the job and wearing your best suit are not enough. It takes a well thought-out strategy, proper mental preparation, and insight into the prospective employer to pull off a winning performance.

To know what your strategy should be, which skills to emphasize, and how to present yourself, you have to know how you will be judged and how hiring decisions are made. This is where even the most savvy job-seekers often fall short. It's easy to fall into the trap of concentrating on what you think the

Unofficially...
Given the rapid rate of change in most organizations these days, employers are often more concerned about your ability to help them achieve long-range goals—some of which aren't even set yet—than your ability to handle the specific duties of a current position.

employer is looking for rather than finding out what he or she really wants. Only when you know the decision-making criteria for a given position can you shape an effective interviewing strategy.

Essential Hiring Criteria

The criteria on which hiring decisions are based depends upon the nature of the organization, the position itself, and the individual interviewer. (Chapter 3, "Research: The Root of All Strategy," discusses research methods that enable you to discern those criteria for each of your target companies.) There are, however, some common threads in what most interviewers are seeking. Anyone trying to fill a position is essentially seeking a satisfactory answer to the following three basic questions:

1. *Can you do the job?* Do you have the skills, strengths, potential, and experience necessary to function in this job, this environment, and this industry or sector? Can you help us succeed in a competitive global marketplace and meet our organizational goals?

2. *Will you fit in?* Can you be one of us? Can you get along with your colleagues, work in harmony with the organization's values, and present the image we want in our employees? Will you fit into our organizational structure and into the budget we have allocated for employee compensation?

3. *Do you want to work here?* Do you know what you're getting into? Are you likely to stay in this job or with this organization long enough to make our investment in you pay off?

To find answers to these questions, recruiters take a variety of approaches. As you'll see in Chapter

8, "Variations on the Interviewing Theme" (which describes in detail the various types of interviews you might encounter) interviews come in all shapes and sizes. But whether an interviewer fires off hundreds of tough questions or simply conducts a casual conversation with you, you can be sure of one thing. He or she essentially just wants to know if you can do the job, if you'll fit in, and if you want the job.

Can You Do the Job?

I often am approached by prospective clients seeking advice on a job search strategy, with particular concern about their resumes, cover letters, and where to find leads to jobs. When I ask whether they need help with their interviewing techniques, I frequently hear, "Oh, I don't having any problem in interviews. I'm comfortable talking to people." Well, unbeknownst to them, being a good conversationalist and having an affable personality is not a guarantee of success in an interview. Though such qualities are important, you can't simply talk your way into a job. You have to provide hard evidence that you can do the job and do it well.

Employers don't hire people just to fill up square footage in the office. They hire people who can make a difference. That means having the skills, experience, and potential to handle the basic job responsibilities—as well as to add extra value that other candidates don't bring to the table.

The value that you bring to a prospective employer can be broken down into several factors: content knowledge, transferable skills, personal qualities, and experience. Let's look at these factors in more detail and examine the rationale for why employers care about them.

> ❝
> With competition more intense than ever, companies can no longer ... carry on their payrolls excessive numbers of employees who do not make a measurable contribution to the competitive effort.
> —Max Messmer in *The Fast Forward MBA in Hiring,* New York: John Wiley & Sons, 1998
> ❞

Timesaver
Before an interview, try to obtain the official, written description of the available position so that you don't waste time preparing to discuss skills and experiences that aren't relevant.

Content Knowledge

The content knowledge that you bring to a job consists of the subjects that you know something about and in which you have some expertise. If you're interviewing for a pharmaceutical sales job, for example, then the relevant content knowledge you have to offer might be an academic background in chemistry, or work experience as a nurse or physician. Sales experience, if any, would be your transferable skill (discussed in greater detail later in this chapter). Similarly, if you are seeking a job with a public relations firm that specializes in promoting clients in the securities industry, then the interviewer would be pleased to learn that you understand the difference between bond trading and option trading and that you can converse intelligently about finance in general. In that case, your content knowledge lies in finance, and your transferable skills might be such functions as writing and media relations.

At a minimum, possessing knowledge of certain content areas assures an employer that you know enough to do the job in question. More important, however, is that your knowledge can help you make a real contribution to the organization above and beyond your basic job duties. Your knowledge base enables you to bring innovation and insight to your new employer, two benefits highly valued as organizations try to thrive in an increasingly competitive marketplace. Chapter 4, "Making Yourself the Top Candidate," tells you how to identify your own content knowledge areas.

Transferable Skills

It probably comes as no surprise that the changing structure of organizations over the past several years has brought about a need for employees with diverse, versatile skill sets. In addition to having specialized knowledge (as described in the previous section), you must have skills that are generic enough to be of value in—or transferable to—a variety of jobs and situations.

The transferable skills can be thought of as the skills that you might preface with the phrase "I can…." Chapter 4 offers many examples of transferable skills and details how to identify yours. The following are just a few examples:

- I can manage people.
- I can coordinate an event.
- I can write well.
- I can solve complex mathematical problems.

Impressing the interviewer with your transferable skills is particularly important if you are changing career fields or industries. In such cases, your content knowledge is likely to be less relevant because it may be too closely linked to your old field. In such a case, your transferable skills become more critical. Transferable skills are also useful when your interview is exploratory in nature—that is, when you are not discussing a specific job opening but are being interviewed to see where you might fit within a given organization. (Strategies for exploratory interviews are described in Chapter 8.)

Personal Qualities

Personal qualities are the aptitudes, traits, and proclivities that—like transferable skills—can be useful in a variety of situations. Your personal qualities are often expressed in statements beginning with "I am…." Some examples include the following:

Unofficially…
Recruiters—the good ones at least—usually have a very specific idea of what they're looking for in a job candidate. Prior to the interview process, many chart job responsibilities and organizational goals, matching those with desired qualifications.

- I am detail-oriented.

- I am a leader.

- I am creative.

- I am calm in the face of chaos.

- I am outgoing.

- I am sensitive to others' needs.

- I am physically strong and agile.

Watch Out!
As the job market has improved and become a seller's market, many companies are scrambling to fill vacant positions. Don't let this lead you to believe that employers have lowered their hiring standards significantly. They still want to make the best match.

As you can see, the personal qualities are not exactly skills; they are the personality characteristics that enable you to acquire particular skills. This is an important point because many employers want to know that you not only have the skills needed for the immediate job, but that you also have the potential to handle the next step in a job—or a future incarnation of it. Your personal qualities are what enable you to adapt to the changing needs of the organization.

As with content knowledge and transferable skills, you'll find more details on assessing your personal qualities in Chapter 4. The objective here is simply for you to be aware of what constitutes the general question of "Can you do the job?" After you have a handle on the basic criteria upon which hiring decisions are based, you can then move on in later chapters to take stock of what you have to offer with regard to those criteria.

Table 1.1 describes more personal qualities, as well as transferable skills, that employers are seeking as a result of trends in today's workplace.

Experience

Employers also make hiring decisions based on your past performance. After all, it's easy to say you possess a certain skill or personal quality; it's another thing to provide evidence. Your work experience

TABLE 1.1: WORKPLACE TRENDS AND SKILLS NEEDED

Trend	Transferable Skills Needed	Personal Qualities Needed
Focus on the future	Goal setting, visualizing, strategic planning, brainstorming, inventing, conceptualizing	Risk-taker, visionary, energetic, entrepreneurial, innovative, creative, perceptive, big-picture thinker
Lean operational and managerial processes	Budgeting, managing people and projects efficiently, systematizing, estimating costs, budgeting, cutting costs, organizing, doing more with less, streamlining, trouble-shooting	Resourceful, disciplined, detail-oriented, organized, efficient, effective
Commitment to diversity	Communicating, negotiating, managing or resolving conflicts, navigating other cultures, supporting others	Open-minded, diplomatic, tactful, patient, flexible, sensitive, tolerant, global in orientation
Less supervision	Managing one's own career development, taking initiative, following through, implementing plans	Independent, self-starter, disciplined
Service and quality	Assessing quality, overseeing production, communicating orally, handling client and customer relations	Conscientious, detail-oriented, ethical, achiever, communicative
Seeking knowledge/intelligence	Accessing the Internet and databases, using research skills, analyzing; interviewing for information; reading; thinking critically	Inquisitive, curious, well-connected, resourceful, technically inclined
Ethics	Working with integrity, recognizing potential ethical breaches, resolving ethical dilemmas, understanding employment discrimination and sexual harassment laws	Honest, moral, responsible, fair, possessing good judgment and common sense

(and, where relevant, your educational and avocational experiences) can provide proof of your abilities.

When discussing your experience in an interview, avoid the common pitfall of focusing only on the responsibilities of your current or past jobs. Instead, spell out for the interviewer the skills and strengths you demonstrated in doing that work. In the "Building Your Case" section of Chapter 4, you'll find more detail on how to do this. For now, just keep in mind that as you begin to prepare for interviews, you must take stock of your accomplishments. In the mind of a recruiter, it is your past patterns of success, not a litany of your previous job duties, that make you a safe bet.

Will You Fit In?

In an employer's ideal world, all positions would be filled through personal referral. People simply like to hire people they know. Doing so eliminates much of the guesswork involved, making it easier to predict what the new hire will be like as a person, not just as a set of skills and experience on a resume.

You may already be aware that the issue of "fit" is a significant one when recruiters are looking for the best candidate for the job. But, if you are vaguely defining "fit" as having the right personality—as many job-seekers do—then you're overlooking some critical elements of the concept.

"Fit" means more than just getting along well with the people you meet during the interview process. It's also more than wearing the right cut of suit or the same color shirt as everyone at your target organization. Personality and appearance are a part of fit, but you also must have values and a work style that are congruent with the place where you

Bright Idea
If you've been out of work for a considerable period of time, start doing some volunteer work, or help out in a friend's business—anything to get some recent accomplishments under your belt, even if they are in areas not directly related to your target job.

want to work. And, you need to meet some fairly objective criteria such as "Can we afford you?" and "Do we have a place for you?".

Regarding the former point—the issue of your personality, appearance, values, and work style being congruent—this idea of "fit" is one of the more subjective variables to enter into the interview success equation; it is nonetheless possible to make those variables more tangible, and therefore, more controllable. When I first began career counseling some years ago, I worried that there was not much I could do to help clients address this issue when preparing for interviews. They either had it—whatever *it* was—or they didn't. The more I spoke with people on the other side of the interview desk, however, the more I realized that there were certain tangible factors within the concept of "fit" that my clients could address. This seemingly elusive criterion can actually be broken down into factors that you can partially control: values, work style, image, and personality.

Values

Just as with individuals, organizations operate from a fundamental set of values that drive their objectives, aspirations, and daily behavior. In your own career, you may value such things as making a certain amount of money, helping society, or being creative. You may place the utmost importance on customer service, innovative problem solving, or producing top-quality written materials.

Organizations, too, place importance on some actions or results more than others. You might interview one day with a corporation that is obsessed with quality in their products and services, and the next day with a company focused solely on cutting costs.

Moneysaver
If you'll be interviewing for a type of job or organization in which you've never worked, don't invest a lot of money in interviewing attire until you find out what people in that occupation or setting tend to wear.

Bright Idea
When consider-
ing how you fit
with an organi-
zation's culture,
be sure to take
into account the
values and style
of any outside
people and orga-
nizations with
whom you'd be
working, such as
clients, vendors,
consultants, and
collaborators.

Some organizations' values are clearly stated in their published mission statements or orientation manuals. (Chapter 3 discusses ways to research organizations to ascertain their values.) Be aware, though, that organizational values fluctuate and that the "value of the week" is not necessarily reflected in the company literature. You may have to speak to people familiar with the organization or, ideally, with people who already work there. Then there are values that are common to most organizations these days—at least the savvy ones. As you saw in Table 1.1, issues such as a commitment to diversity, focus on long-range planning, and a desire to be competitive globally are just a few of the trends in organizations these days.

Work Style

A second important element within the concept of "fit" is the issue of work style. Everything from the hours you expect to work to whether you keep your office door open (assuming you have an office) must be consistent with the policies and practices of your target employer. If an interviewer gets the sense that you expect to leave at five o'clock most days, but the job calls for significant overtime, then a big red flag has obviously been raised. Consider the following checklist of work style issues on which you may or may not be in sync with your target employers.

- Work ethic. How seriously do you take your job, and how strong of an allegiance are you willing to make to your employer?

- Schedule. What kind of hours do you expect to keep? Are you a clock-watcher ready to leave at the stroke of five, or are you willing to sacrifice nights and weekends for your job?

- Formality. Do you fit best into a staid, conservative, and serious office climate, or one in which cartoons adorn cubicles and jokes circulate through email?

- Team orientation. Do you believe that more is merrier when tackling a project, or do you prefer to go it alone?

During interviews, be on the lookout for questions or directions in the conversation that indicate the interviewer is trying to discern your work style. Remember, though—as mentioned in the introduction to this book—that the best approach to interviewing is to be yourself, and this issue of work style is no exception. If you try to conform to an environment that conflicts too much with your preferred way of working, then you are not likely to be satisfied or successful—even if you *do* land the job.

Image

Work style refers to the way you do your actual work, while *image* is defined as the way you look and the impression you give while working. Interviewers aren't necessarily looking to hire clones of themselves and their colleagues, but they do usually want to hire people who have a similar air about them. So, one important element that determines whether you seem like you will fit in is that of your image.

Social psychologists have found that the impression you make in about the first seven seconds of an interaction is the lasting one. Chapter 6, "Presenting the Right Image," covers how to dress for an interview to make a positive first impression, but as a way of introduction to that chapter, consider now which other factors make up your image besides your attire.

> **❝**
> When I was hiring account executives and administrative staff, I would walk through the reception area before interviews. If I found that a candidate didn't meet our standards for professional image—the three Ds: dress, demeanor, and dialogue—I went back to my desk and typed the rejection letter before the interview even started.
> —Barry Cohen, career consultant and former Director of Recruiting and National Sales Manager for Snapple Beverages
> **❞**

While it is certainly important to dress appropriately, many job-seekers spend too much time worrying about their wardrobe and not enough about the overall image they convey. The way you speak and the way you carry yourself are just as important as what you're wearing. Your accent, speech patterns, tone of voice, and volume of speech are reflections of you—for good or bad. Your comportment—including your posture, pace of walking, and air of confidence (or lack thereof)—also figure into an interviewer's decision about whether you will fit in.

Personality

Moneysaver
To assess your personality type without having to take expensive tests, read some of the books in the "Personality" section of Appendix C.

A final element is that of your personality. The interviewer has to feel confident that you will get along well with your bosses, subordinates, coworkers, clients, and anyone else connected to the job. Of all the elements within the concept of "fit," personality may be the most hit-or-miss. Instead of simply having to come across as a pleasant and reasonable person, you must convey the particular personality type needed to deal with specific people in that job.

Take the case of Lydia, who was in the final round of interviews for a position as Director of Special Projects in the development office of a major not-for-profit organization. She knew that the position required that she be extremely assertive in order to boost the fundraising efforts of the organization. She needed to be politically astute, well-connected, and a tough manager. Lydia not only possessed those qualities, but she also was able to present evidence of them in her past career accomplishments.

After three meetings with various people in the organization, the pool of candidates was narrowed to Lydia and one other person. When she ended up not being the one selected, she was surprised and disappointed. To determine what went wrong, she asked a colleague who knew people in that organization to do some checking. Much to her dismay, she found out that the person hired actually had less relevant experience and less of a proven track record.

So what made the difference? It was personality. Lydia learned that the Director of Development, to whom the Director of Special Projects would report, was a rather insecure sort who was threatened by strong, self-assured types. He wanted to hire someone a bit malleable and willing to put up with his micro-management style. Though Lydia was actually a very flexible, easy-going person, she had played up her assertive side in the interview, assuming that was what they were seeking. After that experience, she knew never to make assumptions again about the personality characteristics sought in the ideal candidate.

Fitting into the Organizational and Salary Structure

When purchasing a product, you probably make the decision to do so based on both subjective and objective criteria—does this item appeal to me and can I afford it? Employers do the same thing when considering hiring you. They have to know that the salary and related compensation—bonuses, benefits, and other perks—are within the budget they have allocated for the position. They also need to know that the level of responsibility you are seeking and the title you would require fit with the needs of a given department, group, or functional area within the organization. If your requirements do not fit what they can offer, you may not be able to reach an agreement and will have to look elsewhere. Fortunately, however, there is usually some leeway

Unofficially...
The average cost of hiring a new employee (exempt status) is approximately $8,500, according to a 1997 study by the Saratoga Institute, a human resources think tank. This figure does not include hidden costs such as the time managers spend recruiting and interviewing— away from their regular responsibilities.

when it comes to these matters, and with effective negotiating tactics, you can make yourself fit. (Negotiating the terms of a job offer, including salary, are discussed in Chapter 14, "Evaluating and Negotiating Offers.")

Do You Want the Job?

Of all the criteria on which employers base hiring decisions, the issue of whether you really want the job is the one that most job-seekers completely overlook. Now, you might say, "But I always express my interest in the position and show enthusiasm both during the interview and throughout my follow-up efforts." Well, those efforts are appropriate and useful, but they are far from being strategic moves that will make or break your success.

Watch Out!
While expressing your interest in working for a particular organization, don't go overboard with your enthusiasm. Employers these days can't make a promise of life-long employment, so they'll be turned off if you sound like you're already too attached.

Most of your competitors will be expressing interest and saying that they want the job. What they won't necessarily be doing, however, is convincing the interviewer that they know what they're getting into. Employers want to hire people who are going to stick around long enough to make their investment worthwhile. They don't want you to come on board only to discover two weeks or two months into the job that it's not what you expected or that it doesn't fit with your long-term career goals.

The only way someone will have complete confidence in the statement, "I want this job," is if you can say something to the effect of, "I know everything there is to know about this job, this organization, and this industry, and I have given careful thought to how my own goals will be met and my skills utilized."

There is also an element of ego-massaging at work with this hiring criterion. Employers want to know that you targeted them because of something unique they have to offer and that you haven't just chosen them as part of a random sampling of prospective employers. The research techniques suggested in Chapter 3 can help you identify aspects of your target organization and position that you can mention in the interview as being particularly attractive to you. These, of course, should be organizational qualities that do genuinely have some meaning for you.

Behind Closed Doors with the Decision-Makers

In many organizations—particularly medium-sized and large corporations and not-for-profits—recruiting, interviewing, and hiring procedures are more complex and sophisticated than ever. As discussed in the introduction of this book, the increase in global competition and the aftermath of the early 1990s workplace turmoil have made employers much more conscious of every dollar expended on their human resources. Each person hired must not just occupy a desk but must work to occupy a place in that company's history, in a sense.

As a result, many employers have revamped their hiring procedures to ensure that everyone brought on board can contribute to bottom-line profits in the short-term and help the organization meet its goals in the long-term. This is the concept of strategic staffing discussed in the introduction. This means that you, the job-seeker, may actually benefit from a decision-making process that is systematic, careful, deliberate, and, therefore, more likely to be fair and efficient.

Of course, such model systems are not universal. You may still come up against a hiring process that is slow, random, and biased. (Discriminatory hiring

Unofficially...
About 12 million businesses (97 percent of the private sector) have fewer than 100 employees.

practices are discussed in Chapter 12, "Interview Curve Balls.") Larger, progressive organizations with established human resources departments are more likely to use strategic staffing methods. A large percentage of the employment opportunities exist in smaller organizations, however, so you may need to deal with a wider range of hiring practices. In some small businesses, you are likely to find that an office manager or a director of the organization does the interviewing and hiring—and may not have any specialized knowledge or training in recruiting.

Regardless of the methods used, all employers must do three basic things: collect data on candidates, review the data, and make a decision.

How Data Is Collected on Candidates

With any particular employer during the course of your job search, you might have just one interview and be given an offer on the spot—or you might be subjected to several rounds of interviews with a variety of people, take a full day of tests, have every reference checked, and still not get an answer. The way information is collected about you will vary from place to place, but you can be sure that the data will be gathered in any of four basic ways:

- *Interviews.* An interview is certainly the most common way to collect information about an applicant. It can be one-on-one, group meetings with multiple candidates and one or more interviewers, or panel interviews with one candidate and multiple interviewers. You may be screened by an inexperienced personnel assistant or by a seasoned human resources professional. You might meet with the person who would be your boss, or the people who would be your subordinates or team members. Interviews can be conversational and friendly or stressful and intimidating. They can take place at a variety of venues, including college campuses, the employer's offices, conferences, via telephone, or even over the Internet. The various types of interviews are described more in Chapter 8; typical questions and discussion topics are addressed in Chapters 9, "The Fifteen Trickiest Interview Questions," and 10, "Fifty More Questions You Might Be Asked."

■ *Observation of behavior.* Instead of just asking you about who you are and what you're capable of, some employers want you to show them who you are and what you can do. Observing you in situations that simulate the workplace is an excellent way to assess issues of skill, fit, and personal character. Some observation may take place in an interview, particularly in a group interview in which the group may be given a task to accomplish and everyone is observed while working on that task.

Bright Idea
To figure out what kind of decision-making process a prospective employer uses to make hiring decisions, simply ask him or her.

You may also be asked to make a presentation of some sort, particularly for sales, training, or consulting jobs. You might even be invited to come on board for a trial period to do the actual job with the understanding that your performance will be assessed and, if satisfactory, you will be hired formally. (This last method was more common when the job market was tighter. Job-seekers offered to work without pay for a matter of days, weeks, or months to demonstrate what they could do. Now that it's a seller's market, most job-seekers don't have to volunteer their services to get a foot in the door, unless they are seriously lacking experience or basic qualifications.) And, finally, an indirect way that recruiters can observe your behavior is to ask your former employers about their observations of you.

- *Assessment.* The use of tests as a way of evaluating candidates has been on the increase in the past several years, despite the fact that the validity and reliability of much of the test data is questionable. Many large companies send candidates to an in-house or external assessment center to sit through tests of personality, psychological makeup, intelligence, integrity, aptitudes, and/or specific skills. The results are obtained and reviewed by psychologists and other qualified professionals and are reported to the hiring authorities for use in their final decision. Assessment is discussed in more detail in Chapter 11, "Passing Muster: Tests, Observation, and Other Ways You'll be Assessed."

- *Paper credentials.* Some employers rely heavily on basic data on paper when making their decision. They pay close attention to the content and presentation of your resume, to work samples and "kudos" provided in your portfolio, and to documents such as school transcripts and standardized test scores. You'll find more information on these documents in Chapter 6.

Six Styles of Decision Making

After the information about you is collected and the interviewing process is complete, the hiring authorities turn to the task of reviewing the data and making a decision about which candidate should receive an offer. As with everything connected with hiring, the methods for review and decision making vary widely. I have found, however, that there are basically six types of decision-makers when it comes to hiring:

- *Model decision-makers.* Model decision-makers use a process that is so balanced and fair it seems straight out of a human resources textbook. They begin with a clear idea of their hiring criteria. Then they carefully evaluate all the applicant data from a variety of sources—interviews, credentials on paper, assessment results, references, portfolio, personality, and observation—and make a carefully thought-out decision. They are likely to make the decision a team effort so that no one person's opinion weighs too heavily, and they are swift and expedient in coming to a conclusion and notifying the candidate of an offer. If only they could all be that way!

- *Quantitative decision-makers.* These decision-makers can't make a move until the test results are in. Instead of using formal assessment to complement data gathered in interviews, they rely heavily—often too heavily—on what the tests tell them. This type also has a tendency to be a keen student of research showing correlations between various applicant characteristics and future job performance or retention. While few studies have revealed any clear correlations, the quantitative decision-maker keeps hoping for the magic answer. If you suspect you're dealing with a quantitative decision-maker, you need to pay particular attention to the strategies suggested in Chapter 12.

Unofficially...
While figures vary from study to study, research has shown that the average cost to replace an employee who leaves after being on the job for less than six months can be as high as two times that person's annual salary.

- *Gut-feel decision-makers.* At the opposite end of the spectrum are the gut-feel decision-makers. They reject most hard data and prefer instead to rely on their intuition. They prefer a subjective, go-with-what-my-gut-tells-me approach over a more methodical evaluation of objective data. This approach is common among managers and business leaders with extensive experience, as well as anyone who has the utmost confidence in his or her ability to judge people. Sometimes this random process works, and sometimes it doesn't.

- *What's-your-pedigree decision-makers.* Some employers are overly concerned with who you are on paper, usually wanting to hire people who meet some elitist standard of an ideal employee. They might want to hire only someone who attended an Ivy League college or who has an M.B.A. from a Top Ten school, or who has worked for only the most prestigious firms. They might even care about your social status or whether you belong to the right country club. Not only does this practice venture dangerously close to the edge of employment discrimination laws, but it is at the very least simply frustrating for job-seekers. There is very little you can do to sway someone who has such rigid criteria.

- *Who-do-you-know decision-makers.* These decision-makers only want to hire through personal referral. If you don't know someone in the company or have a mutual acquaintance, then you may not have much of a chance. If you think you're dealing with this kind of interviewer, then you need to pay special attention to the "Don't Go It Alone" strategy, recommended in

Timesaver
If you find out that you are unlikely to get a particular job offer because of factors beyond your control, don't waste time pursuing that employer. Accept it and move on.

Chapter 2, "The Biggest Mistakes Interviewees Make," which shows how to create a connection when one is not already there.

- *Just-get-me-a-warm-body decision-makers.* Some recruiters need to fill a position so quickly that they throw all traditional hiring methods out the window and take the first warm body who comes along who reasonably fits the bill. This type of decision-maker may at first seem to be a job-seeker's dream come true, but savvy job-seekers know it's a trap. If you get an offer that seems to come too quickly or to be based on insufficient information about you as an applicant, think twice before accepting. The offer may very well be something fantastic, but an offer made prematurely can cause problems down the road.

  Such a cavalier approach to staffing may reflect a lack of professionalism in the people with whom you'd be working or throughout the organization in general. If no thought goes into a hiring decision, then what does that say about how the organization conducts the rest of its business? An indiscriminate choice may also mean that after you get started with the company, they may find that you are not exactly what they were looking for and send you back pounding the pavement. Those who hire in haste are likely to fire in haste as well.

Wildcard Variables that Affect Hiring Decisions

Unless you are lucky enough to get the first job for which you interview, it is inevitable that at some point in your search you will come up against some insurmountable—or seemingly insurmountable—obstacles. I'm not talking about relatively minor

"

Something most job seekers don't realize is that when screening and interviewing applicants, recruiters generally end up weighing one applicant against the others, rather than the applicants against the job itself. If you have a weak pool of responding applicants, the result is hiring a relative 'superstar' rather than a true expert.
—Marc LeVine, Director of Technology Staffing Solutions, InfoPro Corp.

"

objections employers might have to your candidacy, such as a lack of a particular skill or an unexplained six-month gap on your resume. These can be dealt with, as you'll see in Chapter 12, "Interview Curve Balls."

Instead, I am referring to forces that tax the limits of even the most powerful interviewing strategy or the most savvy job seeker. Much of the time, these are immutable forces beyond your control, but there are occasional times when you can regain some control. Following are several of the most common wildcard variables.

Hiring internally. In many cases, employment law dictates that positions must be advertised to the outside world. They can't be filled with a current employee of that same organization until candidates from the outside have had an opportunity to apply for the positions. (One notable exception occurs in the case of some union positions in which union members must get the first crack at a job.) So, if you think that you have a particular job in the bag only to find out that you didn't get it, the reason may be that the employer hired internally. They may have planned to do so all along and were just going through the motions of interviewing others to meet the legal obligations.

Nepotism. Similar to the issue of hiring internally is that of nepotism. I use this term loosely in that I do not necessarily mean hiring a relative. In fact, many companies have policies that prohibit relatives from working for the same organization. In its looser sense, nepotism here describes a situation in which one person at a given organization has enough power to persuade all the decision-makers that his or her friend or colleague must be hired.

Sometimes upper-level managers owe favors, and as a result, need to offer jobs to friends' sons, daughters, spouses, or the like. Or, sometimes a manager comes on board at a new company and wants to bring his or her former colleagues along. Regardless of who is involved, the point is that someone who has the power to override others' opinions—and who has a pet candidate—might interfere with your ability to get hired.

Opting for a temporary employee. A major development of the past several years has been the dramatic growth in the temporary staffing industry. Employers find the use of temporary workers—for clerical as well as managerial and technical functions—to be an efficient way to allocate resources. If an organization needs more people to handle a temporary increase in workload, hiring permanent employees leaves the company carrying a heavy payroll burden after the work is done and the employees are no longer needed. Some companies have used lay-offs as a way of trimming the excess at that point, but more are finding that doing so is an inefficient (not to mention inhumane!) way of dealing with the problem. So, hiring temporary employees is one solution.

This affects your interviewing process because you may come across an employer who is very interested in you, but who can't justify the expense of bringing you on permanently. In that case, you may need to work extra hard at proving how you could make a contribution in the long run, not just with the immediate needs of the organization, so that you—not a temporary employee—will be chosen.

Also, you need to be aware that the employer might try to get *you* on board in a temporary or

Unofficially...
According to the National Association of Temporary and Staffing Services, the average daily number of people working as temporary employees more than doubled from 1990 to 1997, increasing from 1,165,200 to 2,535,220.

consulting capacity instead of in a permanent staff position. If you agree to those terms, make a careful assessment of the probability that the temp route will turn into permanent employment (that is, find out how many of the current staff made that transition). Though there are federal laws regulating the use of temporary employees, enforcement of them is sloppy; many employers get away with using temps on a long-term basis, never having to make a particular position permanent.

Outsourcing. As with using temporary workers, outsourcing has become an increasingly popular way to cut costs. Outsourcing refers to the process of contracting with outside firms to handle certain functions such as payroll administration and other accounting areas, recruiting, printing, desktop publishing, technical support, and more. Some of these functions require equipment so expensive that the cost of purchasing, maintaining, and operating it far exceeds the cost of paying for outside vendors to provide that service or product. Other organizations outsource because they believe that the quality delivered by outside specialists surpasses what is possible for the company's existing employees to provide.

Just as you can possibly convince an employer that you are a better buy than a temporary worker, you might be able to compete with the idea of outsourcing. Be aware, though, that decisions to outsource versus set up an internal system are often made after a lengthy, careful cost-benefit analysis. So you may be up against quite a strong brick wall if a company has made up its mind to outsource rather than hire you.

Whether you're dealing with the wildcard variables or a model decision-maker, and whether the employer just cares about skills or fit, it helps to be aware of how you are being judged and how the final decision is made. You'll find a further discussion of hiring decisions in Chapter 13, "Following Up to Get to 'Yes'," which offers advice on follow-up techniques that can sway the decision in your favor. In Chapter 2 and many other chapters, you'll find more detailed advice on strategies for showing employers that you meet their hiring criteria.

And, of course, this chapter would not be complete without mentioning that most elusive of all factors: luck. Just as that tennis player trying to ace a serve can benefit from the help of a strong tailwind, your success at interviewing will no doubt be affected by a little luck. There's nothing like a good strategy and some hard work, though, to get the luck pouring in your direction.

Just the Facts

- All questions asked in any interview get at three bigger questions: Can you do this job? Will you fit in with us? Do you really want this job?

- Hiring decisions are based in part on an assessment of what you know, what you can do, what you have accomplished, and what you have the potential to do.

- How you will fit into an organization is determined by subjective factors such as your values, work style, image, and personality, as well as by tangible criteria such as your desired compensation and title.

- Don't assume that a winning personality alone will enable you to ace an interview.

- Time, effort, and money go into hiring and training a new employee, so interviewers must have confidence in your commitment to them before they'll make a commitment to you.

- Hiring decisions are based on methods that range from sophisticated and systematic to random and subjective.

GET THE SCOOP ON...
Common pitfalls to avoid ▪ Distinguishing
yourself from the competition ▪
Taking control of the interview ▪ Networking ▪
Winning interview strategies

The Biggest Mistakes Interviewees Make

Chapter 2

Now that you know how hiring decisions are made, you're equipped with the necessary knowledge to craft a strategy for your interviews. You might believe that you're well qualified for the job, skilled at establishing rapport, and comfortable conversing with most anybody, but as discussed in Chapter 1, "How Hiring Decisions Are Made," it takes more than credentials and personality to be an effective interviewer. It takes an approach based on a thorough assessment of your assets, clear communication, evidence of your capabilities, and an understanding of the employer's needs. In other words, it takes a strategy. Interviewers have a strategy—the well-prepared ones do at least—and you must as well. You must have a game plan that dictates the right moves to make and anticipates potential pitfalls.

Unfortunately, many job-seekers take a can't-see-the-forest-for-the-trees approach to interviewing. They focus on the nitty-gritty aspects of interviewing

Timesaver
Instead of preparing answers to all the hundreds of possible questions you may be asked in an interview, group the most typical interview questions into several main categories and prepare answers for each category, not each question.

and overlook the bigger picture elements of strategy and preparation. They might, for example, exhaustively try to anticipate every possible question they may be asked. They may even prepare and rehearse scripts for answering those questions. Some fuss over their attire and spend hours in the library or online scouring sources for every last fact and figure about the prospective employer. They go into the interview feeling well prepared and confident.

What's so bad about that approach? Such focus on details means these people may lose sight of the forest. When the interview doesn't conform to their expectations, they get rattled. They have no overall strategy or operating principles to guide them through the inevitable twists and turns that interviews will take. Unexpected questions, an adversarial interviewer, an interview that is much shorter or longer than anticipated, or any other change of plan can be disconcerting. To avoid being thrown by such curves, focus on adopting a set of principles or tactics that enable you to be more flexible and to handle any question that comes your way.

This chapter focuses on the elements of such a strategy. By learning about the most common mistakes interviewers make, you'll see which pitfalls you need to avoid and what tactics to employ. On the pages that follow, you'll find extensive reference to other chapters. The objective of this chapter is to give you an overview of interviewing strategy—a prelude of sorts to the rest of the book. Then later chapters provide the details you need to develop and implement your own strategy.

The Five Worst Mistakes Job-Seekers Make

While there are many danger spots when interviewing—areas where unsuspecting job seekers can get tripped up—there are five primary areas of concern. Each is detailed in the following sections.

Interviewing Mistake #1: Bowing to Authority

Many job-seekers think of an interview as a one-sided activity. The interviewer has all the power—power to direct the course of the conversation and to determine the outcome—while the interviewee has none. Not only is that assumption erroneous, but it is unfortunate. Job-seekers can have considerable control over the interview. When they exercise that control, they're more likely to get not just an offer, but an offer they know how to evaluate.

Successful interviewing requires going in with a mental attitude that says, "I am going to be a full and active participant in this interaction, and I will attempt to maintain an equal balance of power." You must go in with clear objectives for information you want to convey and be ready to counter any objections. It's all about being assertive without stepping on the interviewer's toes. I'm not advocating being pushy or rude—just be an equal player in the encounter.

Taking some control enables you not only to convey the information that will encourage the interviewer to see you as a viable candidate, but also to get the information you need to assess the prospective employer. You're there to interview them as much as they're there to interview you. You must assess the employer's stability, culture, opportunities for growth, and any other factors that may

Unofficially... Contrary to popular belief, interviewers rarely set out to interrogate applicants. Their objective is simply to get to know the candidate well enough to make a good match with the position to be filled, so they actually want the interviewee to take an active role in the interaction.

be important to you. Waiting until the end of the interview when you're given the opportunity to ask questions is not sufficient for collecting the relevant information. You must be proactive in directing the course of the conversation before that point to get the answers you need. Ways to achieve this balance of power are discussed in Chapters 5, "Developing the Right Attitude," and 7, "Strategic Communication for Interviews."

Interviewing Mistake #2: Thinking Like a Job-Hunter

Related to the idea of control is the problem of thinking like a job-hunter—with emphasis on the word "hunter." Companies don't want to hire people who are desperate. They want to hire people who can help them solve problems, improve their products or services, grow, and reach any other sort of goals on the horizon. You're being hired to be a colleague, a team player, and a peer—someone who can fit in and make a difference. To position yourself best for that role, you should come across during the interview almost as if you already work there. Doing so helps the interviewer actually visualize you in the position; otherwise, you remain in the lowly stratum of job-hunter.

Another drawback to thinking like a job-seeker is that job hunting makes one very self-centered. Phrases such as "I want…," "I need…," and "I'm looking for…," become the mantra of the unemployed or the unhappily employed. This attitude can lead to an egocentrism that makes the job-seeker overlook the needs of the target employer. Rather than focusing on your own needs and wants, you should try to think from the perspective of the interviewer. Considering the prospective employer's needs and wants enables you to come across as a consultant, problem-solver, or trouble-shooter— which, in turn, enables the interviewer to see you as someone worth hiring.

Chapter 3, "Research: The Root of All Strategy," describes ways to conduct research to get a sense of the job requirements and the organization's needs before the interview so you can adopt that posture. You'll also find more on how to stop thinking like a job-hunter in Chapter 4, "Making Yourself the Top Candidate," Chapter 5, and Chapter 7, "Strategic Communication for Interviews."

Interviewing Mistake #3: Not Being Distinctive

As a career counselor, I usually begin sessions by having clients tell me a little about themselves—particularly their work history—so I can know enough about them to help them. I consistently find that even the most articulate, personable people unwittingly describe their experience in a jargon-laden, detached manner, forcing me to ask the follow-up question, "Yes, but what do you *do?*" They often sound as if they're reading the official job description, not describing an endeavor in which they spend most of their waking hours.

While employers are certainly interested in knowing what your responsibilities and day-to-day tasks are—or have been on past jobs—they are usually more interested in hearing about your accomplishments, skills, and abilities. In other words, they care more about your performance at a given task than about the task itself. By hearing about the outcomes of your past efforts and the skills you bring to the table, they can envision how you could be of benefit to them. That way, if other candidates have essentially the same descriptions on their resume, you distinguish yourself from the pack.

Bright Idea
Before an interview, if you find that you are saying (aloud or to yourself) anything like "I'm being interviewed for a job at XYZ," replace that thought with the consultant's approach: "I'm going to speak to the people at XYZ about how I might be able to help them reach their goals."

Another strategy that helps make you distinctive is to describe your experience as if it were an actual story, not a recitation of bland facts and figures. Instead of saying, for example, "I learned a great deal about the business of art on that job, particularly how to develop a client base and how to market a luxury good," add some flavor to your description. An interviewer is much more likely to remember that job seeker if the statement is something like, "At that job, I got a crash course in marketing a luxury good and managing client relations with everyone from people who'd been collecting art for generations to newcomers with a real passion for art, like Sylvester Stallone." You'll then be remembered as "the candidate who sold paintings to Sly Stallone" instead of "the applicant I interviewed at nine o'clock Wednesday morning."

Even if your work experience is not quite so colorful that you can drop the names of major movie stars, don't worry. Most people don't have such experience. I pulled this example from the case of an actual client I worked with, changing the name of the celebrity to protect his confidentiality, but I'm the first to admit it's not the norm for job experience. The point here is not to show that you've hobnobbed with celebrities but simply to mention actual people, places, products, events, or organizations to make your account more real. Little tidbits of reality can make a big difference in making you memorable.

In Chapter 4 you'll learn how to put together asset statements that help you convey your skills, knowledge, and positive personal qualities in a way that is relevant and meaningful for a prospective employer. Then, in Chapter 7, "Strategic

Communication for Interviews" you'll find more on techniques for powerful communication.

Interviewing Mistake #4: Being on Your Best Behavior

Most job-seekers go into an interview planning to be on their best behavior. With shoes polished, smile fresh, and a firm handshake, they greet the interviewer with an amiable, professional demeanor. They start the meeting with polite chit-chat, dutifully answer questions throughout the meeting, sit with an erect posture, and try to do everything just right.

While the person I've just described might sound overly docile, I have found that even the most self-assured and gregarious people become downright robotic when interviewing. Being stiff or overly formal is no way to ace the interview. Not only does doing so mean you're less likely to be in control, but you are also less likely to connect with the interviewer.

Remember that you're being interviewed by a fellow member of the human race. So to connect with that person—and to be offered a job—your best bet is to be down-to-earth, personable, genuine, and even humorous when appropriate. (See Chapter 7 for more on establishing rapport with the interviewer.)

Interviewing Mistake #5: Trying to Go It Alone

Job searching can be a very solitary activity. You don't take your best friend, your spouse, or your mother into an interview. It's just you against all the potential employers out there. As a result, the interviewing and overall job search process can be lonely, frustrating, and, at times, confusing. You're on your own to get through it. Or are you?

Bright Idea
To remember that interviewers are people, too, try this trick: Think about how well you know your current or former bosses or coworkers. Then remember when you were interviewed by them and how they seemed like such unknown commodities. An unfamiliar interviewer today may be a close colleague and friend tomorrow!

By turning to your network of friends, family, and professional colleagues, your job search success—and, specifically, your interviews—will be greatly enhanced. Plus, the process will be more manageable and even enjoyable as members of your network can provide emotional support and encouragement throughout your search.

"
I use not only all the brains I have but all I can borrow.
—Woodrow Wilson
"

As you prepare for an interview, members of your network can help you take stock of your skills and strengths as you prepare your asset statements (as described in Chapter 4). They can also help you recall examples of your accomplishments to discuss in interviews. Some people need an objective third party to point out their positive qualities or to recognize their achievements, so consulting people who know them well is key before interviewing.

Networking is also useful in the research stage. As you'll see in Chapter 3, preparing for interviews requires more than reading a company's annual report and glancing at their Web site. You have to talk to colleagues, friends, and family to find out what they know about your target employers. And getting the inside scoop on your target employers is just one benefit of networking. You might also find that someone you know—or can get to know—knows someone at the place where you'll be interviewing. Being able to drop a relevant, respected name during an interview is a sure way to jump to the head of the class of applicants (as long as the name-dropping is not done in a pompous manner).

Your network can also serve as a useful sounding board during the job search. There are invariably times when you have questions about when and how to follow up after an interview or about whether to accept an offer. Having input from others can help you make good decisions.

Pitfalls to Avoid in Interviewing: the Runners-Up

The five mistakes described up to this point are the big ones. Being aware of them and employing the strategies I recommended for avoiding them (here and in the chapters that take them up more specifically) enables you to adapt successfully to most any interview situation. There are, however, plenty of additional pitfalls to avoid—and these are discussed in this section. While these aren't quite on the macro level of the previous five, they are serious matters that require your vigilance. As with the other mistakes, strategies for dealing with these remaining pitfalls are offered here briefly and then elaborated on in subsequent chapters.

Not Having Your Act Together

Your behavior during an interview—and during pre- and post-interview interactions—is a reflection of how you might conduct yourself on the job. Besides your resume, references, and account of your accomplishments, a recruiter must rely on observations of your behavior as an indicator of how you'll act on the job. You'd better have your act together during all encounters with a prospective employer.

"Having your act together" implies having a professional air about you and a professional approach to tasks. Be aware, however, that "professional" means different things to different target employers. The term usually brings to mind an image of pinstripe suits and a buttoned-down attitude, which is not always the norm as many workplaces become increasingly casual in both dress code and atmosphere. I discuss this issue of professionalism more in Chapter 3 and Chapter 6, "Presenting the Right

Moneysaver
If you have trouble getting and keeping your act together and are currently employed, ask your human resources department if your company can pay for you to attend any seminars on time management and organization.

Image," so for now just keep in mind that the term "professional" describes behavior that is appropriate for a given target employer rather than referring to a narrowly defined standard.

Some of the ways to convey that you have your act together include being organized and punctual and following through on tasks. Gaining entry to a prospective employer, completing the interview process, and negotiating the terms of employment are like any business transaction. Documents are faxed and mailed, e-mails are sent, appointments are set, and loose ends must be attended to. For example, you may have an initial screening interview by phone and promise to fax a resume after that conversation. Or, you might have an on-site interview and have to follow up with additional information such as a college or graduate school transcript, phone numbers of your references, or a sample of your work. If you are late in doing any of these things, or if you don't do them at all, you seriously jeopardize your candidacy.

Not having your act together is not only inconvenient and annoying for the prospective employer, but it also has implications for how you could handle the job in question. Many workplaces these days are busier than ever, requiring employees to handle multiple tasks and engage in long-range planning, not just put out fires as they erupt. If you can't handle the relatively simple challenges of the job search, what message are you sending employers about your ability to handle the job itself?

Letting the Stress Get to You

"Never let 'em see you sweat" is an expression that certainly applies to interviewing. As with "not having your act together," showing your nerves or hinting that you're buckling under pressure raises a red flag with prospective employers. While some degree of nervousness is normal, getting obviously rattled is simply not acceptable. Employers want to hire people who can think clearly when the going gets tough and who can remain rational at all times.

Chapter 5 deals with ways to offset nerves before they get the best of you.

Not Researching Your Target Employers

You can't have a strategy for your interview if you don't know the prospective employer's needs. As stated previously, you must think from the perspective of the employer, considering his or her needs and wants, not just yours. The only way to understand that perspective is through research.

Sometimes a job description gives some clue to those needs. An ad or listing that reads "Seeking a self-starter with five years managerial experience to oversee the development of a new West Coast sales territory" makes it clear that the company is looking to grow and is seeking management skills, knowledge of sales and business development, and a go-getter personality. The problem with knowing only that much, though, is that all the other applicants for that job have the same information.

To distinguish yourself from the crowd, you must dig deeper to uncover what is going on at a particular organization and to see how you might be able to help them solve problems and achieve goals. You need to use a variety of print, online, and people resources to do so. We all have more information accessible to us than ever from all three of those sources, so the ante has been upped when it comes to research. You must assume that other candidates will be conducting extensive research prior to an

> 66
> Today's organizations face simultaneous, unpredictable changes in many domains— technological, economic, regulatory, social, and political. They need employees who can not only cope with these changes, but respond to them in an innovative fashion. Employers want candidates who will flourish, not wilt, under stress.
>
> —Lori Rosenkopf, Wharton School of Business
> 99

Unofficially...
Many recruiters
and hiring man-
agers don't have
time to keep up
with develop-
ments at their
own organiza-
tion, so making
even a small
extra effort in
your research
can impress
interviewers with
information they
themselves didn't
have (as long as
you do so in a
subtle way that
doesn't make
them feel
foolish).

interview to keep up with the competition. For that reason—and because many job seekers don't know where to begin such research or when to stop—Chapter 3 of this book is devoted entirely to that subject.

Showing a Flat Demeanor

The success of that pop culture item, the little yellow smiley face, over the past 30 years or so is a testament to the power of positive expression. I once worked with a client who was having a tough time finding a job despite excellent qualifications. After doing a little trouble shooting to identify any problems with her strategy, I realized her problem was simple. She rarely smiled. I had her start concentrating on smiling as she walked into each interview—not a phony, Cheshire Cat grin, but just a pleasant expression with the corners of her mouth slightly upturned. From that point on, she started getting call-backs from first interviews, and the dramatic turnaround seemed more than a coincidence.

If you don't radiate enthusiasm and energy, then the interviewer is not likely to take much interest in you. I'm sure you've heard a million times that enthusiasm is contagious. Well, that old adage is particularly applicable to interviews. If you forget to smile, or if you speak in a monotone voice, sound tired, or walk slowly or with slouched posture, you'll turn off the interviewer immediately. No matter how well you've prepared for an interview, and no matter how effectively you communicate who you are, a flat demeanor can negate all your hard work.

Using Poor Communication Skills

Related to the importance of demeanor is the idea that your communication skills can make or break your success. If you don't speak and write clearly with proper grammar and syntax, no one will pay attention to what you're saying because they'll be too distracted by how you're saying it. This particular problem is a tough one to deal with, not because the solutions to it are difficult, but because most people don't even realize they have a problem. If you are a poor writer or an inarticulate speaker, chances are that no one has had the nerve to tell you so. You must take it upon yourself to determine whether there is a problem—and then to fix it. Chapter 6, "Presenting the Right Image," discusses how to find out whether your written materials for the job search are holding you back and to find ways to improve them. Chapter 7 then addresses the issue of oral communication.

Wearing Sloppy or Inappropriate Dress

Whether you like it or not, your appearance has an enormous impact on how you are perceived. As with poor communication skills, no matter what you say or how well qualified you are, a sloppy or inappropriate appearance will lead the interviewer to reject you immediately. Chapter 6 deals with the issue of attire and grooming in more detail. For now, be aware that, even if you're not typically concerned about your appearance or are interested in clothes, you must pay special attention to them when interviewing.

Not Following Up and Following Through

Maintaining contact with the prospective employer until you get to an answer of yes, no, or maybe is your responsibility. Time and again, I hear job-seekers say, "I had an interview with XYZ company a few weeks ago and wrote a thank-you note right

Moneysaver
To save money on interviewing clothes but still look polished, choose just two basic, core outfits (most likely suits). You'll get more mileage out of them by varying the ties, shirts, or accessories you wear with them.

Timesaver
Before you leave an interview, ask how many more people are to be interviewed, when a decision is likely to be made, and when you may follow up. That way, you'll know what you're dealing with and won't waste time following up too soon—or lose time checking in too late.

away, but I haven't heard back, so I guess nothing's going to happen there." Not necessarily. You don't know until you follow up and find out what's going on. The passive approach of sitting back and waiting to hear won't get you anywhere. Just as I advocate taking control during an interview, you should maintain some control after an interview as well. Chapter 13 offers many suggestions for ways to follow up appropriately and effectively, and to manage the tricky issue of keeping in touch without being a pest.

Not Practicing, or Over-rehearsing

If you think you can wing it when it comes to interviewing, think again. Interviewing effectively is like speaking a foreign language fluently. You will find yourself talking about your experience, strengths, and goals in ways that you probably don't do in the course of a routine day. The only way to speak a new language effortlessly is to practice it.

To be a proficient interviewer, you not only must prepare what you are going to say and how you'll conduct yourself while saying it, but you also need to practice. Whether you simply practice your replies out loud (perhaps in front of a mirror) or formally in a videotaped mock interview, you must simulate the interview process in some way before it actually takes place.

It is important, however, that you not go overboard with your practice and turn it into a rehearsal. Practicing implies that you are simply getting used to some of the communication and behavior that might be needed in an interview. Rehearsal implies that you have a script to memorize and an act to perform. Remember that an interview is not a theatrical production. Be yourself. If you write scripts for your replies to anticipated questions and rehearse reciting them verbatim, you'll not only get rattled when the interview doesn't go the way you had expected, but you also will come across as robotic or insincere.

Not Listening

You'd be amazed at how many people lose out on jobs because they didn't listen. They either flubbed responses to questions because they simply didn't listen carefully to what was being asked, or they alienated the interviewer by seeming detached or self-absorbed. Listening attentively is critical to your success. Only then can you pick up on interviewers' needs, answer questions effectively, and come across as focused and engaged. When asked if they're good listeners, most people say that they are, when, in fact, they're not. Listening is not just waiting for your turn to speak. It means really hearing what is being said. Listening is discussed more in Chapter 7.

Missing Important Personality Cues

In addition to listening to what the interviewer is saying, you must listen to nonverbal communication as well. Body language and personality style provide clues to who the interviewer is and how you are being received. Half the battle in interviewing is to get along well with the people you meet, so picking up on nonverbal cues is essential. Doing so helps you avoid personality clashes and moves you one step closer to acing the interview. Ways to address this issue are suggested in Chapters 6 and 7.

Being Negative

No one likes a whiner, or someone who even hints at being negative, angry, or bitter. If you've had a nightmare boss, a dull job, a rocky career, financial woes, or personal problems, you cannot bring them

Watch Out!
A sure sign that you're not listening to the interviewer is when you lose eye contact. While you shouldn't stare down the other person, do make sure that your eyes don't drift away too often. Otherwise you'll look like you're bored or not paying attention.

into the interview. Discussing an unpleasant experience or saying anything negative about a person or organization may seem harmless enough when all you think you're doing is telling the truth. What happens, however, is that negativism can mushroom in the mind of the interviewer, leading you to be perceived as someone who can't get along with people or who is plagued by failures. As you'll see in Chapter 7, the power of language is such that one seemingly innocuous word or phrase can be received by the listener as a major red flag.

Nonetheless, it is true that there are times when you have no choice but to tell the truth about a personality clash with a former boss, a job that didn't work out, or a business of yours that failed. If you must do so, certain techniques enable you to balance the negatives with more positive information so that you don't sabotage the interview. Such methods are described in Chapter 12.

Lacking Confidence

Interviewing can be tough on the ego. You're being judged, evaluated, and, at times, rejected or ignored. Doubts about your qualifications or uncertainty about how to promote yourself can shatter even the steadiest confidence levels. This problem not only puts you on an emotional roller-coaster, but it also shows through during interviews and interferes with your ability to be seen as a strong candidate. Everything from your handshake and posture to your way of speaking and the content of what you say conveys your level of confidence.

If you expect the interviewer to have enough confidence in you to hire you, then you must show that you have confidence in yourself. Being well-prepared for interviews is one way to feel better about yourself and your abilities. Also compile asset statements, address gaps in your qualifications (see Chapter 4), and develop an understanding of the psychology of interviewing (see Chapter 5).

Being Insensitive to Diversity Matters

Cultural diversity is a much touted buzzword of the '90s—so much so, in fact, that I expect some of you to roll your eyes at the sound of it. When it comes to interviewing, however, being sensitive to the world view of others is not just giving in to the political correctness fad; it is simply good old-fashioned tact.

In the course of a job search, you will undoubtedly come across people who are different from you in some significant way, or who make reference to coworkers or others who also happen to be culturally different. While few professionals these days are so ignorant and provincial as to make blatant slurs toward people of other groups, many do display cultural insensitivity without even realizing it. Chapter 7 discusses ways to recognize and address your weaknesses in this area.

Lying

I shouldn't even have to say it, but I will. Never lie in an interview! You will most likely get caught—and even if you aren't, you'll have to live with the lie throughout your career. Enough said.

Accepting an Offer Too Quickly

Rarely is a job offer extended on the spot in a first interview, but when it is, you may be caught off guard and tempted to take it. Doing so can be a mistake because, like any big decision in life, you need time to weigh your options and often need more information. The same is true if you are offered a position after a lengthy evaluation process. You may

Unofficially...
Cultural insensitivity can be expressed in more subtle ways than the blatant racist or sexist joke. For example, personal space—the distance between people that must be maintained for comfortable interaction—is defined quite differently across cultures. Violation of that space, even unintended, can seem intrusive or oppressive to others around you.

be tempted to accept the offer right away just to get the ordeal over with, but this, too, can be a mistake. You need to take a step back—whether for hours, days, or weeks depending on the employer's time frame—and carefully study the offer. You also owe it to yourself to negotiate favorable terms of employment, such as salary, title, responsibilities, and other factors. Evaluating and negotiating offers—including determining how quickly is too quickly to give an answer—is the focus of Chapter 14, "Evaluating and Negotiating Offers."

Developing a Strategy that Steers Clear of the Pitfalls

The common mistakes outlined in this chapter should give you a sense of what to avoid and the tactics for success in interviewing. To help you implement these suggestions, I've summarized the steps in interviewing strategy into a checklist, which I recommend you consult frequently during your job search to keep you on track.

1. Conduct research to determine the employer's needs.

2. Identify your assets and prepare memorable, distinctive, and specific accounts of experiences that demonstrate those assets.

3. Develop an attitude in which you are confident, forthright, and cognizant of the power you have to direct the course and outcome of the interview.

4. Attend to your appearance, making sure you are dressed appropriately and are well-groomed.

5. Concentrate on projecting enthusiasm, energy, and interest.

6. Identify any flaws in your oral and written communication style, and take steps to correct them.

7. Seek feedback from your network about your personal presentation, and seek input on your target employers.

8. Make a concerted effort to be organized, punctual, and efficient in all your job search logistics.

9. Learn how to be a good listener.

10. Plan what you are going to say in interviews (how you'll answer anticipated questions), and practice—but don't over-script or over-rehearse.

11. Be prepared to put a positive—but not dishonest—spin on any negatives in your background.

12. Address any gaps in your knowledge of cultural diversity issues and discrimination laws.

13. Follow up politely but persistently after interviews rather than passively waiting to hear the outcome.

14. Make a promise to yourself that you will take the time to evaluate carefully any offers that are extended to you.

15. Relax and be yourself!

Just the Facts

- Effective interviewing requires a strategy based on guiding principles that dictate your behavior no matter what form the interview takes.

- Rather than seeing yourself as powerless in an interview, operate from a position of strength, maintain an equal balance of power, don't act desperate for a job, and follow up until you get an answer.

- Establishing and consulting with a network of friends, family, and professional colleagues enhances your interview preparation and process.

- Lying, displaying cultural insensitivity, and being negative seriously jeopardize your candidacy.

- A successful and manageable interview strategy follows a logical, step-by-step process.

What to Do Before the Interview

GET THE SCOOP ON...
The importance of pre-interview research ▪
Determining the employer's needs ▪
Avoiding wild goose chases ▪ Conversation
topics for your interview ▪ Keeping track
of research information

PART II

Research: The Root of All Strategy

Chapter 3

I t probably comes as no surprise that an important first step in preparing for an interview is to do some research. You wouldn't dream of going into the interview cold, without knowing at least a little something about the prospective employer, right? Well, before you assume that you know all there is to know about pre-interview research and decide to skip over this chapter, consider whether you really know how *much* information you need to gather and how to *use* that knowledge strategically.

Most job-seekers don't have the time or patience for more than a cursory glance through a prospective employer's annual report or Web site. Such corner-cutting can have unfortunate consequences. I can't begin to count the number of times clients have reported to me that they received a job offer simply because they impressed the interviewer with some seemingly trivial bit of knowledge that showed they had done their homework beyond the basics. In fact, you're more likely to ace the interview

> **"** With the revolution in career and business resource collections, job seekers have access to more information more easily than ever before. Research is vital to speaking intelligently during interviews and to keeping up with the competition.
> —Georgia Donati, Career Resource Consultant and former Director, New York Public Library Job Information Center **"**

knowing where the interviewer went to college or what type of community service the company's employees do than with recitations of obscure financial statistics from the annual report.

This chapter shows you how to research strategically so you won't waste your time chasing down useless information—and so that the information you do obtain will help you answer those three critical questions discussed in Chapter 1, "How Hiring Decisions Are Made": Can you do the job? Will you fit in? Do you want the job? With thorough research, you can set yourself apart from competitors who are likely to have done only the basic homework.

Six Degrees of Information

Almost everyone else interviewing for the job you want will know whether the prospective employer makes widgets or Web sites, is expanding or shrinking, and is global or local. To distinguish yourself as the best candidate for the job, you need to be conversant on a broader range of topics that are both directly and tangentially related to the job. A thorough pre-interview research process involves gathering information in the following six areas:

- Information about the organization itself
- The nature and responsibilities of the job
- Biographical data about the interviewer(s)
- The nature of the profession or occupation
- Trends in the industry or sector
- Current events and general interest areas

Each of these six areas is explained in more depth on the pages that follow.

What You Need to Know About the Prospective Employer

At a minimum, you need to know what the prospective employer's products or services are, where their offices or branches are located, how long they have been in existence, how the organization is structured in terms of divisions and areas, and who the top management is. But you can set yourself apart from the pack by digging a bit deeper to find out a little about these topics:

- The corporate culture
- Characteristics valued in employees
- The organization's goals and vision for the future
- Projected areas of growth and expansion
- Difficulties facing the organization

As I've mentioned before, when you go into an interview, you are not a job candidate but a potential problem-solver and contributor. To show that you could be effective in those areas, you must get at the heart of the employer's needs. What problems do they need solved? What new contributions could they use? In what areas do they need innovation and a new way of thinking? What are they looking for in the way of personnel? Fresh faces or established, proven types? Independent thinkers? People with contacts, or specific areas of expertise? Entrepreneurs or intrapreneurs? Only when you know the answers to these questions can you position yourself strategically.

What Does the Job Itself Entail?

To interview strategically, you must know as much as possible about what the job entails and requires. Of all the research areas, this is the one to which you're

Watch Out!
Research takes time! You'll need anywhere from a couple of hours to a couple of days to conduct sufficient research for each interview. Keep this in mind when scheduling an interview, and allow ample time before your appointment to visit the library, browse the Internet, or call your contacts.

most likely to find answers during the interview instead of before it. The job of a marketing executive at Coca-Cola, for example, differs somewhat from that of a marketing executive at Pepsi, so even if you are a seasoned marketing professional, you won't fully know the ins and outs of the job until you get to the interview.

That said, you should, at the very least, know what your target position would typically entail. You need to know what the usual job responsibilities are, what qualifications are needed, where this job fits into a departmental and organizational structure, and what a typical compensation package includes. Many of the resources in the section "Who Has the Information You Need" are good sources of such data.

Watch Out!
Knowing about the job itself is particularly important if you are new to the work world or are transitioning into a different career field. You have to convince the interviewer that you know what you're getting into. You also need to link your transferable skills to those needed on the job, and you can't do that effectively without knowing what the job entails.

Beyond those basics, you should make the effort to find out what you can about the specific position at the organization where you'll be interviewing. You may be able to determine some of the following key points:

- Who previously held the job, and why he or she left (or is leaving)
- To whom you would report if you held the position
- Whom you would supervise in that job
- Which other departments or offices you would interact with
- Which skills and personal qualities are needed for success on the job
- The biggest challenges of the job

To find answers to these questions, you'll need to turn to your network to track down any current or former employees of that organization, as well their clients, customers, or vendors. Tips on developing your network are discussed later in this chapter.

Who Is the Individual Interviewer?

As discussed in Chapter 1, an interview is essentially a conversation between two human beings. Employers don't hire resumes, and they don't hire robots. The more you come across as a colleague, a peer, or even a potential friend—not as some anonymous job-seeker—the more comfortable the interviewer will feel with you.

It's ideal if you can discover something you have in common with the interviewer to address the issue of how you'll fit in the organization or the department. You need to find out about the interviewer's educational background, past work experience, professional interests, hobbies, family, geographic background, and any pet causes or charities. It also doesn't hurt to have some inkling of interviewers' religious affiliations and political leanings so you can avoid putting your foot in your mouth in case those subjects come up. (Except in special cases, you should never raise the topic of religion or politics in an interview; you'll find more advice on this point in Chapter 7, "Strategic Communication for Interviews.")

Even if you find that you don't have much, if anything, in common with the interviewer, you will at least get a sense of his or her interests, values, and personal style so that you can conduct yourself accordingly.

What's Happening in the Profession?

A common pitfall when preparing for an interview is concentrating all your research efforts on the organization itself and the individual interviewer(s), forgetting about the big-picture context.

Bright Idea
Whenever possible, obtain the bios of people who will be interviewing you. You can request a bio through the interviewers' administrative assistants or the organization's public relations department. In addition, some of the books listed in Appendix C include biographical data on the key players in various organizations.

That context is the overall career field or profession in which the position could be categorized, as well as the overall industry or sector of which the position or organization is a part. (The latter is discussed in greater detail in the section "What's Happening in the Industry or Sector," later in this chapter.)

Being a savvy, visible member of your profession is a real plus when you're being evaluated by most any type of organization. Awareness of trends and developments in your career field and contact with people from comparable organizations enables you to bring innovation and knowledge to your new employer.

Watch Out!
If you are interviewing for jobs in a career field or industry in which you've never worked, pay special attention to the jargon of that field as you do your research. Speaking the "language" of your new occupation will help you sound more like an insider during the interview.

This area of research is especially important if you are attempting to make the transition into a new career field. In that case, you have to prove that you know what you're getting into. Most career-changers focus on identifying their transferable skills so they can convince prospective employers that they can do the job, even if they haven't done that exact kind of job before. What they often forget to do is to convince the employer that they really know what they're getting into. If you can show that you have learned what there is to know about being in marketing, sales, banking, not-for-profit management, or whatever, then the prospective employer will have more confidence in your ability to make the transition. You must be able to discuss typical career paths, trends in the field, and skills needed to be a success. You should also be able to do a little name-dropping of people and places you've come across through attending conferences, meetings, and educational seminars or lectures. It's all about sounding like an insider before you even get inside.

What's Happening in the Industry or Sector?

Following the news of the overall industry (finance, real estate, health care, or media, for example) or sector (such as corporate, not-for-profit, or government) also shows that you can add value to the organization. You need to know who has merged with whom, how the economy is affecting a particular product or service, who the major players are, and what the significant trends are.

This research is particularly important for higher-level managers and professionals whose interviews are not so much an interrogation as a conversation between peers. Just as you might discuss general current events at a cocktail party, you need to be up to speed on current events in your industry for the sophisticated conversation that will take place in your interviews.

A useful checklist of tasks to accomplish before each interview follows:

- Read the current and past three issues of any relevant trade and professional association journals, newsletters, or magazines.

- Read the current and past two issues of magazines such as *U.S. News and World Report*, *Newsweek*, and *Time*, as well as any specialized periodicals relevant to your field.

- Read your local daily newspaper, as well as a major city newspaper such as the *New York Times* or *Chicago Tribune* if you do not live in a major metropolitan area.

- If possible, attend a trade or professional association meeting or other informative event that would give you insight into economic, political, social, or intellectual issues related to your line of work.

- Have a conversation with at least one of the most savvy members of your network to get the latest inside scoop on what's happening in the industry in which you work (or wish to work).

Current Events and General Interest Areas

Being up-to-date on what's happening in the world at large and having a range of personal interests will make you a more effective interviewee. You should never go into an interview without having read that morning's paper, and, if possible, tuned into a 24-hour cable news show for a last-minute report just before your appointment.

Timesaver
Some Internet service providers (America Online or CompuServe, for example) have a handy feature that enables you to design your own newspaper that appears on your screen each time you log on. You choose the type of news that interests you and can select the publications from which your news is pulled. It's a very convenient way to get all the news you need in a hurry.

You should also make every effort to remain active in your hobbies and interests. A job-seeker who does nothing but read the classifieds and go on interviews makes for a boring candidate. As much as your schedule and financial situation permit, you should go to an occasional movie, read a novel, or do whatever it is that you would be doing if you didn't have to worry about your career. I know of a woman named Linda who was interviewing with the head of a major search firm to be his executive assistant. When he asked what she does with her time when not working, she replied that she sings some weekends in a Dixieland jazz band. Well, it turned out that he spends his weekends as the drummer in a Dixieland jazz band. Now, this coincidence is one of those rare ones job-seekers dream about, but even if the interviewer doesn't share your hobby, you'll at least have something interesting to talk about if you're involved in interesting pursuits. Oh, and Linda got the job, of course.

If your research into the individual interviewer turned up any valuable information about hobbies and interests, then you'll know which current events to focus on. If your interviewer is into tennis, and your appointment is around the time of the U.S. Open or Wimbledon, then don't even think of going to the interview without knowing who's winning, who's losing, and whose backhand is better this year. Even if you don't know what your interviewer is interested in, knowing at least a little bit about current events in sports, film, literature, the arts, finance, and politics will help you hedge your bets.

Who Has the Information You Need

For the most part, the information you need to collect in the six areas just described is easily accessible. With minimal effort, you can uncover the basic things you need to know—but with just a little more perseverance and resourcefulness, you can acquire knowledge that will dazzle the interviewer. You can gain that knowledge from a combination of print, electronic, and people resources found through the prospective employer, professional associations, the Internet and World Wide Web, libraries, bookstores, college and university career offices, and your network of contacts.

The Organization Itself

While not exactly an unbiased source, the organization with which you'll be interviewing is a good place to start for some basic information. Depending on the size and nature of the prospective employer, the company may be able to supply you with reports, brochures, and other printed literature that will give you a sense of what that organization is all about. Typical publications include the annual report, shareholders' or development reports, and promotional literature used for public relations purposes.

Moneysaver
Staying on top of news in everything from sports, to film, to business, to politics can get expensive if you have to subscribe to or frequently purchase copies of magazines and newspapers. Instead, consider reading the publications in their online version. And there's always the periodicals room of your local library.

Watch Out!
The glossy pages of annual reports are not objective sources of information on an organization's fiscal health, growth, and stability. They are written with an eye toward presenting the rosiest picture possible for clients, consumers, competitors, and investors. Take them with a grain of salt, and be sure to consult additional sources to obtain a balanced picture.

Don't stop there, though. Most job-seekers are not aware that many large corporations (and some not-so-large companies and non-profit organizations), have surprisingly elaborate recruitment information packets written specifically for job-seekers. These describe typical jobs and career paths within the company and often provide much more useful information than the rather dry facts and figures presented in the annual report. If you've ever participated in an on-campus recruiting program as a college senior or graduate student, you're no doubt familiar with such publications, as they are usually kept on file in college and university career placement offices. If you've long since graduated, check with the placement office of your alma mater(s) to see whether you can have access to those files.

Also try to get your hands on any in-house publications, such as the employee newsletter. Newsletters give you great insight into the organization's culture and offer clues to handy conversation topics for the interview. For example, you might connect with the interviewer by mentioning recent events such as the company's softball game win over a major competitor, or the fact that the head of the accounting department just became a grandfather. Armed with the inside scoop from the employee newsletter, you'll sound like you already work there, not like a job-hunter.

Where you'll find all of this information is usually through the public relations, community affairs, corporate communications, and human resources departments. If you already have an interview scheduled, you can ask the administrative assistant of the person who will be interviewing you to send a packet of information, or to direct you to the appropriate department to make the request. And, of course, you should visit the organization's Web site, where much of this information will be readily available.

Professional Associations

If you are already participating in professional or trade associations for general networking purposes, then you're aware of the value of such groups for developing your career. In addition to being a good source of job leads, professional associations are quite useful during the research phase of your interview preparations. Their print materials, Web sites, and meetings or conferences can provide insight into developments and trends in your profession, career field, or industry. Whether or not you join a particular group, you can at least receive their introductory membership packet, which gives you an overview of the association as well as some limited information about that profession as a whole.

To dig deeper, however, you must be a frequent visitor to the association's Web site to see which issues are being discussed and to interact with other members online. You should also attend face-to-face events whenever possible. The ideas, innovations, and problems discussed at conferences, regular meetings, seminars, and social gatherings are the sorts of things you should be discussing in your interviews.

Online Sources

The Internet is an obvious and convenient place to conduct your research. With its endless stores of data and frequently updated material (in most cases), the Internet and World Wide Web are likely to be your best sources. That same vast scope, however, can also make them your most frustrating sources.

Bright Idea
When requesting information from a company's human resources or public relations department, you may feel the need to do so anonymously, as if your request were something to hide. On the contrary, asking for their literature shows initiative and genuine interest in working for them, so let them know why you need it. Doing so will also help ensure that they send you the right materials.

Moneysaver
Membership dues in professional associations are often steep, but you can sometimes attend association meetings as a guest at no charge or for a nominal meeting fee. Inquire about such arrangements through the association's administrative office or, better yet, track down a member who might let you tag along to the next meeting.

The key to efficient and productive online searches prior to interviews is to use shortcuts that keep the overwhelming amount of online information manageable and accessible. Bookmarking important sites, using multiple terms instead of single words for keyword searches, and using links set up on sites you already know about to connect with more information are just three ways to save time and effort. Now, if you're conducting a keyword search and don't know the difference between Boolean logic and bowling, then you probably need to turn to the books recommended in the "Internet" section of Appendix C for help with the basics of researching on the Internet.

Assuming you've mastered the basics of navigating the Net, your next challenge is to figure out where to begin your research and how far to go. The following are seven steps for effective online research when preparing for an interview:

1. Start by looking up the Web site of the organization where you'll be interviewing (assuming they have one). The easiest way to get the online address is simply by asking someone at the company. If you can't do that for any reason, then do a keyword search by typing in the organization's name and having a search engine (a portal to the Internet, such as Excite, InfoSeek, or Yahoo) pull up all references to that organization. If you get too many matches to your keyword, refine your search a bit by re-entering the company name, preceded by "www." That way, you'll be more likely to call up the company's actual Web address, not just sites that mention the company name.

2. Conduct a keyword search (as described in step 1) to find any media coverage or other references to the organization itself.

3. In addition to step 2—or as an alternative—you can go directly to the sites of magazines and newspapers that relate to the field or industry in which you're interviewing. Search their archives for recent and past articles that feature the organization where you'll be interviewing, the people you'll be meeting, and any other relevant topics.

4. Visit the Web sites of trade and professional associations relevant to the field in which you work or wish to work. Look for news, trends, and events in your occupation or profession, as well as for opportunities to interact with members.

5. Browse the articles and message boards of career-related Web sites to find tips on interviewing techniques, profiles of career fields or industries, and occasionally even employer profiles.

6. Look up online databases that provide data on private sector companies and non-profit organizations. (See the "Researching Organizations and Industries" section of Appendix C for examples.) Many of these are the electronic version of standard reference books from companies such as *Standard & Poors, Dun & Bradstreet, Hoover's,* and others.

7. Join newsgroups that address topics related to your job search and profession.

Timesaver
It can be time-consuming to check numerous Web sites on a regular basis for new postings or events, even if you have them bookmarked. To save time, see whether the sites offer a service that sends you an email message or electronic newsletter alerting you to new postings or events on the site. You then will know if it's worth your time to visit the actual site.

Libraries

If you haven't done any job search-related research in a while, you might be planning to stop by your local public library, thumb through a hefty business directory to read about a particular company, then call it a day. Well, are you ever in for a surprise! If you venture into one of the newer, high-tech libraries, you're likely to ask, "Where are the books?"

In New York City, for example, I send my clients to the impressive Science, Industry, and Business Library (SIBL), which is part of the public library system. There they find every database, print directory, and CD-ROM they could ever need to research any person, place, or thing.

You may also have access to a branch of the public library with a Job Information Center (JIC), a special section of the library with an extensive career resource collection. Many public libraries around the country house specialized collections like a JIC or SIBL, so check with your local library's main branch to see where you might find such resources. And, of course, don't forget that you can also conduct effective research at a business library within a college or university, and that you can access many libraries on the Internet.

These are among the helpful resources you might find at the library:

- Free access to the Internet, possibly including access to fee-based database services at no charge

- Directories (print and CD-ROM versions) listing businesses of various sizes, with some basic data on each organization

- Professional association journals

- Current and back issues of magazines and newspapers

Moneysaver
If you're not a member of a particular professional association but wish to read their journal or magazine, you can purchase a subscription. These can be expensive, however, so before writing that check, look for the publications you need in your local public or university library.

Bookstores

Some of the information you would find in libraries is also available in the career or business section of bookstores. The important issue here is to know what is worth spending your money on and what you should use for free at a library or online. Most of the business directories you might need to use are expensive reference books best perused in the library or electronically rather than purchasing. In fact, they are rarely even sold at the average neighborhood bookstore.

Instead, you might want to purchase books that describe the career field or profession in which you wish to work. These can help you identify the areas of your experience that you should highlight in the interview (as discussed in Chapter 4, "Making Yourself the Top Candidate,") and can provide valuable salary information to use in your negotiations. Books such as these that give overviews of various fields are listed in the "Career Planning" and "Researching Occupations" sections of Appendix C.

College and University Career Offices

The career counseling or placement office of the college or graduate school you attended (or currently attend) is a good place to find many of the same resources available in public libraries and bookstores. One advantage of conducting some of your research on campus is that the person who will be showing you around the career and business resources will most likely be not only a reference librarian but also a trained career counselor.

Useful resources found in most campus career offices include the following:

- Recruitment information packets describing career opportunities in various companies as part of the on-campus recruiting files

Bright Idea
Books on the lives and careers of prominent people in your profession offer insight into historic or contemporary issues in that field, as well as handy trivia to bring up in interviews. Founders of companies, captains of industry, and leaders in science and technology are often profiled in biographies or have written their own memoirs.(See the "Biographies and Corporate Profiles" section of Appendix C.)

Timesaver
Avoid showing up unannounced at your local university's business school library or career planning office assuming you can use their resources. Instead, call the career planning office of your alma mater and ask whether they have a reciprocity agreement with any colleges or universities in your area. They can often request permission for you to use that school's career information resources.

- Names and contact information of alumni who could speak with you for information in any of the six areas of your research
- Career counselors who may also know about certain companies, recruiters, career fields, jobs, or industries
- A career resource library with many of the books and directories described earlier in this chapter
- Possible access to the Internet or online databases

Your Network

In addition to print and online resources, real people are an important source of information at this stage of your interview preparation. (Recommended books on developing and interacting with a network of contacts are listed in the "Networking" section of Appendix C.) Your current and past professional colleagues, family, friends, professors, and fellow alumni of your alma mater(s) may know something about the places where you'll be interviewing or the people you'll be meeting.

It's important to go beyond the basics, however, and consult with the sorts of people who, by virtue of their own positions, are likely to have in-depth or cutting-edge knowledge of key people, places, professions, and industries. Such people can include: stock brokers, accountants, and financial analysts; consultants (particularly management consultants); attorneys and investment bankers; Better Business Bureaus and Chambers of Commerce; regulatory agencies with which companies must make public filings; journalists; and scholars.

To make the best use of networking, do the print and online research first before contacting people. That way, you'll know where the gaps in your knowledge are and will have focused questions to ask.

Researching the Hard to Research

Not all of your target employers will have thousands of citations on the Web, slick brochures describing the exciting career opportunities they offer, and a staff that fills the pages of *Who's Who*. Small businesses, some non-profits, individual entrepreneurs, and privately held companies can be difficult to research.

In those cases, you need to be persistent and resourceful in your research efforts. You must have faith that the information you need does exist and that if you keep digging, you will unearth it. Now is the time to turn to reference librarians and other information specialists who are trained in obtaining data that's hard to find. They can point you toward useful resources such as the *Inc Magazine 1000, Directory of Leading Private Companies*, and *Directories in Print*.

This is also a situation that calls for more networking than book research. Think of who might do business with or otherwise know about the organization from which you need information. For example, foundation officers and grant writers would know about not-for-profit organizations. Small Business Administration staff might be familiar with a certain small business you're researching. And, certainly the Internet is a useful way to cast a wide net for the information you need.

Bright Idea
Even if you're going on an interview that you arranged on your own, headhunters might be willing to tell you what they know about the place you'll be going. You can then get back to them after the interview with valuable information about what's happening at that organization.

Watch Out!
When networking for information on the Internet, remember that you may not be as anonymous as you think. If you need to keep your job search confidential, be extra careful when venturing into chat rooms or posting on message or bulletin boards. You might not recognize the personal screen name for your boss or nosy coworker, but they may recognize yours.

What to Do With the Information You Collect

All the research in the world is useless if your results come in the form of random notes on scratch paper, vague recollections of phone conversations, and file folders too stuffed to wade through before an interview. You'll make your life easier and will be more successful in your meetings if you take the vast amounts of information you collect and put them in a format that is easily accessible and quickly scanned. Before that, however, you need to know when to stop researching so that you don't end up wasting your time chasing down unnecessary information.

Knowing When to Stop

When preparing for an interview, you may wonder how much research is enough and how much is too much. Do you need to be able to recite every statistic in the organization's annual report? Do you really have to know where the daughter of the company's CFO attends college? Maybe, but maybe not. Research is important, but you don't need to go overboard. You will find yourself overwhelmed if you try to memorize too many facts and figures or stay on top of too many subjects. Plus, nobody likes a show-off; the interviewer will just want to see that you are reasonably well-informed, not a walking encyclopedia.

The suggestions presented in this section are just that—suggestions. The key is to strike a balance between conducting thorough research and also devoting enough time to the other tasks of your job search. If you feel that the knowledge you have gained is reliable, accurate, up-to-date, and

WORKSHEET 2.1: INFORMATION GEMS

Organization name: Year Established:

Interviewer(s) name and title:

Products/services:

Office/branch locations:

CEO or director:

Other key managers/officers:

Organizational culture/style/philosophy:

Goals/vision:

Growth areas:

Problem areas:

Skills/expertise/personality needed for the job:

Interviewer's biographical data:

Profession or industry developments:

Current events/news:

Best book I've read lately:

Best film/theatrical production I've seen lately:

Personal interests/hobbies worth mentioning:

← Note!
Don't list every piece of information you've collected. Just put down the key points, especially those that other candidates may not have uncovered.

Bright Idea
To gain some insight into the employer's perspective and get a jump on the competition, visit the Web sites that human resources recruiters and headhunters frequent. Some of these are listed in Appendix B.

unbiased (or at least reflects a variety of opinions), then you have probably done enough.

Organizing/Note-Taking

To distill the information you collect down to a manageable amount and accessible format, complete a form such as the sample in Worksheet 2.1 for each interview, and review it before every appointment. This form is called "Information Gems" because it should contain only those data bits that will help you dazzle the interviewer with your knowledge.

Just the Facts

- Don't just research the organization where you'll be interviewing. Research the position itself, the interviewer(s), the overall career field, and the industry or sector.

- Never rely solely on the usual sources such as annual reports, business directories, and company home pages; always dig deeper.

- Consult with people—not just books, Web sites, and databases—when seeking information.

- Be prepared to discuss topics not directly related to the job, such as current events or your hobbies and interests.

- Be persistent and resourceful when looking for hard-to-find information.

- Prepare an Information Gems form for each organization, and review it before each interview.

GET THE SCOOP ON...
Taking inventory of your strengths ▪ Linking
your strengths to employers' needs ▪
Building a case that makes you the top candi-
date ▪ Blowing your own horn without bragging
▪ Why you need to identify your weaknesses

Making Yourself the Top Candidate

Chapter 4

Conducting research to craft an effective strategy and to sound knowledgeable during the
interview is just the first step in your preparation. You now have to work on sounding knowledgeable about yourself. To convince the interviewer that you can do the job, that you will fit in
well, and that you want the job, you must convey
who you are and what you have to offer. You must
provide a clear picture of your skills, capabilities,
areas of expertise, and personal qualities as they
relate to the job in question to prove that you would
be an asset to that organization.

As discussed in Chapter 2, "The Biggest Mistakes
Interviewees Make," a common pitfall in interviewing is the Bowing to Authority problem—not taking
some control over the direction of the conversation.
This problem is particularly relevant to the issue of
your skills and experience. If you don't take the initiative to tell the interviewer what you bring to
the table, you run the risk of giving an incomplete

66

As an executive recruiter, if I don't screen out applicants for my client, then I'm not doing my job. It is therefore incumbent on candidates to demonstrate first to me, then to the prospective employer, that they have the skills and personal style necessary for the job.
—Michael Aronin, Vice President, Fisher-Todd Associates

99

picture of your assets. And if you're dealing with an inexperienced or unskilled interviewer who doesn't ask the right questions, you may have to make an extra effort to direct the conversation in a way that lets you bring up your most marketable qualities.

Because you can't assume that the interviewer will bring to light your best qualities, you must go into the interview with a strategy that includes specific skills and characteristics you want to discuss and a plan for how you will convey them. Of course, to develop that plan, you must have conducted adequate research (as described in Chapter 3, "Research: The Root of All Strategy") to learn which of your assets are relevant to a particular job and employer. It does you no good to say you can offer apples when the interviewer is looking for oranges. In this chapter you'll learn how to lay the foundation for developing just such an agenda that will powerfully convey your assets.

You'll also learn how to provide evidence of those assets so that you're not just making empty claims about your qualifications—you need to prove them by discussing your past accomplishments. You may recall from "Interviewing Mistake #3: Not Being Distinctive" in Chapter 2 that too many interviews end with the recruiter not having a clear sense of the person behind the applicant. All the candidates for a job begin to blur together in the mind of the interviewer, with no distinguishing characteristics. The section "Building Your Case," later in this chapter, shows you how to ensure that you will be remembered long after the last candidate is out the door and the final decision is being made.

By the way, this is a working chapter. It's your chance to start taking action and develop an interviewing strategy based on the concepts and facts discussed in Chapters 1 and 2. Where appropriate, I have provided space for you to complete exercises directly in this book, but you may choose to do your work on separate paper or on a computer. Whichever way you do it, the important thing is that you get something down. Too many job-seekers think they have such a good handle on their strengths and skills that they don't need to write them down—or that doing so is too elementary. If that happens to be your attitude, then consider whether you'd approach a bank or venture capitalist for money to start a business without a written business plan. Probably not. The same principle is at work when asking for a job. You need to get your plan out of your head and onto paper.

Preparing to present yourself as the most qualified candidate involves five main steps:

1. Take stock of your content knowledge.

2. Identify your transferable skills.

3. Assess your positive personal qualities.

4. Compile asset statements.

5. Address your weaknesses.

Taking Stock of Your Content Knowledge

As defined in Chapter 1, your content knowledge consists of the subjects and topics with which you are familiar, as well as your areas of expertise or specializations. Your content knowledge not only enables you to do your job, but it also brings an added bonus to your employer.

Consider the case of Fran, a corporate attorney who wished to make a career change into

Watch Out!
When trying to come across as knowledgeable, don't overwhelm the interviewer with irrelevant statistics and trivia. Say enough to demonstrate your knowledge but not so much as to be a show-off or bore.

Bright Idea
A fun way to identify your content knowledge is to imagine you've been invited to take a year off and travel on a world cruise for free. The only catch is that you have to lead a shipboard seminar or discussion group once a week. What topics would you choose?

investment banking. Though she had not worked directly in that field, she had worked on financial transactions from the legal perspective. The fact that she could discuss subjects such as commercial lending, corporate restructuring, and bankruptcy in her interviews made her seem less like a career-changer and more like someone who could hit the ground running. In addition, Fran had lived in Spain for a year and had traveled in Central and South America. Her knowledge of Latin American culture and business would be an added bonus to prospective employers involved in financial markets in those countries.

Some of your content knowledge areas will be obvious, especially those that relate to your job. A real estate broker, for example, might know something about mortgage banking, interior design, engineering, and architecture. A social worker might be familiar with public policy, psychiatry, and nursing. Other content knowledge evolves out of your hobbies, personal interests, and academic background.

The sources for this knowledge are endless and vary widely from person to person. To identify yours, take a look at Worksheet 4.1 and see if any of the questions reveal your areas of expertise. A sample answer has been provided for Question 1 on the worksheet to help you get started.

Identifying Your Transferable Skills

The next step in taking stock of your assets is to identify your transferable skills. Unlike content knowledge—which consists of subjects, topics, or areas of specialization—transferable skills are things that you actually do. You can think of them as functions, actions, or behaviors. These skills are also not

WORKSHEET 4.1: CONTENT KNOWLEDGE

1. Consider your current employment (or most recent, if not currently employed). What do you have to know to do your job, or what have you learned as a result of doing your job?

2. Now do the same for past jobs you have held.

3. Think about any hobbies or activities you are involved in outside of work. What do you know about as a result of those involvements?

4. What topics do you discuss with friends or family, read about in books or magazines, or follow on the Internet?

5. In what subjects are you conversant or proficient as a result of your academic background—whether from a full degree program or just a course or two?

← Note!
Be sure you're not confusing content knowledge areas with transferable skills. If you need some clarification, read ahead to the next section of this chapter to see over a hundred examples of transferable skills.

linked to any one job, project, or employer—they're generic enough to be of interest to most anyone.

That attorney interested in working in investment banking, for example, did not go into interviews using legal jargon and focusing on skills unique to the law, such as drafting and filing motions, analyzing appellate briefs, or conducting hearings. Instead, she spoke about her ability to analyze quantitative data and text, problem-solve, work in teams, write reports, and maintain good relations with clients.

Timesaver
For a shortcut to identifying your transferable skills, ask colleagues who have similar experience to yours if you can see their resumes to get ideas of skills they've highlighted and terminology they've used.

To identify your own transferable skills, review the lists that follow and put a check next to any skills you possess. When you've gone through all the lists, go back and circle (or highlight in whichever way you prefer) the 10 to 15 skills that are likely to be most marketable and relevant to your target job or employer.

Uncovering Additional Skills

Reviewing these checklists is just one way to identify your transferable skills. You also need to tackle the problem from the opposite perspective—thinking about your experiences and accomplishments and pulling skills from those.

Take the case of Leon, who had been a high school English teacher for five years since completing a master's degree in English literature after college. Leon decided that he wanted to make a career transition and enter a management training program with a major insurance company. When he first reviewed skills checklists similar to those on the preceding pages, he was concerned that he had little to offer a corporate employer.

But when he carefully analyzed his background by breaking down his job as a teacher and his

CHECKLIST 4.1: BUSINESS & MANAGEMENT SKILLS

Appraise value _____
Assess/oversee quality control _____
Bargain _____
Barter _____
Compete _____
Conduct meetings _____
Consult _____
Delegate _____
Develop a business plan _____
Direct _____
Estimate costs _____
Fund-raise _____
Handle office politics _____
Improvise _____
Interview candidates _____
Make decisions _____
Manage people _____
Manage projects _____
Negotiate _____
Plan strategy _____
Reprimand _____
Set goals _____
Supervise _____
Train employees _____
Trouble-shoot _____

Moneysaver
If you're concerned about lacking particular skills, avoid the temptation to sign up for expensive courses or training programs until you're certain that the skills you would learn are an absolute prerequisite for the job you want.

avocational activities into generic functional areas, he was relieved to find that he possessed more transferable skills than he had imagined. He had demonstrated management skills while supervising student clubs; used his quantitative abilities as treasurer of his cooperative apartment building's board;

Watch Out!
Beware of aptitude testing centers offering expensive, lengthy test batteries. While they may do a good job of measuring general aptitudes such as spatial relations, verbal reasoning, and musical ability, most job seekers need to identify their more tangible, specific, job-related skills with the help of a career counselor.

CHECKLIST 4.2: COGNITIVE SKILLS

Analyze situations/problems/facts   ____

Assess needs   ____

Concentrate for long periods of time   ____

Conceptualize   ____

Develop theories/hypothesize   ____

Employ logic   ____

Extrapolate   ____

Memorize/recall information   ____

Observe   ____

Read carefully and critically   ____

Research   ____

See the big picture   ____

Synthesize/integrate ideas or information ____

CHECKLIST 4.3: CREATIVE SKILLS

Brainstorming   ____

Create works of art   ____

Design programs or procedures   ____

Develop marketing campaigns   ____

Invent products or services   ____

Make spaces/objects aesthetically pleasing ____

Perform   ____

Use imagination   ____

Visualize   ____

CHECKLIST 4.4: INTERPERSONAL SKILLS

Advise _____

Advocate _____

Build teams _____

Coach _____

Collaborate _____

Console _____

Counsel _____

Educate _____

Empathize _____

Entertain _____

Facilitate others' development _____

Facilitate groups _____

Guide _____

Host _____

Influence people _____

Interact effectively cross-culturally _____

Listen attentively _____

Mediate conflicts/disputes _____

Mentor _____

Motivate others _____

Network/keep in touch with people _____

Nurture _____

Orient newcomers _____

Persuade _____

Provide constructive criticism/
  critique work _____

Serve/assist customers or clients _____

Teach _____

Train _____

CHECKLIST 4.5: ORAL COMMUNICATION SKILLS

Be humorous   _____

Debate   _____

Explain things to others   _____

Interpret   _____

Interview others for information   _____

Lead seminars or workshops   _____

Learn/speak foreign language(s)   _____

Make conversation   _____

Mediate disputes/conflicts   _____

Moderate a panel of speakers   _____

Speak in public   _____

Unofficially...
In studies commissioned by the federal government to identify workplace skills needed in the 21st century, that old standby—reading—has been cited as one of the most important due to the increased role technology and information play in most jobs.

CHECKLIST 4.6: ORGANIZATIONAL SKILLS

Coordinate projects or events   _____

Coordinate schedules   _____

Handle details   _____

Handle multiple tasks simultaneously   _____

Implement plans/follow through   _____

Monitor the flow of a project   _____

Oversee a production effort   _____

Process documents   _____

Reorganize systems/procedures   _____

Set up and maintain
   record-keeping systems   _____

CHECKLIST 4.7: QUANTITATIVE SKILLS

Administer accounts payable   _____

Administer accounts receivable   _____

Analyze data   _____

Calculate/tally numbers   _____

Conduct statistical analyses   _____

Cut costs   _____

Generate financial reports   _____

Handle collections   _____

Plan and work with budgets   _____

Solve complex mathematical problems   _____

CHECKLIST 4.8: SALES SKILLS

Close sales   _____

Conduct sales presentations   _____

Convince   _____

Develop new markets   _____

Identify prospects   _____

Make sales calls in person   _____

Maintain client/customer accounts   _____

Negotiate   _____

Persuade   _____

Telemarket   _____

Bright Idea
To identify more of your transferable skills, check the written job description for your current or past positions (usually available from Human Resources if you don't already have a copy).

CHECKLIST 4.9: TECHNICAL SKILLS

Build/construct things   _____

Fix/repair things   _____

Make installations   _____

Operate machinery or equipment   _____

Troubleshoot malfunctions   _____

Use physical strength   _____

Use tools   _____

Watch Out!
If you tend to be a bit self-deprecating, you might make the mistake of selling yourself short when taking stock of your skills. Before assuming you don't have adequate skills, make sure you aren't setting your standards too high. You don't have to be a world-renowned expert to say you have a particular skill.

CHECKLIST 4.10: WRITTEN COMMUNICATION SKILLS

Copywrite   _____

Edit   _____

Proofread   _____

Translate   _____

Write for business   _____

Write creatively   _____

Write journalistically   _____

Write grants   _____

was a proven team-player through participation in numerous faculty committees; and obviously used presentation, public speaking, listening, and analytical skills as a teacher and graduate student.

Think about your work, academic, and personal experiences and the skills that you have demonstrated throughout them. If you find any skills not already checked off on the lists provided above, by all means add them.

Assessing Your Personal Qualities

The final step in taking stock of your assets is to assess the positive personal qualities that may be of value to your target employer. (If you don't have a particular type of job or employer targeted, then you need to take a temporary step back and refer to some of the books in the "Career Planning" and "Job Search" sections of Appendix C for help in defining a focus.) As discussed in Chapter 1, certain personality characteristics—such as flexibility, vision, and creativity—are widely valued in organizational settings these days, while other personal qualities sought are unique to a particular setting.

Read through the checklist that follows and place a check next to any characteristics that you think describe you. Then go back and circle the five to seven characteristics that *best* describe you out of all the ones checked.

Building Your Case

As with stocks and bonds, real estate, and a bank balance, your professional assets—skills, content knowledge, and personal qualities—have value in the eyes of others. Most wise investors wouldn't purchase property without seeing it, and they wouldn't buy stock in a company they know nothing about. They need proof that an investment has a certain value or value potential. The same holds true in the hiring process. For a prospective employer to see value in you and want to invest in you, you must provide evidence of your worth.

Anyone can make claims about having the necessary qualifications for a job. Not everyone can, or will think to, back up those claims with evidence.

Bright Idea
Make copies of the Personal Qualities Checklist for at least three friends, colleagues, or family members before you complete it. Have them check off the qualities that they see in you, then compare all the results to see how the perspectives vary.

Unofficially...
Employers these days care less about the old workhorse qualities—such as being faithful, dependable, and loyal—and more about energy, enthusiasm, creativity, and vision.

66

If the applicant cannot provide some concrete, credible examples of performance, I reach the conclusion that either the experience is not there, or the person is not able to articulate the experience. Generally, the person is dropped out of the viable candidate pool if it is a critical skill or experience.
—Susan Lamb, Human Resources Director, ISA, the international society for measurement and control

99

CHECKLIST 4.11: PERSONAL QUALITIES

Adaptable	____	Mechanically-inclined	____
Aggressive	____	Musically-inclined	____
Artistic	____		
Assertive	____		
Athletic	____	Observant	____
Calm	____	Open-minded	____
Communicative	____	Optimistic	____
Conscientious	____	Organized	____
Considerate	____	Patient	____
Creative	____	Perceptive	____
Dependable	____	Persevering	____
Detail-oriented	____	Persuasive	____
Diplomatic	____	Poised	____
Disciplined	____	Practical	____
Discreet	____	Punctual	____
Driven	____	Quiet	____
Effective	____	Reserved	____
Efficient	____	Resourceful	____
Energetic	____	Responsible	____
Enterprising	____	Scholarly	____
Enthusiastic	____	Self-aware	____
Ethical	____	Self-confident	____
Expressive	____	Self-disciplined	____
Faithful	____	Sensitive	____
Flexible	____	Serious	____
Funny	____	Sincere	____
Gregarious	____	Tactful	____
Honest	____	Technically-inclined	____
Independent	____		
Loyal	____	Thoughtful	____
Mathematically-inclined	____	Visionary	____

Most anyone who gets past the initial screening process and into an interview will have met the basic requirements for the job. The way to distinguish yourself from the competition at that point is to instill confidence in the interviewer by showing, not just saying, that you have what it takes to make a difference. This is particularly relevant at higher levels, where it's a given that you have the basic strengths and experience to do the job. What's not so obvious, however, are the details of what you've done in the past and exactly how those past accomplishments could help you meet their current and future needs.

The Importance of Asset Statements

Too many interviewees get caught in the trap of simply describing their experience. They believe that all the interviewer needs to hear is an elaboration of their brief job descriptions on the resume. Instead of just detailing those responsibilities or projects, spell out the assets you demonstrated while carrying them out .

Another common pitfall is to bombard the interviewer with a laundry list of assets. A statement such as, "I am detail-oriented, analytical, mathematically-inclined, a strong manager, and proficient in three languages" is not only likely to go in one ear and out the other, but it also has no substance to back it up.

To distinguish yourself from other candidates who may recite the same list of assets, and to make the discussion of your experience richer and more relevant, prepare asset statements. These are carefully crafted statements prepared before you get to the interview that tell the prospective employer how you could add value, how you've done so in the past, and how you can do so more effectively than other candidates.

How to Develop Asset Statements

Developing asset statements is a five-step process. For each interview, you should ask the following questions and then record the answers in a format like that of the "Asset Statement Development Form" at the end of this section.

1. What does the employer need or the job require?

2. What assets do I have that enable me to meet those needs?

3. How would I use those assets to the employer's benefit?

4. How have I proven in the past that I can do what I claim to be capable of?

5. How do I differ in this regard from other candidates?

Let's look in more detail at what each of these steps entails.

Identify the employer's needs: From the research you will have already conducted before preparing asset statements, you should have a sense of what the employer is looking for in an ideal candidate, and what the problems, goals, and philosophy are of the prospective employing organization. You may already have this information recorded on your "Information Gems" worksheet from Chapter 3 under the headings "Organizational Culture/Style/Philosophy," "Goals/Vision," "Growth Areas," and "Problem Areas." You can now transfer those information gems to the first section of the Asset Statement Development Form.

> *Example:* Frank is applying for a position in human resources management with a major commercial bank to handle the recruiting of

information technology (IT) specialists. Through his research he has identified the bank's needs as: expanding the IT staff significantly; solving an employee retention problem; decentralizing IT recruiting from the general human resources function to line management; and smoothing relations among an increasingly ethnically diverse staff.

Identify which of your assets can meet the employer's needs. For each problem to be solved, growth area to contribute to, or other need of the employer, identify one or more of your assets that enable you to meet that need. Whether it's a skill, content knowledge, or personal quality, the asset should be relevant and beneficial to the job and the organization.

Example: Frank first chooses to focus on the bank's retention problem. He realizes that a few of his assets would help with that dilemma. He is knowledgeable in cutting-edge human resource practices that have been proven to reduce turnover rates; his macro-management style enables him to have a vision of how employees should be treated in the long run, not just during the orientation period; and, having worked for two computer companies, he has a solid handle on the information technology industry as a whole. So, his content knowledge areas here are the IT industry and advanced HR practices, while his transferable skills relate to management. These are the assets he would list in the "Relevant Assets" portion of the development form.

State the benefit of your assets to the prospective employer. The next step is to think of how your

Timesaver
Keep in mind that many organizations will have similar needs—those universal ones such as vision, ethics, creativity, team players, and so on. You can prepare asset statements that will be useful in most interviews so you don't have to reinvent the wheel every time.

Unofficially...
Conventional wisdom among those who dispense interviewing advice has been to focus on the outcomes of past efforts— how you've solved problems and met challenges. That's important, but even more relevant to future employers is how you can solve *their* problems, not those of former employers.

strengths can be of direct benefit to the employer, either immediately or in the near future. Instead of offering vague promises, be sure to specify and quantify what you can do. Instead of saying something like, "I could increase your sales in the Southeastern region," you would say "I am confident that with my contacts and track record, I could double your sales in Florida and Georgia by the end of the fiscal year and in the remaining territories over the following year."

> *Example:* Frank could tell his interviewers that he would reduce their turnover rates by certain percentages within the first year and in subsequent years, based on his experience with proven retention techniques. He could also tell them that his contacts in and knowledge of the IT profession would enable him to stay on top of the competition and developments in the field so that he could foresee why the bank's employees might want to go elsewhere.

Give an example of a past accomplishment. Immediately after making the claims that Step 3 advises, back them up with some evidence. Examples of how you've solved problems in the past, met challenges, overcome obstacles, reached goals, and otherwise achieved success give credence to your claims. By showing that you have accomplished something similar in the past, you are not making empty promises, but are demonstrating solid evidence of your capabilities. Plus, you're telling a story of sorts, which gives flavor to your discussion and makes the interviewer's encounter with you more meaningful. Whenever possible, to make it even more memorable, enhance your story with "props" that further illustrate the past incident or accomplishment you are describing. Kudo letters, commendations, reports, photos, or other relevant documents from your portfolio can be powerful evidence of your achievements. (Portfolios and their contents are discussed more in Chapter 7, "Strategic Communication for Interviews.")

> *Example:* To prove that he could reduce turnover, Frank would discuss his role in a major retention initiative at a former company. He had brought in consultants to assess why employees were leaving the company in large numbers after short tenures. He analyzed the findings and then used his management skills to develop and direct progressive but cost-effective procedures for recruitment, orientation, and training, as well as employee development and coaching. To supplement his account of this effort, he could also show interviewers a concise report he had prepared for the senior management at his former company to document the positive results of his work. He would also show a letter from the company's CEO praising him for his contribution.

Compare and contrast your assets. A final step in preparing asset statements is to find a way to distinguish yourself from others who might have skills, knowledge, and personal qualities comparable to yours, or who have equally compelling evidence for their assets. While making your asset statements during the interview, it is helpful to put those statements into some sort of context, giving the interviewer a frame of reference by which to judge you. That frame of reference might be past or present coworkers, bosses, fellow students, or personal

Bright Idea
If you've ever had what is called a 360° review in which your peers—not just your bosses—rate your performance, you have valuable data you can use to distinguish yourself from others in your asset statements.

contacts. The key here is not so much to whom you're comparing yourself, but to what extent you do things faster, better, more inexpensively, more creatively, and so forth than others doing the same kind of work.

It has been my experience that this is not only something job-seekers usually don't even think to do, but it is something they are often reluctant to do. This is not surprising, considering that our culture doesn't like a show-off, a tattle-tale, or a harsh critic. Also, most interviewees know they're not supposed to say anything negative about any past or current colleagues, and they don't know how they could pull off a comparison to others without sounding negative.

While these concerns are understandable, they are unfortunate. When worded carefully and couched in the appropriate context, contrasting yourself with less capable or effective peers is a powerful interviewing technique, not the rantings of an egomaniac. First of all, you make the comparisons anonymously, not just by omitting the use of any names or even initials, but by giving absolutely no identifying information. Second, you make it clear that the statement is not a personal attack but is merely designed to point out a difference of style or opinion. You might even say something positive about the person in question to show that you're not making a blanket criticism, just highlighting one aspect of that person's work. Finally, you objectify the statement whenever possible by showing that the comparison is not just your opinion but has been made by others.

> *Example:* To further emphasize how outstanding his retention turnaround was, Frank could say, "It seems I have a real knack for

taking a complex problem and finding solutions that are complex enough to meet the challenge, but simple enough that they can actually be implemented. In working on that retention effort at my former company, I found that some of my colleagues who were ordinarily quite skilled and accomplished seemed to be making the project more complicated than it needed to be. I think there must be something unique about my analytical abilities that help me take the massive amounts of data from the consulting firm and swiftly convert them into cost-effective solutions for our problems. At least that's what the CEO told me, and she had been managing recruitment and retention functions for 30 years, so I was gratified by her feedback."

> 66
> I've never been much of a self-promoter or felt comfortable blowing my own horn, but when I started talking about my strengths in terms of how others have recognized them, I no longer felt like I was bragging. I was just stating a fact.
> —Marilyn, management consultant, 42
> 99

Common Concerns When Developing Asset Statements

Many job-seekers face certain common questions and issues when attempting to draw up their asset statements. Here are a few I've encountered in my work, along with advice and answers:

- *Is it much more effective to draw my asset examples from professional experiences than from personal ones?* As often as possible, you should pull examples from professional experiences since those will undoubtedly be more relevant for the interviewer. Remember that these experiences can include not just current or past jobs but also involvement in trade and professional associations, as well as community business activities such as boards of trustees, Chambers of Commerce, leadership in Junior Achievement, or related groups. There are times, however, when you do not have a work-related example with which to demonstrate a particular asset, so you must draw from your personal or academic life. Doing so is acceptable if the example is relevant—point out how your participation in a sport shows leadership skills, or tell how you've gained knowledge of a particular subject through a personal hobby. If the example is especially strong, you might even be better off using it rather than a professional one.

Bright Idea
As much as your schedule allows, keep participating in non-work-related activities during your job search so that you have current examples of your assets to discuss during interviews.

- *How old is too old when it comes to choosing examples?* A rough rule of thumb is that the more recent the example, the better. This is certainly true if the accomplishment you are describing relates to an industry, product, or type of job that has changed significantly since the event took place. For example, if the best evidence of someone's marketing skills in the computer industry comes from a time when the world was using DOS, not Windows, then your story will sound dated and will be taken less seriously, no matter how outstanding your accomplishment was. On the other hand, if you want to use an old example that is much more powerful than anything you've done recently, then by all means use it as long as it still has some relevance.

- *What if I know I possess a particular asset but can't think of any example that demonstrates it?* This is a common dilemma that I find most people can get past if they just put some thought into it. It's often difficult to think of great examples off the top of your head, so don't worry if nothing comes to mind right away. You may need to jog your memory a bit by walking yourself through your resume to recall incidents worth talking about in an interview. You can also enlist the help of others, particularly current or past coworkers who may remember your successes better than you do.

- *What if I have more than one example that demonstrates an asset?* Great! You will most likely have more than one accomplishment in your past that provides evidence of a particular asset. If so, just jot down notes about a few of them in the "Asset Evidence" portion of the development form. You will then have a repertoire of sorts from which you can pull the best example for the occasion. By the way, the reverse can happen as well—you have one example that demonstrates more than one asset. This is especially common because we invariably use multiple skills, personal qualities, and knowledge bases to accomplish any one task.

- *What if I can't discern the organization's needs despite a concerted research effort?* If you simply cannot get the inside scoop on a particular organization, don't despair. You can always prepare asset statements for the needs that are universal to most employers—needs such as integrity, vision, teamwork, communication skills, technology proficiency, and the like.

Asset Statement Development Form

Use the following form to record the information that will form the basis of your asset statements. You can type up a similar form on your computer for easy use as a template or might prefer to write these notes on index cards that you can discreetly review just before each interview.

Note! ➔
Use one form per organizational need instead of listing all needs for one employer on one form. Because each target employer will have multiple needs or problems to be solved, you should end up with several forms for each interview.

ASSET STATEMENT DEVELOPMENT FORM

Organization's need

Relevant assets

Benefits to the target employer

Asset evidence

Comparison with others

Watch Out!
When developing asset statements based on personal qualities—not tangible skills or knowledge—be particularly careful to use a solid example and objective (third-party) evidence. It's one thing to say "I am well organized" or "I am resourceful." It's another to back up those claims with evidence.

Making Up For Deficits

Many job seekers find that one of the most difficult interview questions to address is "What are your weaknesses?" Not only is it difficult to answer for obvious reasons—you want to sell the interviewer on your positive qualities, not your negatives—but most job-seekers haven't given much thought to their weaknesses. They spend so much time taking stock of their accomplishments, skills, and stellar personality characteristics that it doesn't even occur to them to analyze their deficits.

Doing so is critical so that if you are faced with that dreaded what-is-your-weakness question, you can give a well-prepared, meaningful answer. But even if you aren't directly asked about your deficits, giving some thought to them before an interview is nonetheless important. By identifying gaps in your skills or knowledge, or personal qualities that could use some improvement, you can anticipate—and be ready to counter—recruiters' objections. Doing so also gives you time to make up for your deficits by taking classes or doing whatever you need to do to get up to speed.

How to Identify Your Deficits

Some deficits are easy to identify. You hear about a position that requires a master's degree, but you have two years of college. Your deficit in this case is education-related. You read a classified ad that calls for a marketing manager with knowledge of Web site marketing. You have years of experience in marketing and management, but you're an Internet neophyte, so you have the skills to do the job but not the content knowledge. Or perhaps you want to work for a very conservative company known for its rigid ethical standards, but you once worked for a company that was sued in a widely publicized case for its shady business practices. Even though you had nothing to do with those problems, the company's name stands out on your resume like a big red flag.

While none of these situations is a certain dead-end (you may be able to talk your way around gaps in your credentials), they can be difficult challenges to overcome. Chapter 12, "Interview Curve Balls," provides much more detail on how to deal with such obstacles, including ways to put a positive spin on them in conversation as well as substantive ways to acquire new skills, further your education, or smooth personality flaws. For now, though, I'd like you to take a preliminary inventory of your skills deficits, gaps in credentials, or personal weaknesses.

Moneysaver
If you need to acquire a particular skill set to obtain the job you want, don't assume you have to go back to school for a full degree. Instead, consider taking courses through a university's school of continuing education or professional studies division.

In going through the checklists and exercises earlier in this chapter, some problems may already have come to mind. If not, or to be more thorough, consider the following methods:

Watch Out!
If you're not having any success in your job search, don't automatically assume that you have skills or knowledge deficits requiring major "repair work." You might just need to improve your interviewing technique and the way that you communicate the assets you do have.

- Be objective. Make sure you haven't inflated your qualifications in your own mind. It's great to have high self-esteem and positive self-regard, but you don't want to overestimate your candidacy. Doing so will only lead to disappointment when you find out that you weren't as qualified for the job as you had thought. While I do not advocate going to the opposite extreme and being overly negative about your qualifications and pessimistic about your chances, a little humble caution never hurts. So be honest with yourself and ask what an employer might want that you don't have.

- Seek feedback from others. Turn to your network of friends, family, and professional colleagues to get some honest feedback about yourself. Seek out the friend who knows you well enough to say, "John, you talk too much," or the former boss who'll say, "Maria, you need to develop better management skills." Also ask career consultants or headhunters for input into your credentials. They may not know you personally, but they can often tell you where the gaps are in your education, training, and work experience as related to the type of job or employer you've targeted.

- Read old performance reviews. Pull out any performance reviews or evaluations you've saved from past jobs or from your current position. Look for comments about your work style, demonstrated skills, and areas needing improvement. Are there any patterns to the reviews that alert you to a chronic problem?

- Refer to your pre-interview research. Before assuming that you lack the necessary credentials or qualities for a particular job or employer—or before assuming that you do have everything needed, when in fact you don't— consult the findings of the research you conducted, as described in Chapter 3. Review the typical qualifications needed for the type of job you're going after, along with the culture and needs of the organizations where you'll be interviewing, and see how your credentials stack up.

When you've assessed where your deficits might lie, you have some decisions to make. Are they so problematic that you'll have difficulty getting hired, or are they minor glitches that you can talk your way around? You may be able to answer those questions by referring to your research findings, but you may also need to ask someone who would know. Here's where your network comes into play again. Before assuming that you have to go back to school, enter a costly training program, or consult a therapist for a personality issue, speak with knowledgeable people who can let you know just how big a gap you're facing between what you have to offer and what the job or the employer requires. If you do find that you have some major obstacles to overcome, don't despair. You have plenty of options for doing so. You'll find examples of these in Chapter 12.

Bright Idea
You can also seek feedback about your weaknesses from people who have interviewed you earlier in your job search. Ways to encourage such feedback are discussed in Chapter 13, "Following Up to Get to 'Yes'."

Just the Facts

- Knowing yourself—your skills, knowledge, and personal qualities—is as important as knowing about the prospective employer.

- You have to take the initiative to communicate what your assets are. Don't assume the interviewer will deduce them from a basic discussion of your experience.

- To build a case for why you're the best candidate, you must provide evidence of past accomplishments, problems solved, and goals attained.

- Employers are more interested in the skills, knowledge, and character you demonstrated on past jobs than on the basic nature of the jobs themselves.

- Take stock of your deficits so you can take constructive steps toward overcoming skill and knowledge gaps or smoothing the rough patches in your personal style.

GET THE SCOOP ON...
Being confident but not cocky ▪ Calming your
pre-interview jitters ▪
Confronting stage fright ▪ Riding the emotional
roller-coaster of interviewing ▪ Preparing yourself mentally

Developing the Right Attitude

Chapter 5

You can go into an interview prepared to answer any question thrown your way and to showcase your strengths and experience powerfully—but if you don't have the right mental attitude to back it all up, then those efforts are wasted. Preparing your psyche prior to an interview is just as important as researching the company and identifying your relevant skills, yet it is often the most overlooked area of preparation. Too many job-seekers rush off to an interview, become frazzled along the way, decompress for a minute or two in the elevator, then take a few deep breaths in the waiting room and hope for the best. Not only does such an approach increase the likelihood that a bad case of nerves will strike, but it also contributes to the emotional roller-coaster nature of job hunting and interviewing.

Throughout the course of a job search, you are likely to go from feeling confident to cursed, optimistic to hopeless, and capable to ineffectual. You may also find that your mental state affects your physical demeanor, taking you from a broad smile and tall shoulders to sweaty palms and slumped posture. Such ups and downs are normal for a process in which you are being judged, in which you face significant consequences for your personal and professional life, and in which you often must face rejection. Attending to your mental state with some simple techniques described in this chapter can help make interviewing less of a thrill ride and more of a smooth one.

The Psychology of Interviewing

The process a recruiter undergoes to identify the best candidate and the process a job-seeker undergoes to find employment are both ripe for psychological analysis. In fact, interviewing is really more about psychology than it is about principles of human resources or the nuts and bolts of career development. It is, essentially, a social interaction; second, it is a business meeting.

Focusing on the content of an interview—what questions might be asked, what you should say—is important, but to interview strategically you must focus on the dynamics of the process as well. Whenever two or more human beings interact, the psyche of each participant becomes an ingredient in a sort of group dynamics stew. As with a real stew, the ingredients can mesh well to create something delicious, or they can clash so that you never want to combine them again. Your goal in interviewing is to have all the involved parties want to get together again, either for more interviews or as colleagues on the job. For that to happen, the social interaction must be pleasant and comfortable for all who take part in it. The psychological ingredients must meld well.

As the interviewee, you do have considerable control over the success or failure of the interaction with your interviewer(s). First, by paying attention to your own thoughts and feelings prior to the interview, you can develop a winning attitude and not succumb to self-doubt, nervousness, or false confidence. I call this task the power of balancing. Second, you can contribute to a favorable social exchange during the interview, employing tactics that give you control over the outcome without steam-rolling over the interviewer's authority. You can think of this as dealing with the balance of power.

The Power of Balancing

Going into an interview with the right attitude is like walking a tightrope. You have to come across as confident but not cocky, and positive but not starry-eyed. You must convey enthusiasm but show studied reserve as well. You should let yourself enjoy the experience while maintaining a healthy dose of fear to keep you on your toes. And, you need to seem eager without seeming desperate. Easier said than done? Not at all.

It's a little like the ancient Greeks' admonition of "Everything in moderation, nothing in excess." You can, for example, allow yourself to be apprehensive but not let the fear overcome you. Or, if you tend to err on the side of overconfidence rather than concern, you need to let that confidence work for you, but not to the point that it distorts your good judgment and makes you blasé. It's all about balance. Trying to banish all negative thoughts and feelings as you anticipate an interview is pointless. Fear, doubt, concern, and false confidence are normal, healthy emotions. Instead of attempting the

Unofficially... Attending to your emotions is particularly important if you're interviewing after being fired or coming off a difficult work situation. Outplacement firms, for example, require that clients deal with their grief and pain before letting them move on to the business of a job search.

impossible task of squelching them completely, you simply need to keep them in check so that no one thought or feeling overpowers another.

In addition, you can replace the negative or self-sabotaging thoughts and emotions with more positive and productive ones. Cognitive psychologists advocate the use of positive self-talk as one way to do just that. Every time you find yourself in a behavior or action that you want to change—getting nervous, let's say—you should think of what thought preceded that action. Was it something like, "I know I'm going to blow it," or "What if they grill me with unexpected questions?" After you've identified the offending thought, you should replace it with something more positive. You might say, for example, "Remember the last time I thought I was going to make too many mistakes in the interview but was pleasantly surprised at how well I did?" or "Even if they throw tough questions at me, I've prepared so well for this interview that I can handle most anything." Even if nervousness is not a concern, I suggest that you monitor your self-talk before each interview to be on the look-out for any potential attitude problems.

The Balance of Power

You need to strive for balance not just within your own mind but in social interactions as well. Coming to the interview with the right mental attitude is the first step. Once you get there, you should adapt your attitude to fit the dynamics of the situation. While group dynamics is a complex topic ("group" here can refer to as few as two people), you should be aware of two main factors: control and attraction.

As mentioned before, you do have the right to take some control in the interview. You are there to

> 66
> Remember—error is an inevitable part of life. That is why pencils have erasers on them. Most everyday errors are manageable, provided you act like a problem-solver. From this perspective you see that making mistakes is understandable and, more importantly, that the essence of you remains acceptable.
> —William J. Knaus, Ed.D., in *Change Your Life Now* (New York: John Wiley & Sons, 1996)
> 99

TABLE 5.1: DEVELOPING THE RIGHT ATTITUDE FOR INTERVIEWING

Attitude Element	How to Get It	How to Keep Balance
Confidence	Review your asset statements; recall past successes; realize you've already beat out some of the competition just to get to the interview stage. If it helps, call upon your religious or spiritual faith for strength.	Avoid getting blindly confident, cocky, or arrogant; be prepared for a tough interview that could shake your confidence.
Optimism	Remember that the current job market favors the job-seeker; keep in mind that the interviewer wants to make a match and would prefer to favor you than to screen you out. Your chances for success are good.	Be aware of what could go wrong. Don't dwell on the potential for failure, but be alert to possible pitfalls.
Positivism	Try to minimize feelings of bitterness or frustration you may have as a result of prior job experiences or a difficult job search. Focus on the positives: the fact that you're making an effort to advance your career, or that each interview brings you one step closer to a new job.	Don't try to deny or hide your negative feelings completely. If handled carefully, you can sometimes be candid about negative experiences when talking to a recruiter. Remember, putting too much of a positive spin on some inherently negative situations can look dishonest. Chapter 9, "The Fifteen Trickiest Interview Questions," offers more advice on this tricky issue.
Enthusiasm	Treat each interview as an interesting opportunity to learn something about an organization, other people, and even yourself. Look at it as an enjoyable experience, a chance to have a pleasant conversation with a fellow human being. Most importantly, treat it as a chance to start an exciting new chapter in your career and your life.	Don't confuse a pleasant social interaction with a serious meeting of the minds. Remember your agenda and be strategic. Don't get lost in unfocused conversation. And don't overwhelm the interviewer with too much enthusiasm and energy—it can look phony.

interview the prospective employer, not just to be interviewed. Only when you have some of the power in the interviewing relationship can you collect the information you need to assess whether you want to work there. You also need control to get your point across, to make your asset statements as described in Chapter 4, "Making Yourself the Top Candidate." So what does all this have to do with psychology? Well, there is perhaps no trickier issue in the psychology of groups than that of control.

Bright Idea
Ask current or former bosses how they perceive your ability to handle the balance of power in a working relationship. Then apply their comments to your role in the interviewing relationship and see where you could use some improvement.

Chapter 8, "Variations on the Interviewing Theme," and Chapter 9 address in more detail the issue of how to achieve and maintain a proper balance of power in interviews. For now, simply be aware of how important control, power, and authority are in the outcome of an interview. If your attitude is one of "I must be in total control of this interview," you will not only be sorely disappointed when you find out that's not possible, but you will also turn off the interviewer. Coming on too strong upsets the delicate balance of power. You will threaten the interviewer's authority if you're too assertive, but if you hold back too much, you will not be seen as an active participant in the problem-solving and trouble-shooting that are cornerstones of an interview.

The other issue that calls for balancing is that of attraction. Everyone from ivory-tower social psychologists to relationship gurus who teach seminars on flirting knows that the more desperate you seem, the less attracted others will be to you. In some ways, an interview is a little like a first date. You're checking each other out to see whether you want to spend more time together—and, possibly, to develop a relationship. When an employer and a candidate meet, basically the same thing is going on.

So, to navigate the psychological aspects of attraction and the interview, be sure that you don't seem overly eager for the job. Showing interest and enthusiasm is important, but doing so must be balanced with a certain amount of reserve. Not only do you not want to come across as desperate, but you also don't want to seem indiscriminate—that is, being wildly enthusiastic about the prospective employer or job before you know all the facts.

A friend of mine once experienced a perfect example of the psychology of attraction. She had relocated to a new city at the height of the recession in the early 1990s and had a difficult time finding a job in her field—sales of particular financial products—despite her excellent credentials. Her search took so long that she became very frustrated and was about to move back home when she got a call from a company she had contacted several weeks earlier inviting her to interview. She considered not even going on the interview because she had already made up her mind to throw in the towel and had begun making arrangements to move.

With a what-the-hell attitude, though, she decided she may as well go on the interview. So, she did go, but with a much different attitude than before. This time, she was completely relaxed and unconcerned about the outcome. To outside observers, however, she was professional and convincing as always—plus, she had something extra. Her internal laissez-faire attitude translated into confidence and a refreshing candor on the outside. She was essentially saying to the interviewers, "Here's what I have to offer. Take it or leave it." They loved it. She was given an offer within a few days with the comment, "We like your attitude."

Timesaver
Bring letters of recommendation with you to the interview so that you won't have to take time to send them afterward. Doing so also may nudge the interviewer toward finding you more appealing from the start.

Unofficially...
You might be surprised to know that many recruiters expect, and will excuse, some nervousness. They realize it's unrealistic to expect you to be completely calm and relaxed—especially students interviewing through on-campus recruiting, or anyone new to the work world.

While you don't necessarily have to go to the extreme that this job seeker did (too casual an approach can backfire if it's interpreted as lack of interest or professionalism), you may be able to take something from her example.

Anxiety and the Interview Process

Becoming nervous before or during an interview is such a pervasive problem that a significant portion of this chapter is devoted to dealing with nerves. Some degree of apprehension or anxiety is part of the normal range of emotions you may experience throughout your job search. While the introduction of this book stressed that interviewing is not a game or an act, it's true that it can seem at times like a first grade school play. You may feel that you're going to be on a stage of sorts having to deliver a stellar performance. For that reason, it is not at all uncommon to experience some pre-interview performance anxiety or to be struck by stage fright once the meeting is underway.

To deal with nervousness, you need to know why it occurs in the first place so you can possibly prevent it from happening. Then you can employ some strategies recommended a little later in this chapter to calm and compose yourself when they do strike.

Why You Get Nervous

Viewing the interview as a performance is one common cause of interviewing anxiety. A classic definition of performance anxiety, or "stage fright," is that offered by Mark Leary in *Understanding Social Anxiety* (Beverly Hills, CA: Sage Publications, 1983):

$$\text{stage fright} = \frac{\text{the importance of the consequences of the performance}}{\text{the prediction of a successful performance}}$$

In other words, if you have your heart set on working for a particular company and you worry that you're not going to do well in the interview there, then you are likely to experience stage fright. When the stakes are high and you have a lot to lose, you'll probably be nervous. But if you expect to give a peak performance, then you may not be so nervous, even if the stakes are high—much like an Olympic athlete who doesn't choke under pressure.

Related to the issue of performance anxiety is the idea that you are putting yourself on the line to be judged. Being evaluated as a candidate for employment is not the same as having your worth as a person assessed, but many job seekers confuse the two. Certainly, an interview is, nonetheless, an assessment in some sense (but not necessarily of your personal worth), it also brings the possibility of rejection or failure. Any doubts about your ability to interview well or the strength of your qualifications can lead to such fears.

Interviewing is a wild card, in many ways. You can prepare and practice all you want, but there will still be variables outside your control. Knowing that the hiring authorities' decision is subject to personal whims, organizational politics, and even large-scale factors such as the economy or fluctuations in your industry can be daunting. There's no denying that interviewing involves an element of luck, and that realization can be nerve-wracking.

Timesaver
To save time *and* reduce stress, consider joining a job search group, such as the Five O'Clock Club (see Appendix B). Attending regularly scheduled meetings and seminars for job-hunting and interviewing advice helps you structure your time wisely. The support of the group and expert coaches also help minimize anxiety.

A Special Word About Nerves and Group Interviews

Nervousness is especially common with group inter-views, either ones in which you are a single candidate interviewed by a panel or in which you are part of a group of candidates interviewed by one or more people. (Group interviews are described in more detail in Chapter 8, "Variations on the Interviewing Theme.") Group inter-views are anxiety-provoking simply because they are often more difficult from a social psychological perspective. Establishing rapport, meeting needs, maintaining eye contact, and reading body language are just a few of the challenges.

It has been my observation, however, that the biggest problem people have with group interviews is that they are akin to public speaking. You are expected to answer questions in front of other candidates and/or to address your replies to an audience of more than one. Sometimes you might even be required to conduct an actual presentation if you are interviewing for a training job or a position that would require making sales or management presentations.

Countless studies have shown that public speaking consistently surpasses death as Americans' No. 1 fear. So, it's no wonder that the thought of a group interview can get those gastrointestinal butterflies fluttering.

Fortunately, you don't have to let yourself be bullied by group interviews. If you find yourself suffering from stage fright, I recommend finding a "friend" in the group. Choose the interviewer (or fellow candidate) who has the most inviting demeanor—perhaps a friendly face, open body language, or positive reactions to your comments—and

Watch Out!
Some anxiety you experience before an interview may have nothing to do with your job search at all. Think about what other aspects of your life are causing you stress, and take action against the problems. You need all your mental energy for interviews.

glance at that person whenever you feel the sweaty palms coming on. Say to yourself, "He likes me" or "She seems to agree with what I'm saying." If you can also block out any negative thoughts about how the others are reacting to you, the positive self-talk will be even more effective. Many of the additional tips for dealing with nerves on the following pages will also work well in group situations.

Strategies for Combating Pre-Interview Nervousness

Simply telling yourself not to be nervous or having well-meaning friends or family say "Oh, I know you'll do fine" just isn't sufficient when nervousness strikes before an interview. The thoughts and feelings that accompany anxiety are powerful, and the physical symptoms are all too obvious. To combat these, you must learn, practice, and employ proven strategies. Many surefire approaches to dealing with nerves are provided on the following pages.

- Channel your nervous energy into positive action. Instead of wallowing in self-destructive thoughts and feelings, do something. Pour more time and energy into research or taking stock of your assets, and less time into unproductive worrying. You can also practice for your interviews, rehearsing what you might say and how you'll say it.

- Reflect on your accomplishments. If you dutifully prepared your asset statements but then put them aside, it's time to pull them back out. Reviewing the strengths, skills, and accomplishments that you have to offer an employer can give your self-confidence the rejuvenating boost it needs to calm your nerves.

Bright Idea
Video- or audio-tape yourself in a mock interview to see how you come across and to give yourself a chance to work on any problem areas. You'll then feel more confident going into an actual interview.

- Try to have other irons in the fire so that not too much rides on any one interview. There will undoubtedly be times when one interview takes on monumental proportions and you feel as if getting the job (or) not will make or break your career. It is normal for such situations to come up occasionally, but if you approach every interview as if it were the first, last, and only one that mattered, you're putting too heavy a burden on your shoulders. I suppose there is a reason why the maxim "Don't put all your eggs in one basket" is such a ubiquitous one. It really does make sense. At any given time in your job search, you should have at least several opportunities in the works. Never go into an interview knowing that if you don't succeed, you'll be back to square one. Your job search should be a bit like the ocean tides; when one set of waves hits the beach and disappears, another should follow. If one interview doesn't work out, you can look forward to the next one—or at least should have lots of feelers out to get more interviews.

- Take a break from your preparation the night before an interview. As you may have experienced during college, it usually doesn't pay to cram right up until the last minute. You need some time to decompress, relax, and let the information you've studied sink in. This downtime also lets you assess how prepared you are for the interview and can calm your nerves if you discover that you are in good shape.

- Similar to the last point is the strategy of distracting yourself shortly before an interview. Try to do something enjoyable and not work-related just before the appointment. You might get together for coffee with a friend, browse in a bookstore, go for a walk, or do whatever your schedule and location permit. Spending time with a friend is a particularly good way to distract yourself. Doing so not only helps reduce your anxiety level by taking your mind off the impending event, but it also warms you up for the interpersonal interaction aspect of the interview. (If you'll be rushing to an interview straight from work in the afternoon, at least try to do something enjoyable at lunch time; the benefits may last until the appointment.)

■ **Don't rush getting to the interview.** No matter how you spend your time just before the interview, it is absolutely essential that you avoid a last-minute rush to make the appointment on time. There may be nothing more nerve-wracking than worrying about traffic, a public transportation delay, or getting lost on your way to an interview.

■ **Use classic stress-reduction techniques** such as controlled breathing, muscle relaxation, and visualization. These include:

Take deep, slow breaths, focusing on and feeling the air entering and leaving your body. For an added benefit, breathe in through your nose and out through your mouth, hearing the air almost whistle its way out through your teeth. Be sure not to take such deep breaths that you start to hyperventilate.

To relax yourself physically—which usually leads to mental relaxation—close your eyes

Unofficially...
Approximately 23 million Americans—13% of the population—suffer from an anxiety disorder, according to the National Institute of Mental Health.

Moneysaver
Rather than paying for private sessions with a massage therapist to relieve stress before an interview, see if the city in which you're interviewing has a storefront chair-massage business, such as The Great American Backrub. You can stop in for a quick and inexpensive back or foot massage to soothe your frazzled nerves.

and concentrate on relaxing every part of your body. Start with your toes and work your way up to the top of your head. It sometimes helps to tighten each muscle first, then loosen it so that you can feel the relaxation in a more pronounced way.

You can guide yourself in a simple visualization exercise by closing your eyes and picturing yourself in a position that you would define as success. You might see yourself shaking the hand of the interviewer at the end of the meeting, satisfied that you've done your best. You might also see yourself placing the phone call to accept a job offer or entering your office on the first day of the new job.

What to Do When Stage Fright Strikes

You might make a concerted effort to minimize nervousness before an interview, only to find that an anxiety attack strikes once you're in the meeting. Even the most seasoned professionals and well-prepared job-seekers can become nervous during an interview. You may find that the interview is nothing like what you had anticipated or that the interviewer is a different person than the one you had expected to meet. You might also find that you're not as well prepared as you had thought. Or, you may be caught in an interview that is intentionally stressful and designed to intimidate you. (Stress interviews are discussed in more detail in Chapter 8.) In other cases, the interview might be moving along swimmingly, but you panic at the end because the very fact that you are doing so well creates more pressure than you can handle. Regardless of the cause, it is helpful to have a few tricks up your sleeve in case an unexpected—or expected—case of stage fright hits. The following strategies might come in handy:

- Don't make assumptions. Panic often sets in during an interview because you assume that the meeting is going badly. Don't fall into that trap! If you are lacking in confidence to start with, or if you're a bit shy with strangers, then it is easy to assume that you are doing or saying something wrong. You might think that the interviewer is bored, disinterested, displeased, or even angry, when, in fact, things are going fine. So, before you assume that the interview is taking a nose-dive, ask yourself if you could possibly be reading the signals wrong.

- Maintain that balance of power. Nervousness during an interview may intensify when you feel yourself losing control. If you're being grilled with tough questions or interrogated on difficult topics, you might feel yourself sinking into that lowly role of "job-seeker," slipping out of the role of confident problem-solver. If that happens, see what steps you can take to regain some control. Do a quick mental review of your agenda, and try to redirect the conversation to get your point across and to focus on positives instead of negatives. This is similar to the strategy mentioned previously for channeling nervous energy into positive action. If you can get your mind working on how to regain some power, you'll distract yourself from what made you nervous in the first place.

- Zero in on your environment. Have you ever come out of a situation in which you had been extremely nervous and felt like it was all a

Bright Idea
Keep in mind that employers have competition, too. Just as you are concerned about beating out other applicants, they are concerned about losing their best candidates to their competitors.

blur—almost as if you had blacked out, but you hadn't? When you get nervous, your brain stops focusing on your environment, so to combat nerves, it helps to zero in on something in your line of vision. Take note of a painting on the wall, the color of the curtains in the room, or the pattern in the interviewer's tie or scarf, saying to yourself, "That's an abstract painting," or "Those curtains are blue." Doing so helps bring you back to reality and sharpens your senses, counteracting the blurring of the senses that nervousness causes.

■ Employ some of the same breathing, muscle-relaxation, and visualization techniques that you used before the interview. You obviously can't close your eyes, wiggle your toes, or take noticeably deep breaths during the interview, but you can modify each of the techniques in a way that is unobtrusive. Keep in mind that the most important of all those methods is breathing. Simply remembering to breathe is critical to your composure. When you get nervous and are talking a lot, you might have a tendency to hold your breath without realizing it. Keep an eye on how you're breathing, and if necessary, pause to take in some air.

■ Address your anxiety openly, if necessary. Sometimes your nervousness is so overwhelming that trying to hide it only makes you more stressed and overtly affects your ability to communicate effectively. In those cases, it may be appropriate to address the nervousness openly. Let's say you really fumble a reply to a question or just go blank. As a way of explanation, you might say something like this: "You'll have to forgive me. I'm usually much more composed

Watch Out!
Never admit to nervousness when you're interviewing for high-level positions or for jobs such as sales or consulting, where you are expected to be able to handle the stresses of pressured situations and social interactions.

than this, but I'm so interested in this position that I've gotten a bit more nervous than I thought I would be." Only bring up the nerves, however, when you feel that you have little to lose by doing so. In other words, you have to weigh which is worse: admitting to being nervous, or having the interviewer assume that you are just inarticulate, unintelligent, or ill-prepared. Often, the former is the lesser of two evils. And, the very act of addressing the nervousness head-on shows some composure and confidence in and of itself.

Keep Some Perspective

As mentioned before, some job-seekers get their hearts and minds set on a particular job and feel that their entire future rides on one interview. What a burden! If you find yourself becoming anxious midstream, try to put the interview in perspective. This is not the last interview you will ever have. You are not interviewing at the last company on earth or with the greatest company on earth. If you fail, you will not lose your friends, your spouse, or your dog (and if they do leave you over one lousy interview, then you wouldn't have wanted them around anymore anyway!). True, you may have a great deal riding on one potential job. You may be in a dire financial situation or at the tail end of a long, frustrating search. Even given those circumstances, though, you do yourself a disservice if you put too much pressure on any one meeting. Remember the example of my friend who did her best interviewing when she finally let go of the pressure and just let things happen.

We become habituated to responding to anxiety with self-destructive and dysfunctional behaviors that are passed down from one generation to another. As a result, one out of four Americans (65 million) has experienced the crippling effect of clinical anxiety symptoms.

—Robert Gerzon in *Finding Serenity in the Age of Anxiety,* New York: Macmillan, 1997

Just the Facts

- Developing the right mental attitude is just as important as researching the prospective employer and preparing your asset statements.

- To interview strategically, you must understand how your thoughts and emotions affect your performance.

- The psychology of group dynamics is a critical element in interviewing.

- Being nervous before and/or during an interview is normal, and if you get too worried about it you'll only make it worse.

- In an interview, you are being evaluated as a potential employee; your worth as a human being is not being judged.

- To combat anxiety, replace your negative "self-talk" with positive statements, and channel your nervous energy into constructive action.

Making a Good First—and Lasting—Impression

PART III

GET THE SCOOP ON...
Creating your image from the inside out ▪
Dressing and accessorizing to your advantage ▪
Interviewing etiquette ▪ Using references to
make—not break—your image ▪ Communicating
your image on paper

Presenting the Right Image

I doubt I'm the first person to tell you that your nonverbal communication and appearance may have more of an impact on your interviewers than the actual words you utter. This fact is supported in the frequently cited findings of sociolinguist Albert Mehrabian, whose research into interpersonal communication sheds light on how impressions are formed and images interpreted. Through a large-scale study of adults in face-to-face encounters, Mehrabian found that our verbal message (the actual words we say) accounts for only 7 percent of the impression the listener forms about us. How we say what we're saying—that is, the tone, speed, volume, inflection, and vocal quality of our speech—accounts for 38 percent, while our facial expression and body language form 55 percent of the impression.

Add to those dramatic figures the findings of social psychologists, which suggest that a first impression is formed in only about seven seconds, and you may start to wonder why you even need to open your mouth in an interview. The content of your interview dialogue is critical, of course, but there's no denying that your overall image enhances or detracts from that content. Let's face it: A well-groomed, appropriately dressed individual with confident carriage will be better received than a less-polished person, even if the exact same words are coming out of their mouths.

The impression you make leads the interviewer to conjure up assumptions about your competence, level of sophistication, integrity, social standing, and even intelligence. The image you project to the interviewer in part comes from what's going on inside your head—your attitude and confidence level. Added to that is your outward appearance, which obviously conveys a particular image. Then there's the reflection of you through the eyes of others, namely current or former bosses, colleagues, or clients who serve as your references. Finally, you project your image through written materials—your resume, portfolio, and correspondence. This chapter addresses each of these aspects of image; we move to the related topics of oral communication and establishing rapport in Chapter 7, "Strategic Communication for Interviews."

Image From the Inside: How You Feel About Yourself

We usually think of clothing, hairstyle, the car we drive, and other external trappings as the most obvious symbols of our image, but the fact is that our true image comes from the inside. How you feel about yourself manifests itself in your outward appearance. To convey the right image when interviewing, you must be confident, well-prepared, and comfortable in your own skin. And, even if you have those factors under control, you must go one step further and make sure that your body language and manners bolster rather than detract from your image.

The Power of Nonverbal Communication

If you've ever studied how to communicate effectively, you know that nonverbal communication speaks volumes. What you do with your hands while speaking, how you carry yourself, and whether you make eye contact are just a few elements of the language our bodies speak. As a quick refresher before your interview, review the following checklist of tips for successful—that is, unobtrusive—nonverbal communication.

- Posture: Stand and walk with your head erect and shoulders back, and keep your gait lively.

- Hands: Keep your hand gestures to a minimum, but don't feel you have to sit on your hands and do nothing with them. Some movement of hands while speaking is natural; just be sure they're not flailing about wildly. Also be sure to keep your hands visible at all times, as not doing so can send a subliminal message that you are untrustworthy.

- Handshake: Shaking hands well is an art. Of course you know not to give a limp, fishy handshake, but are you sure you're not doing so without realizing it? All too often men who are usually not the least bit chauvinist in the ordinary course of the day unwittingly shake a woman's hand gingerly, as if it will break. Everyone should receive a firm but not bone-crushing handshake. Also be sure not to pump

> 66
> The receiving person is bombarded with symbols and signals from you. Everything you do in relation to other people causes them to make judgments about what you stand for and what your message is...unless you identify yourself as a walking, talking message, you miss that critical point.
> —Roger Ailes in *You Are the Message* (New York: Doubleday, 1988)
>

the other person's hand and arm too vigorously or for too long. A quick one or two pumps will suffice. And use only one hand; the two-handed shake (with your second hand patting the top of the two clasped hands) should be reserved for the receiving line of weddings and funerals.

Bright Idea
Carry with you an index card on which you've jotted down a few words or phrases that remind you of a past occasion when you were successful or were rewarded for your accomplishments. Review the card before each interview whenever you need a confidence boost.

■ Facial expression: As mentioned in Chapter 2, "The Biggest Mistakes Interviewees Make," smiling can work wonders. If the image you want to convey is of an upbeat, energetic, capable person, then you must have a pleasant expression on your face. A face that looks relaxed—no furrowed brow, tense jaw, nervous twitches, or stern expression—gives the interviewer the impression that you are not only a pleasant person to deal with, but a confident one, too. You don't have to smile widely and incessantly, but you should make sure that the corners of your mouth are slightly upturned the majority of the time, or in a neutral position when you need to look serious or contemplative.

■ Head movement: A common problem for people who are anxious is to nod their heads excessively. I remember the first time I saw a tape of myself from a live television talk show on which I had been discussing career issues. My head was moving up and down so much I looked as if I was playing the old children's game of bobbing for apples. I was clearly so eager to please—and so nervous about my ability to do so—that I was using the nodding to compensate for my insecurities at that moment, as many people do in such situations. When interviewing, be sure that your head-nodding is subtle and appropriate to the interviewer's comments.

- Eye contact: No list of tips on nonverbal communication would be complete without the mention of maintaining good eye contact, but do you really know what that means? It's often easier said than done. You must balance looking other people in the eyes without staring them down. To do so, concentrate on making eye contact most of the time but breaking it up with an occasional glance away. Just make sure that you don't look down when glancing away or you may be seen as shifty or untrustworthy. A gaze that goes slightly upward, on the other hand, usually signals that you're thinking. Also, try shifting your gaze back and forth between the other person's two eyes. The subtle shift will keep the interviewer from feeling that you're staring.

- Miscellaneous gestures: Watch out for such unnecessary and unprofessional gestures as tapping your foot, fiddling with a ring or other jewelry, twirling your hair, and drumming your fingers on the chair arm or desk. Not only are these movements distracting, but they imply that you are nervous, impatient, and/or bored.

Etiquette is More Than Table Manners

We live in an age that is less formal than any time in recent history, both in society and in the workplace. As a result, the mention of etiquette may, for some, conjure up outmoded images of calling cards and shoes that match pocketbooks. Such an attitude can be devastating in the professional world, however. Having good manners and following accepted protocol is more than a nicety; it is a necessity.

Though I have recommended that you be relaxed and down-to-earth in your dealings with

> **"**
> There is a new informality at work in how we meet and great, entertain, dress, and socialize with one another, and yet a new formality as we deal with a diversity of people and in other countries.
> —Letitia Baldrige in the *New Complete Guide to Executive Manners* (New York: Simon & Schuster, 1993)
> **"**

prospective employers, I do not mean to advocate abandoning all sense of protocol. It is possible to do both: to follow rules of etiquette and to be comfortably informal. In fact, when you know how to conduct yourself properly and don't have to agonize over which fork to use, you are liberated in a way that enables you to relax and be yourself. Plus, good manners show respect for others, and knowing the rules of etiquette helps you come across as self-assured. When you don't have to worry about how to conduct yourself in a social situation, you are free to concentrate on the business at hand and not on trivial matters.

Unofficially...
Good manners are not just for people who wine and dine clients. Corporations have increased their use of etiquette consultants in recent years, indicating an emphasis on protocol and courtesy as important skills for all employees.

It's worth it to take some time and get an etiquette lesson if you've never learned such things or are a bit rusty. To that end, I've listed a number of good books in the "Business Etiquette" section of the bibliography in Appendix C. You should consult them, or perhaps an actual etiquette expert, for more thorough instruction on the subject than the scope of this book allows. In the meantime, the following are a few quick tips on etiquette:

- Defer to, and show respect to, others who hold a higher position than you or who have more authority, rather than basing those gestures on gender or age. This applies to such circumstances as holding doors open for others and deciding whom to address first when you approach a group of people.

- When introducing yourself to others, do so in about 10 seconds or less. Don't monopolize the conversation before it even starts.

- Don't invade other people's personal space. Be sure that you are roughly arm's length—about 3 to 5 feet—from anyone you're speaking to.

- When you're in a group and a new person approaches, take the initiative to introduce yourself and others in the group to that new person (unless another group member is clearly in charge).

- Make "thank-you" a standard part of your vernacular. From the person who fills your water glass in a restaurant, to the receptionist who greets you before an interview, to the person who conducts an interview, you should make it a point to express your thanks.

- Stick to neutral, noncontroversial topics when making small-talk, and don't ask personal questions.

- When entering the room for a meeting or interview, wait to sit until you are invited to do so.

- Be an attentive, active listener. It is inconsiderate to be preoccupied with what you are going to say next rather than focusing on what the other person is saying at that moment.

- Be cordial to everyone you meet at all times.

- Be discreet. Don't reveal secrets of your former employer, such as confidential projects, future plans, proprietary information, or personal matters of people with whom you've worked.

- Keep your technology in working order. A fax that doesn't work or is always busy, e-mail you forget to check, or an answering machine that cuts callers off after 10 seconds is frustrating to people trying to communicate with you. What's more, this sends the wrong signal about whether you have your act together.

- Be punctual. Allow extra time to get to interviews to guard against unforeseen delays; if you

Timesaver
Always get the business card of anyone you meet when interviewing so that you can send your thank-yous and follow-up notes promptly without having to chase down spelling of names, titles, and addresses later.

are going to be late, call to let them know. Being punctual also applies to keeping telephone appointments, returning calls in a timely manner, and promptly sending any necessary documents (perhaps a resume, school transcript, reference list, or other materials interviewers may request before or after you meet).

Watch Out!
If you're trying to obtain a job at a higher level than any you've held in the past, be sure your image is congruent with that higher level, even before you have the job.

Image on the Outside: How You Look

When I had my first professional photo shoot, the photographer and stylist asked me what kind of image I wanted to convey. I was taken aback by the question because I really hadn't thought about it. I knew that I didn't want to look like I was having a bad hair day and that I wanted to look slim, but beyond that, I wasn't sure. They told me that most women they photograph want to look like Diane Sawyer—professional and serious, yet soft and feminine. I said that I wanted to look like myself, which raised the unnecessarily existential question—unnecessary for the occasion, at least: "Who am I?"

Whether male or female, when you find yourself selecting clothes to wear on an interview or considering a new haircut, you may be surprised to find that this is a question you are asking yourself as well. "Should I wear the white shirt or the blue one, the gray suit or the beige one?" is really the same thing as saying "Who do I want to be today?" Outfitting yourself for an interview raises the issue of your personal style, and how that style conforms to or conflicts with that of the environment in which you'd like to work or the job you want to hold.

No matter what you look like, it is important to communicate a clear image or style through the variables over which you do have some control: the color, cut, and style of clothes you wear; the accessories you choose; and your personal grooming. The image you radiate must be appropriate for your career field, career level (or level to which you aspire), industry, geographic location, type of organization, and nature and level of the job for which you'll be interviewing. More importantly, it needs to fit you.

I knew I was no Diane Sawyer when I had that photo shoot, but I understood what the photographer and stylist meant when they made that comment. They weren't suggesting that I be someone I'm not. They were saying that with the right makeup, hairstyle, facial expression, clothing, and lighting, they could incorporate elements of a respected and admired professional into my own natural look. They could create an image. You can do the same for yourself without a great deal of effort or expense. Let's look at the components of your external image and examine some guidelines for making the most of each.

Color

Before discussing clothing, accessories, and grooming, let's examine the issue of color, which pervades all aspects of your appearance. Color is actually the subject of a scientific movement: chromatics, which explores the physical properties of color and the effects of color on humans.

In 1666, Isaac Newton declared that light is essential for color to exist in the human eye and mind, which raises an interesting question: When the lights are turned out in a colorful room, does the color still exist if no one's there to see it? Apparently, it does if you touch it. Scientists have found that blind people can "see" color by picking up vibrations from colors' wave lengths on human

Unofficially...
In some high-tech companies—particularly West Coast ones—where routine attire is jeans and sandals, a new phenomenon of Dress-Up Fridays has emerged so that technical types can practice dressing like some of their more formal clients and colleagues.

tissue. Sometimes their tongue, earlobe, or tip of nose is even more effective than fingers. It seems that colored light beams transmit energy to humans who come in contact with them.

The length of these light waves and the speed of the vibrations colors emit affect us in various ways. Color can affect our blood pressure, rate of breathing, pulse rate, sensitivity of taste buds, and sense of smell—not to mention our mood.

Watch Out!
We see colors in relation to their surrounding colors (such as ties against shirts, scarves against blouses, and a suit against your skin tone), so keep this in mind when deciding which colors to wear. The power of a particular color will be enhanced or diminished by the color(s) next to it.

As a result, color has been used creatively and strategically in everything from marketing to engineering. Blue, for example, is used for packaging "slim" products such as club soda, cottage cheese, and skim milk. Red is the powerful, energetic color used for colas. And when the makers of sugar-free Canada Dry ginger ale changed their cans from red to green and white (to convey flavor, nature, and purity), sales rose 27 percent in six months. Engineers sometimes paint bridges blue in hopes that the color's calming effect will deter suicides, and architects have changed school walls from orange to blue and found that students' blood pressure dropped. (These examples of the use of color are excerpted from Morton Walker's *The Power of Color,* Garden City Park, NY: Avery Publishing Group, 1991.)

And you thought your spouse was just being difficult when asking disgustedly, "Are you going to wear that?" Colors clearly have a profound effect on the people who see them. This does not mean you need to forget all other preparation for your interviews and agonize for days over the colors you will wear. But it does mean that the careful use of color can be one more tool in your interviewing strategy.

Certainly, choosing colors based on their potential effect on the interviewer's mood or "purchasing decision" is one tactic. But, you should also select colors that are appropriate for the occupation or industry in which you're seeking work and are flattering to you. Some conservative industries and professions such as banking and law require more subtle colors. In fields like advertising, media, technology, entertainment, and education, you can get away with much brighter, bolder hues and interesting color combinations.

The Positive and Negative Powers of Color

The chart on page 130, adapted from Morton Walker's *The Power of Color,* shows what typically comes to mind when we see various hues, including the negative effects of those colors.

Clothing

Besides being careful about the color of your clothing, you must pay attention to which items of clothing you choose to wear. As you probably know, gone are the days when navy blue suits and white shirts were de rigueur for interviews. You have considerably more leeway in how you dress for an interview now, as long as your attire is appropriate for the job, the organizational culture, and the industry or profession.

Jobs in finance, law, management consulting, and many areas of business do still have fairly rigid dress codes—at least for the interview. You almost always must wear a navy or gray suit (brown, black, and beige are occasionally appropriate, but check that out with someone familiar with where you're going before straying too far from shades of blue or gray). A white shirt for men is usually the best option for its clean, crisp, and conservative appearance. Women have a bit more range of possibilities

Bright Idea
If you're interested in learning more about the best shades for you, call 1-800-COLORME for a referral to a color consultant near you who can conduct a personalized color analysis.

Once, the gray flannel suit embodied the ideals of a rigid business era. Now what's called for is a more creative, entrepreneurial attire—one that combines the power suit with the comfort of a casual look.

—Kim Johnson Gross in *Work Clothes: Casual Dress for Serious Work* (New York: Knopf, 1996)

99

COLOR SYMBOLISM

Yellow (when bold)	Positive: Power, joy, wisdom, intuitional insight, youth, merriment Negative: Cowardice
Green	Positive: Nature, healing, peace, regeneration, fortune. Negative: Selfishness, jealousy, laziness
Red	Positive: Power, energy, vitality, strength, excitement for life, passion Negative: Anger, danger, uncontrolled passion, suffering
Blue	Positive: Truth, harmony, calmness, soothing Negative: Depressing
White	Positive: Innocence, purity, perfection, truth Negative: Intolerable to people who are deceitful, malicious, jealous, violent
Black	Positive: Absence of light, strength, power Negative: Emotional drain, loss, death
Indigo (between blue and violet)	Positive: The balance of reason and intuition, discipline and creativity

when it comes to blouses and can venture into blues, yellows, or ivories. They may also wear well-tailored business dresses with matching jackets in lieu of the traditional skirt, blouse, jacket combo.

For jobs in creative or less conservative fields (as well as in education and social services), appropriate attire varies widely. You shouldn't show up for an interview as a social worker or an elementary school teacher in a pinstripe suit, but you shouldn't go so far as to wear jeans or extremely casual attire either, even if that's what you might wear on the job. The rough rule of thumb is to find out what people wear on the job and then err slightly on the side of formality and conservatism while still reflecting the spirit of the setting.

Also make sure that what you choose to wear fits not only the prospective employer and the job, but you as well. Your outfit should enhance your features, coloring, and body shape and size. It should feel like you, not like a costume.

In addition to those rules of thumb, consider the following clothing guidelines:

- Do wear durable fabrics that don't wrinkle excessively.

- Don't wear 100 percent synthetic fabrics.

- Don't ever dress provocatively or in any way that detracts from your professionalism.

- Do wear clothes that are generously cut, not tight or clingy.

- Do make sure that the sleeves of jackets and shirts are long enough.

- Don't have a gap between the back of your neck and your jacket collar.

- Don't wear anything you haven't worn for at least an hour as a "trial run."

Moneysaver
When it comes to clothes, you save money by spending money. If you buy good quality items that fit well and are durable—and also in classic styles that will stand the test of time—you'll save money in the long run.

- Don't wear stockings darker than your shoes (women).

- Don't wear a tie the same hue as your suit or shirt, unless you are a fashion guru and can pull off the look (men).

Watch Out!
When there's a sale on clothes, resist the temptation to buy twice as much just because you're getting a bargain. Instead, buy fewer items of better quality (and, most likely, with higher original prices). They'll last longer, be more likely to stay in style, and will clutter your closet less.

And, finally, be sure to consider the geographic region in which you're interviewing. This is obviously of particular importance if you are attempting to relocate and find yourself in a part of the country—or the world—where you feel a bit like a fish out of water. If you're a woman from the South interviewing in Manhattan you might be surprised to see how many women are sporting black opaque stockings in April while you're in nude or ivory hose. A man from Detroit in a nice pair of wingtips might be taken aback by his Texan interviewer's cowboy boots. A job-seeker from the Northeast may be surprised at the informality of a workplace in southern California. These are just a few of the fashion stereotypes that usually hold true and can trip up unsuspecting job-seekers. Don't feel you can't be yourself; it's a mistake to try to adopt the look of a particular region or city if it's not really you. Be sensitive to the differences, though, and make some small accommodations that let you strike a balance between being yourself and not standing out like a sore thumb.

Accessories

When deciding what to wear, don't overlook the importance of accessories. For women, an attractive silk scarf or carefully selected piece of jewelry can make or break an outfit. For men, the right watch and pair of shoes can enhance your image more than even the more obvious items, such as your tie and suit.

Generally speaking, accessories should subtly accent your overall look, not detract from it. They also reflect your individual style; only so many cuts of suits exist, but you can choose from a seemingly infinite selection of watches, jewelry, bags, and scarves. When taking stock of your accessories, make sure that each of the following items meets the requirements of quality, style, taste, subtlety, and appropriateness:

- Jewelry
- Watch
- The pen you carry and may use during an interview
- Briefcase or portfolio
- Any other bags you carry (all should be in good condition and uncluttered)
- Overcoat or raincoat
- Shoes
- The car in which you arrive (if you drive to interviews and your car is a rolling wreck, try to borrow a car or park out of sight of the interviewers' offices)

Grooming

No matter how busy you are or how disinterested you are in your looks, there's no excuse for cutting corners when it comes to personal grooming. A clean, tidy, fresh appearance goes a long way toward presenting the right image in interviews. Good grooming leads to forgiveness of any flaws in your natural appearance and shows that you care enough about yourself and about the occasion of your interview to make an effort. I probably don't have to tell you to have clean fingernails, take a bath, and make

Watch Out!
Don't forget that your wallet is an important accessory. If you are dressed impeccably but pull out a tattered, overstuffed wallet, what does that say about your image?

Bright Idea
Some amazing products available in drug stores and department stores conceal blemishes or under-eye circles. These substances appear green or yellow in their containers until you apply them to your skin, where they make flaws practically disappear. These products aren't makeup — men can use them as well as women.

sure your makeup is subtle, but for the record, I've provided the following grooming checklist:

- Nails should be clean and trimmed, and skin moisturized to avoid a cracked, dry look. Women should keep nail polish to a neutral color for conservative jobs and organizations, or in a bolder but stylish, tasteful color for more creative or fashion-oriented settings.

- Your hair should be styled so that it's flattering to your face and body size, and not outdated. Any coloring should be subtle and well-maintained. Most importantly, hair should be clean.

- Do your best to keep your skin clear and fresh by watching what you eat, getting rest and exercise, and using non-irritating cleansing products and cosmetics.

- Most women should wear makeup to an interview even if they don't typically do so. When applied well, it looks natural but enhances your own looks. If you are already a big fan of makeup, make sure you are not heavy-handed. The effects should be subtle, well-blended, and flattering. Consult a makeup artist if you have any doubts.

- Your safest bet is to wear no perfume or cologne at all, but if you do, put it on with a light touch. And, remember, cologne is no substitute for a good hot shower.

- Don't assume your breath is fresh; be extra vigilant in making and keeping it that way. Be careful what you eat for a day or two before an interview, and always carry breath mints or spray. (And don't forget that a seemingly harmless cup of coffee before an interview can ruin your breath.)

- Never smoke in an interview—and if you smoke beforehand, do so in an open space so that the smell of smoke won't cling to your clothes and body.

How Your References Reinforce Your Image

Job-seekers typically think of their references as people who will say either good things or bad things about them. Fortunately, the issue is a little more complicated than that. I say "fortunately" because, when chosen, requested, and used strategically, references can be much more than people who will put in a good or bad word for you. These current or former bosses, colleagues, and clients can serve as publicists of sorts, helping you shape an image that will be received favorably by prospective employers.

Making Your References Work for You

The way references shape that image depends in large part on information that you give them. Always try to have some input into the content of your letters of recommendation or conversations your references will have with prospective employers. Rather than simply asking a boss or colleague to serve as a reference for you, discuss your career objectives with them and share your asset statements. Even if your references know you well, you'd be amazed at how uninspired and generic a recommendation they can give without realizing it. So, be sure to let them know which of your strengths and areas of experience you'd like them to emphasize, and which personal qualities they should mention. Also remind them of how you distinguished yourself from your peers.

Bright Idea
To make sure your polished image stays that way, always pack an interviewing "emergency kit." Include such items as safety pins, breath mints, a small mirror, an extra pair of stockings for women, an extra tie for men (in case of stains), and anything else you think you might need.

A Reference List or Recommendation Letters?

Job-seekers commonly ask whether prospective employers prefer a list of references who can be contacted by phone or actual letters of recommendation—or both. The answer is both—usually, that is. Sometimes letters aren't necessary because the hiring process is an informal one in which a quick call made to your last boss will suffice. With other interviewers, letters might make no difference because those individuals don't put much stock in them. They may believe that no one is going to reveal any negatives about you in an open letter, so they consider conversations with your references to be a more thorough approach.

Other employers might not want to bother with phone calls to people on your reference list and will be pleased to have a few letters conveniently on hand. You won't always know which method will be preferred, so it's best to have both available. You should have three to five letters of recommendation (photocopies of the originals are fine), as well as a typed list of three to five people who can support your candidacy. The format of reference lists varies slightly according to personal style preferences but usually parallels that of your resume—that is, using the same or similar font style and size, layout, and paper. Remember to include an e-mail address and fax number for your references whenever possible. Figure 6.1 presents a sample reference list.

Conveying Your Image on Paper

Before witnessing on the Internet the various levels of writing skills of people all over the country, I had no idea what a rare and valuable commodity it is to be able to write even reasonably well. Anyone who can construct a sentence that makes sense and that

FIGURE 6.1: SAMPLE REFERENCE LIST

Nancy Burton
5555 First Street
Chicago, IL 11111
(111) 333-3333 (tel)
(111) 333-4444 (fax)
fakeaddress@all.com

References
Molly Craig
Vice President, Corporate Finance
First Capital, Inc.
222 Second Street, Suite 400
Chicago, IL 11111
(111) 444-4444 (tel)
(111) 444-5555 (fax)
mcraig@fc.com
(Emerging Markets Group Director
and my immediate supervisor, 1997 to present)

John Stevenson
Vice President, Corporate Finance
The Global Corporation
333 Fourth Street, Suite 500
Chicago, IL 11111
(111) 555-5555 (tel)
(111) 555-6666 (fax)
(Emerging Markets Group Director,
and my immediate supervisor at First Capital
1992–1996)

Alexandra Gann
Managing Partner
Economic Solutions, Inc.
444 Fifth Street, 6th floor
Lake Forest, IL 22222
(111) 777-7777 (tel)
(111) 777-8888 (fax)
AKG@es.com
(Client at First Capital)

Homer Price
Professor, Finance Department
Graduate School of Business
Wilson University
Rockefeller Hall
Boston, MA 33333
(222) 888-8888 (tel)
(222) 888-9999 (fax)
hprice@wils.GSB.edu

← **Note!**
If any of your references have changed jobs or companies since you worked with them, give their current contact information and add a parenthetical statement that clarifies their past connection to you. It is optional, but recommended, that you do this for all other references as well, to clarify all connections.

is not riddled with spelling, punctuation, and grammatical errors has a real advantage in the workplace—and in life in general. Anyone who can put two or more of those sentences together in a coherent fashion to convey a point, to educate, or to entertain is miles ahead of the pack. So, what does this have to do with interviewing?

The interviewing process inevitably involves written communication of some sort. Often, you get an interview in the first place as the result of a resume and cover letter. Then you have to write thank-you notes and other follow-up communication. Part of building your case depends upon this correspondence. On a more abstract note, every piece of paper associated with you and your job search is a reflection of your overall image.

The Only Advice You'll Ever Need About Writing Well

I have just one thing to say about written business communication: Write in plain English as if you were speaking to the reader.

Writing from this perspective means abandoning most of the commonly held assumptions about how business writing should sound. Just because you're writing in a business arena or for a job search, you don't have to be overly formal or serious, and you don't have to use a cumbersome vocabulary that feels alien. If you begin by thinking of how an idea or point would sound if you simply said it to someone out loud, you can get that information down on paper in a way that will be pleasing and understandable for the reader. This method is so effective that there has been something of a "Plain English Movement" in the corporate world and public sector, with consultants training employees in this homespun approach to writing.

Of course, writing well is a little more complicated than simply writing as if you were speaking. If
you have problems with grammar, punctuation, syntax, and organizing content, you should solve those
problems through a formal course, tutoring, or
some other means. But if you know the basics of
writing, then you are ready to tackle the method of
writing simply and conversationally.

To get an idea of how powerful clean, clear writing can be, consider this excerpt from *The Old Man
and the Sea* (Scribner/Simon & Schuster, 1952) from
the master of plain English writing, Ernest
Hemingway:

> Everything about him was old except his eyes,
> and they were the same color as the sea and
> were cheerful and undefeated.

Now see how that sentence would sound if it had
been written in the stilted, awkward, and choppy
voice of a bureaucrat:

> All features of him were classified as aged.
> Notwithstanding that fact, however, his ocular
> region constituted a noteworthy exception. The
> latter was analogous in color to that of oceanic
> bodies. In addition, it was blithe and had
> resisted succumbing to adversaries.

Now, I'll admit that this version of Hemingway's
prose is a bit exaggerated, but I expect it doesn't
stray too far in style and tone from some actual business communication you have read at some point in
your career. While a little formality is good—it
shows respect for the reader and the circumstances—you can have too much of a good thing.
The beauty of loosening up and relaxing your tone
is that, in doing so, you actually convey more confidence and professionalism than when you write the

other way. Getting to the point and using slightly conversational style shows that you know what you want to say and how to say it. Writing in an awkward, complicated fashion looks like you're hiding something or that you don't really know what to say.

To write in the plain English method, consider the following tips. (For many more, read *The Plain English Approach to Business Writing* by Edward P. Bailey, Jr. [New York: Oxford University Press, 1997].)

- Use an active rather than passive voice for verbs and for your overall tone. For example, instead of saying "It has come to my attention...," say "I have realized that..." Or, instead of "My efforts on that project were well received," say "My boss and co-workers gave me excellent feedback on my efforts with that project."

- Use contractions. Saying "I am" or "I have" becomes monotonous to the reader. Try to break up the monotony by using contractions in your subject-verb combinations occasionally, saying "I'm," "I've," etc.

- Take some poetic license with rules of grammar. There's nothing wrong with taking some liberties with grammatical rules that are often wrongly thought to be etched in stone. It is acceptable to occasionally split an infinitive or end a sentence with a preposition such as "but" or "with" if doing so makes your writing flow more smoothly. And, you may choose to start a sentence with "and" or "but" from time to time to avoid choppiness.

- Use common words. People who truly have an extensive vocabulary don't try to show off their knowledge at every turn but, instead, use impressive words only when appropriate. When you have a choice, it is usually best to opt for the more ordinary word to express a thought, then save the more sophisticated vocabulary for when it's the best—and perhaps only—way to convey what you mean.

Also make sure that the way you organize the content of your writing is effective. Start with your main point in the first sentence or two, then lay out the details. Business communication should be something like the inverted pyramid style of journalistic writing. You begin with the headline and the crux of the story, then fill in the details.

Finally, make sure that the overall look and format of your written communication is pleasing to the eye, clean, and neat. Use adequate margins, space text well too avoid a crowded look, and keep paragraphs short to avoid a dense feel to the text. If your letters or resumes will be sent through regular mail (as opposed to faxing or e-mailing) or will be delivered by hand, use good quality paper in a conservative color.

Portfolios: The Ultimate Reflection of You on Paper

Portfolios have been increasing in popularity over the past few years as a way to provide examples of your skills, talents, and experience. A portfolio is a binder or notebook of some sort in which you have assembled documents that may include any of the following: samples of your work; letters of recommendation; your reference list; copies of award certificates; academic transcripts; favorable correspondence, such as letters of congratulation or thanks from colleagues or bosses; and perhaps an extra copy of your resume.

Unofficially...
Pyscholinguists have found that it takes longer to read less commonly used words, such as "culminate," than more common ones, like "end." The difference may only be a fraction of a second, but that's significant. Considering that the average cover letter or resume is read in about 10 seconds, you don't have any time to spare.

Portfolios also reinforce your image. The fact that you have even put one together makes you seem more professional and shows that you have your act together. Think about what it's like when you are considering a major purchase. Do you enjoy, and find it helpful, to have brochures and other documentation to look through? It's the same for prospective employers. A portfolio gives them something tangible on which to base their decision and puts a nice finishing touch on your overall image.

Just the Facts

- Be aware that your nonverbal communication and appearance have as powerful an impact on the interviewer as do your words—if not more so.

- Learn and follow rules of business etiquette.

- Image begins on the inside. To convey the best image, be confident and well prepared.

- Image also depends on external factors, including the colors you wear, your clothing, accessories, and grooming.

- Make sure that people serving as your references echo the image you want to convey rather than giving a generic recommendation.

- Try to have both a list of references and actual letters of recommendation available to prospective employers.

- Be aware that your written communication is also a reflection of your image.

- The best thing you can do to improve your writing is to write in plain English, as if you were talking.

- Assemble a portfolio of your work and commendations to further bolster your image.

GET THE SCOOP ON...
Establishing rapport ▪ Saying the right things ▪
Using power words and phrases ▪ Identifying
subjects to avoid ▪ Understanding nuances of
cross-cultural communication

Strategic Communication for Interviews

W hen was the last time you listened to something you didn't want to hear? We are often able to be highly selective in what we choose to hear thanks to the mute button on the television's remote control, the VCR's fast-forward command, and personal stereo headsets that tune out the world. As a result, fewer people these days are truly attentive, patient listeners.

Even if you think of yourself as a good listener and as someone who hasn't gotten caught up in this blocking-out-the-world-through-technology phenomenon, keep in mind that the people to whom you'll be speaking in your interviews might not be such skilled listeners. You therefore must communicate in a way that grabs and holds their attention without being slick or insincere.

The way to do this is to remember that an interview is a conversation, not an interrogation or a

> **66**
> Dialogue, by my
> definition, is
> what happens
> when your reality
> connects with
> your audience's
> reality and
> together you
> move toward a
> new common
> reality.
> —Nido Qubein in
> *How to Be a*
> *Great Communi-*
> *cator* (New York:
> John Wiley &
> Sons, 1997)
> **99**

monologue. You are not simply sitting back having questions fired at you, then rattling on with no input from the other person. When an interview is based on dialogue—not one-sided communication—all parties involved are engaged in the discussion.

Five basic steps lead to effective communication:

1. Deliver your message (through verbal and non-verbal communication).

2. Make sure your message is heard.

3. Determine whether your message has been interpreted accurately.

4. Receive a reply, and continue the dialogue.

5. Leave a good feeling behind after the dialogue is finished.

Of course, steps one through four are repeated throughout a conversation. You say something; the interviewer hears that message, processes it, and responds; and then you deliver another message in reply to that response. While going through those steps, you must establish rapport, say the right things, use appropriate body language, and listen to the interviewer. You then must close the dialogue in a way that will maintain the positive rapport you've established after the interview is over.

The objective in this chapter is to point out common pitfalls to avoid and offer strategies to employ as you go through those steps during an interview. For more detailed advice on oral communication techniques, you may want to turn to some of the excellent books on the subject listed in Appendix C.

Delivering Your Message

As mentioned in previous chapters, the message you convey to interviewers is based on both verbal and nonverbal communication. Your overall conduct—

as well as your body language and appearance—count as much, if not more, than your verbal message.

The following pages discuss how you can begin to deliver your message effectively before the interview even takes place. Then we move on to tips for determining the content of your communication, the actual words and phrases you choose to use.

Critical Pre-Interview Interactions

Many job-seekers focus so intently on an upcoming interview that they forget to apply strategy to pre-interview interactions. This can be a damaging oversight, because the process of establishing rapport with the prospective employer actually begins before you arrive for your interview and continues into the first few minutes of the meeting. Some ways to start the flow of communication going smoothly include the following:

- Make scheduling appointments easy. Don't be overly demanding when coming up with a mutually convenient day and time to meet, and don't reschedule unless absolutely unavoidable.

- Follow through on all your promises. As mentioned in the etiquette discussion in Chapter 6, "Presenting the Right Image," if you have to fax a resume or reference list, make a phone call to schedule an appointment, or engage in any other interaction with the prospective employer prior to the interview, be sure that you do things when you say you will. If you can't do so, call, e-mail, or fax, to let him or her know when you will be following through.

- Be considerate with everyone you speak to or meet. Be courteous and appreciative when working with administrative assistants and

Watch Out!
While it is important to be flexible and accommodating when agreeing on a day and time for an interview, don't go overboard and make your schedule sound wide open. You should give the impression that you are active and in demand, even if you're not currently employed.

receptionists to arrange your interview. And, when you arrive for your interview, be pleasant with everyone you meet, from parking garage attendants to the people in the waiting room. You never know who might have input on the hiring decision.

Bright Idea
To arrive at interviews at the right time, aim for being 30 minutes early to allow for unforeseen delays. If you do actually arrive that early, take a stroll around the block, wait in your car, sit in the building's lobby, or pass the time in some other way until about 10 or 15 minutes before your interview time.

- Be on time for your appointment, but not too early. A common error interviewees make, which seems innocent enough, is to arrive more than 15 minutes early. While an occasional interviewer will be happy to meet with you early to get a little ahead of schedule, many will see your premature arrival as an irritating occurrence that feels intrusive.

- Make every entrance count. When you enter the building, waiting room, and office where the interview will take place, do so in a way that balances energy and composure. Be unobtrusive yet confident, and enthusiastic but relaxed.

- Follow instructions cooperatively and completely. One of the biggest mistakes—and easiest to avoid—that job-seekers make is to complain (either very vocally or with a not-so-subtle sigh or grimace) about having to fill out an application. This is particularly true for higher-level, more experienced candidates who may see an application as an unnecessary nuisance best left to applicants for clerical or entry-level jobs. Don't make that mistake. Most organizations require that every applicant complete an application (though sometimes not until after a first or subsequent interview as an afterthought of sorts), so do so patiently and carefully.

- Greet your interviewer with a solid handshake and a smile, as discussed in Chapter 6.

- Introduce yourself first (stating your first and last name), and call your interviewer by name.

- Make the first words out of your mouth positive ones. The small talk you make at the start of the interview—particularly the first statement or two—does more toward establishing or sabotaging rapport with your interviewer than just about anything else. Starting out with a negative statement about how you got lost on the way there, or how rude someone was to you at the reception desk, or how hot or cold the waiting room was immediately gives the impression that you are a difficult or unpleasant person. What can seem like a simple, casual comment to you can have a much more powerful effect than you might think. Instead, say something pleasant and positive. Acknowledging that you're glad to be there is one easy way to do that.

- Be prepared with anything you might need. Always have a few extra copies of your resume, a portfolio, your reference list and/or letters of recommendation, and pen and paper. Forgetting these items or fumbling around for them in a messy bag or briefcase gives a bad impression.

Content

With all the talk of body language, image, delivery, and rapport, it might seem like the actual words that come out of your mouth are unimportant. On the contrary, the content of your message is critical. In Chapters 9, "The Fifteen Trickiest Interview Questions," and 10, "Some More Questions You Might Be Asked," you'll find specific examples of effective replies to many typical—and not so

Watch Out!
While it is usually appropriate to call interviewers by their first names to sound like a peer, be sure to consider cultural differences. In the South, for example, or in European companies, saying Ms. or Mr. and using the last name is sometimes more appropriate.

typical—interview questions. In the meantime, use the following checklist of general guidelines when giving those answers.

CHECKLIST 7.1 EFFECTIVE COMMUNICATION

Make sure everything you say is relevant to the discussion at hand. Don't stray too far from the crux of a question that was just asked or a conversation topic in progress. _____

Don't bring up personal topics or controversial ones, such as politics and religion; stick to business. _____

Create visual images in the interviewer's mind. Saying, "Profits went through the roof," leaves the listener with a more powerful mental image than does the statement, "Profits increased." _____

Avoid vague words and phrases such as "a few," "a lot," "various," "many," or "in the near future." Be specific and precise. _____

Always keep your own agenda in mind, and be sure you are using your asset statements. _____

Never sound negative, bitter, or angry. _____

Be concise; don't ramble. When you've said enough, keep quiet, even if the interviewer doesn't reply immediately. _____

Avoid using jargon or acronyms specific to an industry or job with which the interviewer is not likely to be familiar. _____

The Power of Language

Cognitive and social psychologists as well as linguists have found that certain words and phrases can have a particularly positive or negative effect on the person hearing them. Most job-seekers don't realize how powerful an individual word can be. When holding up their end of the conversation, they make the mistake of focusing solely on each of their statements as a whole. That is, they focus on concerns such as "Am I giving the right answer to this question? Am I sounding reasonably articulate?" instead of being strategic about their use of language within each statement.

For example, compare the following two statements:

> "By working with the production department, I changed our distribution process, leading to a big increase in profits."

> "By collaborating with the production department, I found ways to expedite our distribution process, which sent profits soaring."

By using just a few powerful words (and the strong visual image of profits soaring like eagles), the second statement makes much more of an impact on the listener. As you prepare your asset statements (as directed in Chapter 4, "Making Yourself the Top Candidate"), think carefully about the words you select to convey your message.

Phrases You Should Never Utter in an Interview

When clients meet with me for career counseling, they say many of the same things to me that they have been saying—or plan to say—when on job interviews. Their explanations for why they left a particular job, why they're looking to make a career

Bright Idea
Accomplished public speakers know that asking questions of the audience engages them and keeps their attention. You can do the same in interviews. After making a statement that answers the interviewer's question, follow it up with a question that draws out the interviewer's opinion, experience, or reaction.

change, what they did on past jobs, or any other aspect of their experience are often peppered with phrases that have a devastating impact on the impression they make. I've found that most people who say these things don't realize that they're doing anything wrong. In fact, they often think that what they're saying shows them in a positive light. What they don't realize is that these statements come across as negative or clichéd. Here are some examples of what I'm talking about:

"I'm a quick learner." This phrase is so common that it has become an interviewing cliché, the sort that makes prospective employers' eyes roll and sends your resume directly to that proverbial circular file. What's the problem with it? First, it calls attention to the fact that you don't know how to do something. The mental image that comes to many people's minds when they hear this phrase is that of a learning curve. When I hear it, for example, I picture a cartoon-like image of a job-seeker at the bottom of a steep hill looking up at the top, perhaps contemplating the arduous (despite the use of the word "quick") route to mastery of that particular task or skill. Employers these days need people who can hit the ground running, not ones who need excessive training (unless training is already a formal, established part of the job).

Instead of just saying you can learn that task or skill, talk about how you've done something similar. An alternative statement could be, "I haven't used that particular program before, but it sounds similar to the one I taught myself on the first two weeks of my last job, so I doubt I'd have any trouble picking it up quickly." The phrase "taught myself" has a much more powerful, positive impact than the more passive "I am a quick learner." And, bringing up a past accomplishment distracts the interviewer from the fact that you are lacking in a particular skill that is currently needed.

"I'm a people person." Never, ever, ever utter this statement in an interview, even if you are the most gregarious person on the face of the earth. It is without a doubt the biggest cliché in the history of interviewing. The problem is that it means nothing. With the exception of those who have serious psychiatric disorders of an antisocial nature, every human being has social needs to some degree. Yes, there certainly are some people who have less of a need for social interaction than do others, but even the strongest introverts enjoy the occasional encounter with another human. So calling yourself a "people person" is not a very distinctive moniker.

This statement is also not descriptive, so it adds nothing to the interviewer's understanding of you. You interact with people on the job in a myriad of ways. You might enjoy—and excel at—helping, educating, training, selling to, managing, socializing with, collaborating with, caring for, coaching, serving, counseling, advising, treating, or analyzing people. So, rather than saying "I'm a people person," describe more specifically exactly how you like to interact with people on the job, and use strong action verbs to do so.

"If you'll just give me a chance…." Remember that you are a consultant, a trouble-shooter, and a problem-solver rolled into one. No matter how long you have been looking for a job, or how badly you want to ace a particular interview, you are not desperate. Asking that the interviewer give you a chance not only conveys desperation, but it also

Bright Idea
When referring to a past accomplishment, use the pronouns "we" and "us" to show that you're a team player who shares credit with others. Do the same when referring to ways you could be an asset to the prospective employer. Say, for example, "We could solve that problem by…"

implies that you have not proven yourself in the past. Smart employers don't take chances. They don't like the idea of gambling on anything less than a close-to-sure thing when it comes to hiring. Instead of pleading for the interviewer to give you a break, put more effort into making your asset statements strong and credible.

"I'm going to be honest with you now...." This statement—and the related "To tell you the truth" or "To be perfectly candid"—can raise major red flags in the listener's mind. Does it mean you haven't been honest up until this point? Or, is what you are about to say such a stretching of the truth (or an outright lie) that you have to cover it with claims of honesty? This is one of those statements that many people don't even realize they say from time to time. If you feel the need to say it coming on, skip right over it and just state your case directly without this lead-in.

In addition to those deadly phrases, some individual words can be dangerous because of the negative reaction they often trigger in others. Here's a sampling of words you should omit from your vocabulary before interviewing:

Abandoned

Afraid/feared

Bad luck

Can't/couldn't

Cheated

Fail/Failed

Forgot

Miscalculated/misjudged

Mishap/snafu

Neglected/overlooked

Non-negotiable

Personality clash

Stressed/overloaded/burned-out

Your Delivery Style

A final element in delivering your message is the style with which you say the things you say. All the power vocabulary in the world is useless if the way you present what you have to say is ineffectual. Consider the following tips for your delivery:

- *Be concise and direct.* As with your written communication, start with the main point, then fill in the details as if you were a news reporter giving the headline first.

- *Avoid sounding evasive.* Don't let any hint of hesitation come through in your voice. If you aren't certain how to answer a particular question, pause for a few seconds to gather your thoughts so that you'll be more confident and forthright when replying.

- *Practice in advance.* As advised in Chapter 5, "Developing the Right Attitude," dealing with nervousness, practicing what you are going to say and how you'll say it is important. Getting used to making your asset statements or answering typical interview questions (as described in Chapters 9 and 10) will ensure a smooth delivery.

- *Speak at a normal speed.* Beware of speaking too slowly or quickly. If you get a little rattled, you might start speaking at too fast a pace, so try to stay composed and concentrate on delivering your words at an appropriate speed.

Watch Out!
Avoid two common grammatical errors to which even the most articulate people often succumb. Don't use "at" unnecessarily, as in "I'm just calling to see where you're at with the interviewing process." Similarly, don't use "to" unnecessarily, as in "Where did that resume go to?"

- *Don't forget to breathe!* If you find yourself rattling on and running out of breath, pause and take a deep breath.

- *Avoid speaking in a monotone.* Be sure that your voice conveys energy and enthusiasm, and that it rises and falls to vary the pitch and engage the listener.

- *Don't turn statements into questions.* Some people let their voices rise at the end of a sentence, turning statements into questions. If you're one of those, practice having your voice go down, or stay neutral, as you close a statement.

Make Sure Your Message is Received

"
It is a luxury to be understood.
—Ralph Waldo Emerson
"

Assuming your interviews are primarily face-to-face ones (as opposed to by telephone or video-conference), you may wonder why you have to worry about your message being received. But just because the interviewer is physically only a few feet from you doesn't mean that there aren't miles between you when it comes to communication.

Competing with Distractions

Distractions are a common culprit when it comes to your message not being received. Interviewers often must divide their attention when meeting with you, frequently worrying about the project they need to get back to or the problem they were grappling with earlier in the day. They might also be distracted by interruptions such as coworkers knocking on the door during your meeting or phone calls they must take. Perhaps nothing is more frustrating than seeing interviewers watch the phones on their desks lit up with calls and knowing that they're wondering who's on each line rather than fully listening to you.

These kinds of distractions are particularly common when you're being interviewed by people outside of the human resources department who do not conduct interviews as a regular part of their jobs. The meeting with you is likely to have been squeezed into an already tight schedule.

What can you do in these situations? Unfortunately, you have little control over these distractions. You can't stop the phone from ringing or people from popping their heads into the office. You can do a few things, however, to turn the tables more in your favor. First, you can be prepared for this scenario by simply realizing that it's likely to happen. Knowing in advance that you won't necessarily have the interviewer's full attention will keep you from getting rattled when it does happen. On a similar note, be sure you don't take the divided attention personally. It does not necessarily mean that you are boring the interviewer or that he has already decided against you. Often the distractions are simply too pressing to be ignored.

You can also make an effort to keep the interviewer's thoughts on track. When she turns back to you after taking a phone call or signing a paper the secretary has brought in, she may not pick up the conversation where it left off, but instead start off on a new thread. If you feel that the previous direction of the conversation was important to your case, tactfully work it back into the dialogue rather than letting it go unfinished.

How You May be Sabotaging Your Own Message

Not all distractions can be blamed on other people or unfair circumstances. Some may be the result of your own doing. The body language pitfalls discussed earlier in this chapter and in Chapter 6 can be highly distracting. An interviewer preoccupied by the annoyance of your foot tapping on the floor or your wild gesticulations is going to tune out much of what you're saying.

Your image and appearance may also cause someone not to listen. You want the interviewer to be hanging on your every word, not distracted by that garish tie hanging around your neck.

Dealing with Different Listening Styles

While interviewers—and people in general—are usually categorized as good or bad listeners, the issue of listening is more complex than the good-or-bad designation. Listening is the art of taking in information, and we all take in information differently. How we respond to stimuli in our environment—that is, what we pay attention to—is affected in large part by our personality type. One of the most valid and widely accepted views of personality is that developed by the eminent psychiatrist Carl Jung. Jung's work has been popularized in the Myers-Briggs Type Indicator (MBTI), a personality assessment tool (published by Consulting Psychologists Press in Palo Alto, California), as well as in numerous books. (See the books by Kroeger & Thuesen, Myers & Myers, and Tieger & Barron-Tieger in the "Personality" section of Appendix C for more information.)

According to Jungian theory and the MBTI, we take in information in one of two ways: either as a sensor or an intuitor. Each of us has some sensing and some intuiting in us, but we usually have a preference for one or the other. Sensors are the people who focus on the facts and figures in a message. They are practical and pragmatic, realistic, and detail-oriented. Sensors tend to focus on the present, so they are likely to pay close attention to what you are saying rather than thinking about something else as you talk.

Intuitors, on the other hand, are more theoretical and abstract. They take in the broad brush strokes of a conversation's content rather than the details. They are more future-oriented, so they are likely to be taking what you say and immediately linking it to some other thought or idea; as a result, they may miss some of the nitty-gritty of your message.

While there is no substitute for measuring someone's personality through formal testing, you can look for clues that will help you estimate whether your interviewer is a sensor or intuitor.

Sensors may show particular interest in these aspects:

- The details of your past work experience more than the outcomes
- Statistics and quantitative data
- Organizational charts, structure, and hierarchies
- Dates and times
- Policies and procedures
- Tangible evidence
- The bottom line
- Practical applications of theories
- Information presented in a step-by-step fashion, a logical sequence

Intuitors may show particular interest in these aspects:

- The future, using terms such as "vision" and "goals"

- The "big picture"
- Abstract concepts
- Theories and hypotheses
- Creativity and imagination
- Ideas
- A dialogue that is more circuitory than step-by-step

Bright Idea
To get more familiar with personality style assessment, consider taking the MBTI through a qualified professional such as a career counselor (see Appendix B for referral sources) or a human resources officer. You can also contact the Association for Psychological Type (www. aptcentral.org or tel: 816-444-3500) for a referral.

Keep in mind that no one is all sensing or all intuiting, so you are likely to come across people who express characteristics from both categories. Your goal is not to become an expert on personality assessment during interviews, but simply to pick up on subtleties in the conversation that help you adapt your way of communicating to fit the other person's style of receiving information.

How Your Message is Processed and Interpreted

Once you've been heard, you must determine whether you've been heard correctly. You probably know how easy it is for something you say to be heard incorrectly or misinterpreted. I'm reminded of a friend of mine who was complaining that her husband's hearing was starting to wane a bit. When she asked him if he'd get her a glass of water, he said "Bring you a quarter?" While hearing deficits may not be the issue in your interviews, the same kind of errors can happen. But when a job is at stake, the mix-up is not so amusing.

If you think the interviewer has mis-heard or misinterpreted something you've said, don't hesitate to speak up. Better yet, try to prevent the misunderstanding from occurring in the first place. Be sure you are speaking clearly and slowly (but not too slowly, of course). Also, if you use words with more than one meaning, don't assume your definition is the same as the interviewer's; if necessary, explain what you mean. Be sure not to pack too much information into one statement, or the listener may find it too much to process and not retain any of what you've said.

When It's Not Your Turn to Speak

Once your message is processed, the interviewer will respond with a follow-up question, a related statement, or, in some cases, silence or a long pause. Your job is to listen well and stay alert. It's easy to fall into the trap of concentrating so intently on answering the interviewer's questions that you let your guard down when it's no longer your turn to speak. You may let out a sigh in your mind as if to say, "Whew, I got that question answered; now I can sit back and relax until the next one is fired at me." Remember that you are in a dialogue, not an interrogation, so listening when it's the other person's turn to speak is just as important as concentrating on what you have to say.

Listening is especially challenging if the interviewer launches into some sort of monologue, perhaps a sales pitch for the company, a commentary on the state of the industry or the world today, or an account of his or her own career history. No matter how dull this soliloquy may be, you have to listen intently.

You need to listen to what the interviewer has to say so that you can perform these critical actions:

- Show interest
- Show respect
- Gain insight into the prospective employer's needs
- Ensure the interview is a dialogue, not monologue

Watch Out!
Occasional note taking during an interview is acceptable when you need to write down any information that you're not likely to remember, such as a name or phone number. Limit your note taking, however, because it will distract the interviewer and look like you're not listening.

- Encourage the interviewer's active involvement
- Demonstrate that you're a team player
- Reinforce your stance as a consultant, not a job-seeker
- Have a chance to regroup before speaking next

Leaving Good Feelings Behind After the Interview

When the interview is coming to a close, you want to leave knowing that good rapport has been established, you've gotten your points across, and you've collected the information you need. Following the suggestions offered throughout this chapter is one way to do that. How you handle the actual closing is another. You should leave with confidence, courtesy, and continuity.

A confident departure is one in which you spell out for the interviewer how you think you're right for the position. In a sense, you restate your asset statements in a concise pitch of about 30 to 60 seconds. This serves as a recap of the interview and reinforces the idea that you are right for the job. This proactive approach is more effective than the typical way of closing, which is to say something like, "I'm very interested in the position."

Departing with courtesy means that you thank the interviewer for the opportunity to be considered for the position and that you show your appreciation for her or his time.

The continuity aspect of your departure means that you set the stage for continued communication after the interview is finished. You inquire about how long the interviewing or decision-making process will continue and when you may follow-up. You might also ask if you can provide any further information.

This issue of closing an interview is discussed in much more detail in Chapter 10, which describes how the last few minutes of an interview lay the foundation for your follow-up efforts.

Communicating with Multiple Interviewers

Chapter 8, "Variations on the Interviewing Theme," describes interviews in which you meet with more than one person in what is often referred to as a panel or board interview. For now, consider the following quick tips for oral communication when you're dealing with multiple interviewers:

- Divide your attention equally among the group; avoid directing your comments to the same person each time.

- Alternate eye contact among the group.

- Defer to the person who has the most authority in the hiring decision; if you don't know who that is, defer to the most senior person according to job title.

- Don't try to change your personality or communication style to fit everyone; be yourself.

Cross-Cultural Communication

Within the cottage industry of consultants who earn their living by going into companies or organizations to improve communication among employees, diversity has become one of the hot issues that gets those consultants hired. Diversity has become such a buzzword in the workplace in recent years that it has almost reached cliché status. Regardless of whether you are sick of hearing about "managing diversity" or whether you take it very seriously, the fact is that diversity is a major concern for most every organization today.

Unofficially...
If it's obvious midway through an interview that the position is not at all right for you, you have the option of saying so. Many employers appreciate your candor and the fact that you don't want to waste their time. They will often speak to you about other positions in their organization and refer you elsewhere.

As a result, you must demonstrate during interviews your ability to communicate and collaborate with people who are different from you. If any of your interviewers is from another racial, ethnic, geographic, or religious background, or of the opposite sex, you have an obvious opportunity to do so. Otherwise, you demonstrate your ability to navigate differences through the examples you use in your asset statements.

Ways to demonstrate your skill in cross-cultural communication and collaboration include the following:

- Emphasize the similarities between you and others, not the differences.

- Use gender-neutral language, such as "spokesperson," not "spokesman."

- Don't trivialize or act inconvenienced by matters that are near-and-dear to the hearts of certain groups (for example, saying something like, "I think those people want to be called Native-Americans these days").

- Don't identify someone's race or ethnic origin when they are not central to the point you are making.

Cross-cultural communication also raises some tricky issues when it comes to matters of business etiquette—particularly when you're dealing with people from different geographic regions within your own country or from other parts of the world. The books listed in the "Cross-Cultural Communication" section of Appendix C have excellent tips on this point. Some of the cultural differences you'll find elaborated on in those publications include the following:

Unofficially...
Women and non-Caucasian groups will constitute the majority of the workforce in the 21st century.

Bright Idea
The best way to become proficient in diversity is to bring it into your own life by seeking friendships and collaborations with people who differ from you. Managing diversity is not something to be learned, but to be experienced.

- The importance, or lack of concern for, punctuality

- The exchange of business cards—when and how to do it

- Ways of showing respect

- The appropriate time and place for business

- Making eye contact

- Shaking hands

- Expressiveness

- Questions about the other person's personal or family life

- The definition of hospitality

- The role of humor in business

- Rules of morality

- Interest in sports

- Comfort level with silence

- Pop culture references

- Humility versus brash self-confidence

- Touching

- Head motions that convey yes or no (such as nodding or shaking)

Watch Out!
Be aware of the hidden sexism in the phrases "he or she" and "men and women." Alternate the order occasionally, saying "she or he" and "women and men."

Just the Facts

- Keep in mind that an interview is a two-way conversation, not a monologue or an interrogation.

- The five steps in communication: deliver your message; make sure your message is heard; determine whether your message has been interpreted accurately; listen carefully to the reply and continue the dialogue; and leave a good feeling behind after the interview.

- Pay attention to how you establish rapport before you begin communicating in an interview.

- Strengthen the impact of your side of the dialogue with power words and phrases.

- Avoid clichéd statements such as "I'm a people person," and "I'm a quick learner."

- Listening well is just as important as speaking well.

- Become comfortable with diversity and communication norms in other cultures.

- Close interviews with confidence, courtesy, and an eye toward continuity.

The Interview Itself

GET THE SCOOP ON...
Interviewing styles and how to deal with them
▪ Managing group and panel interviews ▪
Surviving a stress interview ▪ Behavioral interviews ▪ Unconventional interview settings

Variations on the Interviewing Theme

Chapter 8

Most interviews take place in the prospective employer's office and are fairly straightforward dialogues between you and one recruiter or hiring manager. Some exceptions to this rule exist, however, so it's best to be prepared for anything to happen. That way you aren't thrown by the setting or format of the meeting. You can concentrate instead on communicating how you can do the job, why you want the job, and how you'll fit in.

As with any kind of business meeting, no two interviews are exactly alike, but you can expect that your interview will fit into certain typical patterns. This chapter describes the various formats, settings, and styles of questioning that you may encounter and offers strategies for making the most of each one.

Interviewing Styles

Recruiters and hiring managers who know their stuff have a repertoire of interviewing techniques

Bright Idea
Some interview-
ers read ques-
tions from a
standard form. To
get a sneak peak
at what's on the
clipboard in the
interviewer's lap,
take a look at
some of the
books recruiters
read to guide
their work (see
Appendix C).
Many of these
have sample
interviewing
protocols.

from which to choose. Some are gimmicky or trendy, while others are more traditional methods of questioning applicants about their background, skills, and goals.

The following pages describe the most popular interview styles: direct, behavior-based, conversational, and stress. You will most likely find that your interviews combine a little of each style, or perhaps start with one approach then switch gears mid-stream—maybe going from conversational to confrontational. Considerable overlap exists among the styles, but for the sake of explanation, this chapter approaches them as four discrete approaches.

The Directed Interview

Directed interviews are structured. They follow a logical progression and are based more on a question-and-answer format than a conversational one. This is the textbook-style interview in which you may be asked typical questions such as those listed in Chapter 9, "The Fifteen Trickiest Interview Questions," and Chapter 10, "Some More Questions You Might Be Asked." Directed interviews are most commonly found at the early screening stage; they are usually first interviews conducted by a human resources representative. The directed approach may also be used by a manager who has received some training in interviewing.

The typical flow of a directed interview might go something like this:

- The interviewer begins with small talk to put you at ease and to establish rapport.

- Some interviewers next move right into describing the position and/or discussing the organization itself.

- Others start out with a review of your resume, questioning you about its contents, including work experience, education, activities and interests.

- The interviewer may then move into a discussion of your capabilities, asking you to describe your skills and personal qualities.

- The interview closes with a chance for you to ask questions and with an expression of thanks for your coming in.

- As you shake hands and prepare to part company, the interviewer may provide some information about next steps in the process, such as if and when you might be called back for another interview, how many more candidates are to be interviewed, and so on. (Chapter 13, "Following Up to Get to 'Yes'," covers ways you can elicit this information if it is not volunteered.)

Pros: Directed interviews are relatively easy to prepare for and deal with because the line of questioning is straightforward and follows a logical progression. Rarely are these interviews stressful (other than causing the normal amount of interview jitters), nor will you be thrown many curve balls. This type of interview also works in your favor in that it is likely to be thorough, so the interviewer will probably gather most of the necessary information about your qualifications without you having to worry about working it into the conversation.

Cons: Directed interviews can be *too* structured, making it more of a challenge to work your agenda into the interviewer's agenda. This type of interview puts you in the traditional job-seeker versus hiring

Watch Out!
Interviewers are often trained to look for inconsistencies in your story, such as employment dates that don't add up or an incomplete account of why you left a job, so don't count on being able to evade these issues. (Chapter 12, "Interview Curve Balls," helps you deal with these and other tricky situations.)

authority mode rather than that of two colleagues conferring and conversing. Also, since it is not likely to be conversational, an interview based on this somewhat mechanical approach may not let the interviewer get a feel for you as a person.

Follow this strategy for a directed interview:

- Concentrate on being an equal player in the discussion.

- Make an extra effort to work in your asset statements and any other topics you need to address to make your case.

- Find some common interest on which you can build rapport so that you make a human connection with the interviewer.

The Behavior-based Interview

Behavior-based interviewing (also called "behavioral interviewing") has been a much touted approach to hiring for some years now. As a job-seeker, you may have heard the term and wondered what the reality is behind the mystique. The fact is that the term is something of a misnomer, in that "behavior-based" actually refers to the style of questioning, while the overall interview structure itself does not differ significantly from a directed or conversational interview, or some combination of the two.

The interview is based on a line of questioning that elicits information about your actual behavior in a variety of real-life or hypothetical circumstances. More emphasis rests on your accomplishments and abilities than on the basics of your job duties or your opinions. As behavioral interviewing is the most popular style today, most of this book is designed to prepare you for this kind of interview. In fact, solid asset statements are just about all you need to ace a behavior-based interview.

The following questions give you an idea of how this type of interview might sound. After each behavior-based question, a second question shows the alternative non-behavioral—or traditional—way the same issue might be addressed.

> Behavioral: Tell me about a time when you had to manage a team of people who didn't want to work together.
>
> Traditional: Which management style do you espouse?

> Behavioral: What was the most stressful situation you've ever faced, and how did you handle it?
>
> Traditional: How do you handle stress?

> Behavioral: What would you do if you caught a colleague lying?
>
> Traditional: What do you think about ethics in the workplace?

> Behavioral: A customer is threatening to pull his account from our company because of a billing snafu. What would you do to keep him?
>
> Traditional: Tell me about your customer service experience.

As you can see, behavior-based questions require you to give evidence of your skills, experience, and personal qualities, not just talk in generalities.

Unofficially...
A commonly overlooked benefit of behavior-based interviewing from the candidate's perspective is that it provides clues to the employer's concerns and goals because the hypothetical situations posed are likely to mirror the organization's needs.

Timesaver
More often than you might think, employers have to cancel and reschedule interviews at the last minute—sometimes even after you've already arrived on-site. To avoid this inconvenience, try to schedule interviews for the morning rather than the end of the day, as those are less likely to be canceled.

Pros: If you're well prepared—with a solid handle on your skills, content knowledge, and personal qualities—and if you have crafted and practiced powerful asset statements, then a behavioral interview is the best thing that could happen to your job search. In this type of interview, you can be sure that the interviewer will get a complete picture of not just what you claim to offer, but what you really can do. This type of interview can also be more stimulating and interesting, unlike the rather dull format of the directed interview or the less challenging conversational one.

Cons: If you're not well prepared for a behavioral interview, it can be a disaster. Behavior-based interviews require much more preparation than other types. Thinking of examples off the top of your head is often difficult, so you should develop a versatile set of examples in advance before you're put on the spot to come up with them. You also need to conduct sufficient research on the prospective employer and individual interviewer to reply effectively to the hypothetical situations posed. Knowing what the interviewer is looking for helps you know which of your asset statements to use when discussing what you would do in a particular situation.

Follow this strategy for a behavior-based interview:

- Use your asset statements!

- Don't get so caught up in describing your past accomplishments that you forget to talk about what you could do for the employer in the near future.

- Don't go off on a tangent when talking about your past accomplishments. Just because the interviewer says, "Tell me about a time when…."

doesn't mean you have to tell the whole story. Describe the situation briefly, then move on to discussing the results, the qualities you demonstrated in that situation, and how it all relates to the employer. (You may need to review the elements of an asset statement, as outlined in Chapter 4, "Making Yourself the Top Candidate.")

The Conversational Interview

In a conversational interview, you may feel like you're chatting with a friend or professional colleague instead of a prospective employer. Rather than following a question-and-answer format, the interview flows from one topic to the next, as in a typical conversation. The interviewer may talk at length about the position or the organization as a whole and might want to discuss current events in the industry or world at large.

Conversational interviewers are likely to make open-ended requests for information as opposed to asking specific questions. For example, they might say, "Tell me about yourself" instead of "What are three adjectives that describe you?" Or, they may ask, "What was that job like?" instead of asking about an aspect of it, such as "What size staff did you manage on that job?"

Conversational interviews often take a circuitous route with no apparent agenda. They are sometimes conducted by an unskilled interviewer or a disorganized person, or perhaps by someone who was asked at the last minute to interview you and isn't prepared or is preoccupied with other obligations. Conversational interviews are, however, conducted by some experienced, trained interviewers who simply prefer to gather information in the context of a

Watch Out!
Don't assume that conversational interviewers don't know what they're doing. They may be judging you with a more critical eye than you suspect or lulling you into a false sense of security with the relaxed conversation.

conversation rather than a question-and-answer format.

Pros: Conversational interviews are often more relaxed in tone and thus more comfortable for the interviewee than any other type. Rarely are they stressful (unless you find making conversation to be taxing). They don't pose much of a challenge because you aren't being grilled with tough questions. And, the interviewer is likely to get a good feel for you as a person because you're communicating in a more casual way and discussing thoughts and opinions.

Cons: Conversational interviews can lull you into complacency, leading you to forget your agenda and leave the interview with nothing more accomplished than a pleasant round of chit-chat. Furthermore, interviewers who use the conversational approach are often inexperienced or lack knowledge about effective interviewing techniques, so they may not collect the hard data they need to make an informed decision. You might find that they end up selecting a candidate based on congeniality rather than tangible qualifications.

Follow this strategy for a conversational interview:

- Make a concerted effort to work your agenda into the dialogue.

- Use conversation topics as springboards for making your asset statements rather than getting caught up in a conversation that goes nowhere.

- Pay special attention to questions you ask. Ask things such as, "What qualities do you need in the person who will do this job?" By asking the right questions, you force the interviewer to

Unofficially...
Interviewers are often trained to keep a poker face, so don't assume that a neutral expression signals displeasure with your responses. Try to remain confident even if you're not getting any positive feedback through body language.

address the issue of what's needed and how you might meet that need.

- Watch your tongue. The rapport and comfortable atmosphere in a conversational interview may lead you to open up too much or say something foolish.

The Stress Interview

A stress interview is easy to spot. It's the kind that has you squirming in your seat, tugging at your collar, and developing sweaty palms. It is designed to intimidate and to find out how you operate under pressure.

In a stress interview, the interviewer may seem angry, gruff, disinterested, or distracted. You might find that almost everything you say is met with disagreement and that your opinions and claims are challenged at every turn. A stress interviewer might probe for information until you feel like the victim of the week on *60 Minutes.*

Stress might also be created through skillful use of silence. You reply to a question or make a statement, and the interviewer stares at you with a blank expression for longer than the normal pause in a conversation. (See the strategy tips below for ways to deal with unnatural silences.)

Another way to know you are in a stress interview is if the room seems unusually uncomfortable. You might have a harsh, artificial light or sunlight shining in your eyes, be seated in an uncomfortable chair or one that is very low, or find the room extremely hot or cold.

An additional way stress is induced into an interview is through tough questions that seem like tricks. The interviewer might ask you to give a sales

Bright Idea
When faced with a stress interview, don't take the approach personally. Remember that it's just an interviewing method, not a personal vendetta against you.

Watch Out!
Some companies videotape inter-views when all the decision-makers aren't able to interview candidates per-sonally, or to facilitate a care-ful decision. So don't be thrown if your interview starts with "Lights, camera, action."

pitch for the pen in your hand or to open a window that is nailed or painted shut. Or, you might be asked how many manhole covers or cabs there are in your city or town.

Such tactics are fairly common when interview-ing for stressful jobs or for high-level ones in which you are likely to face pressured situations often. They are not unheard of, however, as a way of weed-ing out applicants for jobs that are not at the high end of the stress scale but simply require that you be assertive, confident, and good at thinking on your feet.

Pros: If you handle it well, you can really shine in a stress interview. This format lets the interviewer see you in action, not just spouting pat answers to routine questions. A stress interview keeps you on your toes, so for those who like a challenge, this type of interview can actually be fun.

Cons: For those who don't thrive on the adrena-line rush that stress interviews bring, or those who are the least bit doubtful about their abilities, stress interviews can obviously be quite unpleasant. Also, it can be difficult to determine whether you really are in a stress interview, as opposed to dealing with an interviewer who simply dislikes you or who is in a bad mood.

Follow this strategy for a stress interview:

- Don't panic. No matter which curve balls come your way, retain your composure at all times. The interviewer's primary objective is usually to see how easily you get rattled, not to find out exactly how many manhole covers are in your town.

- Deal with silences by keeping a confident, pleas-ant look on your face and maintaining eye contact until the interviewer speaks again. Don't shift around in your chair, rub your hands together, bounce your foot up and down on the floor, or let any other nervous body language give you away. If the silence goes on to the point of absurdity, ask whether the interviewer would like you to elaborate on the last point you made. Do not elaborate unless directed to do so, however; talking just to fill the silence is a sure way to put your foot in your mouth.

■ If asked a mind-teaser question (such as "How many taxis are there in this city?"), don't worry so much about the answer as about the thought process you use to get to an answer. In fact, you can admit to not knowing the answer as long as you show how you would find it. For example, if the job you're going for depends heavily on strong intellectual skills and logical thinking, show how you might calculate the answer based on something like the population of your city, the average percentage of people who use a cab in the course of the day, and so on. If your job requires that you be resourceful—perhaps in a research or administrative position—say that you don't know the answer but that you would call the Taxi Commission or do a search on the Internet to find the answer.

■ Balance a go-with-the-flow approach with assertiveness. If you are too composed and relaxed, you might come across as complacent. Yes, it's important to proceed as if nothing is wrong, but you also don't want to seem like a doormat. For example, if the room is extremely warm, make a friendly comment such as, "Looks like the air-conditioning here works

> **"**
> A high station in life is earned by the gallantry with which appalling experiences are survived with grace.
> —Tennessee Williams
> **"**

about as well as the one in my office." To pull off a statement like that you must sound like you're just making a casual comment with a touch of humor rather than complaining. (And do so only if the temperature is exceptionally high or low so that's it's obvious that temperature is being used as a stress tactic.) When you do make such a statement, you show that you're assertive enough to say something about an inappropriate situation. Similarly, if the interviewer challenges everything you say, don't just sit back and take it; speak up, especially if the job for which you're interviewing would require you to be assertive or aggressive. You shouldn't turn the interview into a shouting match, but you can engage in a healthy debate.

Interviewing Formats

Just as the style of collecting information varies, the format or structure of interviews varies as well. The classic format is the one in which you interview with just one person at a time at an organization where you've not worked. The techniques suggested throughout this book apply to the classic format as well as to variations on that structure, such as the group, panel, internal, or follow-up interviews described on the pages that follow. Special tips for dealing with these types of interviews are also offered here.

Group Interviews

In a group interview, you and a few other candidates are interviewed simultaneously by one or more interviewers. This approach is often used for positions in which teamwork is particularly important, or where leadership is critical. Group interviews also save the employer time and money. In a group interview, you may be directed to discuss a topic or complete a task, rather than to answer questions. (See Chapter 11, "Passing Muster: Tests, Observation, and Other Ways You'll be Assessed," for more on group observation as an assessment method in interviews.)

Pros: You get to demonstrate your capabilities in a setting that simulates the workplace. You might also find that you don't experience some of the pressure found in a one-on-one interview because the interviewers' focus does not rest solely on you.

Cons: You have to work extra hard to distinguish yourself within the group, and you may have to deal with some overt competition.

Follow this strategy for a group interview:

- Realize that you are more likely being observed to see what role you adopt in the group and how you behave in general than having your specific comments and answers judged too closely.

- Figure out which qualities the interviewers are seeking—such as leadership, teamwork, or organization—and play that part.

- Be courteous and helpful to your fellow candidates.

- Balance a cooperative, collaborative approach to the task or discussion with the more self-serving comments necessary to promote your candidacy. For example, say things such as, "I think John makes a good point. When I've faced similar situations, I handled it by…"

Panel Interviews

In panel interviews, you are the sole candidate meeting with more than one interviewer. These interviews are typically formal in tone and are

Unofficially… Interviews occasionally take place as part of a company or plant tour, particularly in manufacturing or research environments in which there's more to see than cubicles and desks. Employers like this approach because it lets them assess how you observe and react to your environment and how you interact with people you meet along the way.

Watch Out!
When you've had
a panel inter-
view, don't try to
get away with
writing a thank-
you note only to
the head deci-
sion-maker. You
must write to
each person indi-
vidually. (For
more on follow-
up notes, see
Chapter 13.)

usually conducted by an official search committee, as opposed to a collection of colleagues who just happen to be free to speak with you at the same time. You are most likely to come across panel interviews in academia, government, and for high-level positions in the corporate world. This approach is also used in situations in which a job would require you to make presentations to groups of people, such as in consulting, sales, and training. (Tips for conducting mock presentations as part of the interview are provided in Chapter 11.)

Pros: Panel interviews have a logistical advantage over one-on-one interviews. While it may be intimidating to meet with several people at once, chances are you'd have to meet each one individually at some point, so at least you benefit from the convenience of meeting them all together. Additionally, panel interviews are often part of a more formal—and therefore more organized and efficient—recruiting process. As such, you might get an answer sooner than when you have to meet with each decision-maker individually, which often drags out the process. Also, you don't have to keep repeating your story and your asset statements because everyone hears them at the same time.

Cons: Obviously, panel interviews can be intimidating. I'm reminded of a client who told me about an interview he had for a high school guidance counselor position. He found himself seated in a straight chair looking up at a panel of faculty and administrators perched on a dais, even though he had been told he'd just be meeting with the school principal and "might chat with a few teachers." Though he quickly composed himself and did fine, he said he felt as if he were testifying to a grand jury.

Panel interviews are also a challenge in that you must mesh with multiple personality types and communication styles, not to mention various personal styles with regard to formality, seriousness, and dress.

Follow this strategy for a panel interview:

- Follow the advice in Chapter 6, "Presenting the Right Image," regarding how to vary your eye contact and body position to alternate your focus on the different members of the panel.

- Determine who is the head of the panel, if there is one, and defer slightly to that person while paying sufficient attention to the rest of the group.

- When answering one interviewer's question, focus on that person for most of your reply, then vary eye contact.

Internal Interviews

An interesting twist on the issue of interviewing occurs when you're applying for a position in an organization where you are already employed. An internal interview may result from the initiative you take to find a more satisfying position at your company, or from the efforts of a superior who sees your advancement potential and recommends you for a better job.

Pros: Whether you're meeting with someone you know well or someone with whom you've not had contact, you are at least interviewing in familiar territory. This makes the whole process easier for you in terms of research, mental preparation, building your case, and the logistics of scheduling and getting to interviews. Because you already know—or should know—the organization's needs, culture,

> 66
> When you have an internal interview ... take full responsibility to present yourself as impressively as possible and not assume that your current manager or someone else in the organization has already "won" you the job by their endorsement.... Be as fully prepared as for an external interview.
> —Alan J. Pickman, Ph.D., Psychologist and Senior Outplacement Consultant, Career Services Department, Chase Manhattan Bank.
> 99

and goals, you have an advantage over candidates coming from the outside.

Also, the interviewer may see you as a natural choice because you are a known quantity. Hiring from within is good for morale as well, in that other employees may be encouraged when they see that advancement within the organization is a possibility. Plus, hiring internally can also be more cost-effective for the employer.

Cons: Some of the advantages just described may also work against you. The fact that you are a known quantity can be detrimental if your employer is looking for some "fresh blood." No matter how innovative your ideas or how high your energy level, you're not a new face—and that can be a major stumbling block. Organizational politics also might be at work.

If you've ever rubbed anyone the wrong way, whether intentionally or unknowingly, the slight can come back to haunt you when you try to make a move internally. No matter how stellar your track record with your current employer, a coworker with a grudge can do some significant damage to your reputation and candidacy.

Follow this strategy for an internal interview:

- Don't take an internal interview any less seriously than an external one. Build your case with powerful asset statements, as you would with a stranger.

- Don't skip the research phase just because you think you know your company inside and out. Speak to key players in the organization to find out what's really going on in the department where you would be working, or to learn about the concerns and objectives of upper management, if you are not already privy to such information. (If your desire to make a move is confidential, you can still have these conversations without letting anyone know why you want the information.)

- If you are trying to advance to a higher level within your organization, or to transfer to a different functional area, pay special attention to your image. You're already known as someone at a particular level or in a certain role, so you face a more difficult task in trying to get the interviewer to see you as fitting into a new one. Make sure your attire and demeanor fit the culture of the area or level to which you aspire.

Follow-Up Interviews

After you have had an initial interview, you might make the cut and be called back for one or more follow-up meetings. While an offer is sometimes extended after just one interview, more often it is necessary that you come back to meet more people who have a say in the hiring decision.

At the follow-up interview stage, rarely are you asked for basic information about your background. The interview is more likely to focus on the issue of fit. People you meet at that follow-up stage want to get to know you as a person. They already know you meet the basic requirements of the job. Now they want to see whether you'd fit in and if you really want the job. They also want to make sure that their first impression of you wasn't a false one.

Pros: You've gotten through the first hoop and no longer have to prove yourself quite as much.

Cons: You can develop a false sense of confidence, assuming that you have the job offer and that the call-back is just a formality. Or, you may put

Unofficially...
If you are called back for a third or fourth follow-up interview, it's usually safe to assume that the pool of applicants has narrowed to as few as two, or that you are the sole candidate but are just having to go through the formality of meeting more key people.

undue pressure on yourself because you know you're close to an offer.

Follow this strategy for a follow-up interview:

- Stay on your toes, and don't take follow-up interviews too casually.

- Pay particular attention to establishing rapport and showing that you can fit in.

- Be assertive in your requests for information about where things stand, such as how many other people are being considered and when they expect to make a decision.

- Be sure to ask about any doubts the interviewer may have with your candidacy. At this point, you can be knocked out of the running over one seemingly minor deficit that you could easily correct if you only knew about it.

Interview Settings

Where an interview takes place raises important questions about which communication strategies, attire, and etiquette are appropriate for the setting. How you act during an interview in a formal corporate conference room may not be appropriate for an interview that takes place at a bustling job fair or by telephone. The following are typical—and not so typical—sites for interviews and tactics for navigating them.

On-site Interviewing

The most common place for an interview is at the prospective employer's location. Though the employer in this case has the "home court advantage," this setting presents no special challenges; the strategies throughout this book—particularly those related to business etiquette and communication in

Moneysaver
If you're expected to foot the bill for traveling to an out-of-town interview, ask if anyone from the company will be traveling on business in your area around that time, and see if you could arrange for that person to meet with you locally instead.

Chapter 6 and Chapter 7, "Strategic Communication for Interviews"—are applicable to this setting. Just be sure you know where you're going and how long it will take to get there, especially if interviewing out of town.

On-Campus Interviews

If you are in college or graduate school, you may have the chance to participate in an on-campus recruiting program in which you meet with employers who come to your institution to spend the day interviewing graduating students. In this case, you have the home court advantage and may find that meeting in a familiar spot (often the career counseling or placement office or a classroom) is not only convenient but also comforting. On-campus interviews tend to be fairly brief because several interviews are usually tightly scheduled into the day. They also tend to be standardized so that uniform information can be collected throughout the day. You're more likely to find that the interviewer's approach is directed or behavioral rather than stress or conversational.

An important element in your strategy for this setting is to distinguish yourself from the pack. On-campus recruiting becomes something of an interviewing mill for the prospective employer, so all candidates blur together by the end of the day. And, because the format of each of the interviews is roughly the same, there is even less for the interviewer's memory to latch onto.

Be sure to make good use of your asset statements, and also try to steer the conversation away from academic topics such as grades and what classes you've taken. While your academic background is important to address, many on-campus

Bright Idea
If you interview with several people at a particular company on the same day, don't assume that everyone will compare notes in detail at the end of the day. You should be fresh for each new meeting and be willing to tell your story all over again. Never say, "I told that to the last person...."

recruiters do so at the expense of discussing your work history and your extracurricular experiences.

Also, be aware that companies often send their entry-level employees—particularly those who are alumni of the school where they're interviewing—so you may be dealing with an inexperienced interviewer. If so, follow the advice offered in previous chapters (and earlier in this chapter) on how to take control when the interviewer is ineffectual or, at worst, incompetent.

Conferences and Conventions

Watch Out!
If an interviewer at a conference or convention suggests meeting in a non-public place such as his or her private room, and you feel uncomfortable doing so, don't hesitate to suggest a more public spot, or cancel the interview altogether.

At some professional conferences or trade shows, you might have the opportunity to interview at the meeting site with employers from all around the country or the world. Conferences sponsored by professional or trade associations often build a designated time and place for interviews into the meeting agenda. At other conventions or exhibitions, you might have to arrange interviews yourself. This setting is particularly convenient when you wish to relocate but don't have the time or money to travel to out-of-town employers for interviews.

Though you may have to deal with more than the usual distractions—unless the interview is held in a private room—conferences can be a nice place to interview. The simple fact that you're attending the event shows your initiative and commitment to expanding your knowledge, so the interviewer is likely to view you favorably before the meeting even begins. In addition, the shared experience of being participants in the same conference provides common ground with your interviewer and plenty of conversation topics for your encounter.

Job Fairs

Job fairs are not just window-shopping events. They provide the opportunity to have "mini-interviews" with representatives of numerous organizations under one roof. As with conferences and conventions, job fairs are a slightly more relaxed environment in which to talk with prospective employers. You know that the employers are looking to hire—otherwise they wouldn't be attending the fair—and they appreciate the initiative you've taken to attend the event. Instead of just sitting home mailing or faxing cover letters and resumes, you're getting out and making direct contact, which is an effort that many employers appreciate.

If you do get to sit down with a recruiter for 10 or 15 minutes at a fair, keep a few pointers in mind.

- Try to block out the distractions of the noise and people around you, and focus on the person to whom you're talking.

- Realize that the recruiter's time is limited, so you have to make a big impact in a short period of time. Be sure to cut to the chase, and if possible, prepare in advance what you want to say to various recruiters so that you have one or two achievable objectives for each meeting.

- Keep in mind that employers might be meeting with many candidates during the job fair, so you need to make yourself memorable. Review the suggestions in Chapter 6 for adding "flavor" to your story with lively anecdotes and power words and phrases. And, of course, be sure to work in at least one asset statement.

- Find out who else at the organization, if anyone, is involved in hiring for the types of positions

Bright Idea
When following up with someone you've met at a job fair, be sure to send some documentation, such as your portfolio or other work samples—not just a thank-you note—so that the recruiter has something tangible to remember you by.

for which you're looking. Get the names of any key decision-makers with whom you could follow up so that you're not relying just on the representative at the fair to advocate on your behalf.

Interviewing Over Meals

You might find yourself having breakfast, lunch, or dinner with a busy employer who has only those times to interview you, or who uses this as a supplementary activity to a traditional interview in the office.

Interviews over meals take place on neutral territory (unless you are taken to the interviewer's private club or regularly frequented restaurant), so the experience can be less intimidating than in an office. Getting out of the office also creates a more natural atmosphere for getting to know you as a person and for you to learn more about the interviewer.

For those who panic when they have to choose between three different sizes of spoons and face cherry tomatoes that just won't get on a fork, interviewing over meals can be terrifying. The solution is simple: Learn the basics of table manners. The books listed in the "Business Etiquette" section of Appendix C can help you do just that. And for those of you who know your fish fork from your salad fork but still find mealtime interviewing intimidating, consider these quick tips:

- Keep an eye on your drink glasses (and those of your companions) at all times, and limit your hand and arm gestures so that you minimize the risk of knocking over a glass and sending iced tea splashing onto your interviewer's favorite tie.

- Order wisely, avoiding foods that are difficult to eat, including long noodle pastas, some salads, oversized sandwiches, and anything you have to peel or eat with your hands. Stick with simple things you can eat with a knife and fork in small, manageable bites such as vegetables, fish, chicken breast, steak, and so on.

- Don't drink alcohol—at least 99 percent of the time you shouldn't. At times, however, your interviewer(s) may order a drink and you would seem like a non-conformist if you didn't take one. If you usually are a non-drinker, then you don't have to have one. But if you do enjoy a drink and your hosts are having one (and if the meal is at night rather than in the middle of the workday), then there's no harm in doing so as long as you limit your intake so that you can keep your wits about you.

By the way, some books on interviewing suggest that if the circumstances are appropriate for consuming alcohol, you should order something light, such as a white wine spritzer. Well, picture yourself out for dinner at a steak-and-potatoes kind of restaurant being interviewed by a table of robust people downing scotches and bourbons. What do you think they would think if you order a dainty wine spritzer? Remember how important that old issue of fit is. I'm not advocating imbibing hard liquor if it's not your habit to do so, but don't order what would be viewed as a "wimpy" drink just to be drinking something. You're probably better off having a soda— non-diet and with caffeine, of course!

In addition to being careful about what you order and how you conduct yourself at the table, be sure to follow the strategies suggested throughout this book for interviews in office settings. Just because a mealtime interview takes on a more casual, relaxed feel doesn't mean you shouldn't use your asset statements, powerful language, and all the other ammunition at your disposal.

Telephone Interviews

Watch Out!
Just because your clothes won't be seen when you have a telephone interview doesn't mean you should dress like a slob. You may find that if you wear business attire— or at least something fairly pulled together—you will feel more confident and professional, which will come across in your voice.

The telephone is frequently used as a way to screen applicants before devoting precious time to meeting with them in person, and it's also useful for interviewing candidates who are in another city or town. Hiring decisions rarely are based solely on a phone interview, though, so a phone interview is usually followed up by a face-to-face one.

Interviews over the phone not only are convenient for the interviewer, but they can work to your advantage as well. You don't have to agonize over what to wear, you don't have to worry about your body language, and you can't be discriminated against based on your appearance or apparent age. You might also feel more relaxed in a phone interview because you are likely to be doing it from the familiar surroundings of your own home (or your office, if there is adequate privacy).

For every advantage, however, there is a downside. Obviously, all the nonverbal cues that are so important for reading the interviewer or for communicating part of your message are unavailable. Also, rapport is more difficult to establish when you're not looking each other in the eye. And, if you aren't thrilled with the sound of your voice, you may worry—and rightly so—that the interviewer will misjudge you based solely on how you sound.

By employing a few simple strategies, though, you can make the most of this interviewing format. (For more tips on telephone communication, consult some of the books listed in the "Oral Communi-cation" section of Appendix C.)

■ Stand up while talking, to keep your energy level high, but avoid pacing the floor—you might sound out-of-breath without realizing it.

■ Keep notes handy to remind you of your asset statements and other points you want to make.

■ Minimize all distractions by making sure that your background is quiet, and avoid technical interference by disabling call waiting and speaking from a well-functioning phone.

■ Be extra concise, and avoid speech fillers such as "uh" and "um." Using these or being long-winded is more pronounced when you're on the phone because the listener has nothing to focus on but what you're saying.

■ Be diligent in keeping your voice sounding positive and energetic, and be sure to vary your pitch and tone.

Variations on a Theme

While this book focuses on job interviews conducted by prospective employers, you may find yourself needing to employ the strategies in slightly different situations. The following pages describe three variations on the interviewing theme: exploratory interviews, interviews with headhunters, and interviews for graduate or professional school. While most of the tactics suggested throughout this book apply to these variations, each does call for some techniques specific to that type of meeting.

Exploratory Interviews

In the course of any job search, it is not unusual to find yourself meeting with an employer and not knowing whether a suitable job opening exists for you, or knowing that one definitely doesn't exist but could in the near future. This type of interview is likely to come about through your networking efforts. You make contact with someone at an organization where you'd like to work, and that person agrees to meet with you but makes it clear (or hints at the possibility) that you will not be discussing any one specific position.

An exploratory interview is not to be confused with the proverbial "informational interview." You are not seeking basic information about a field or an employer to help you make a career decision or transition. Instead, in an exploratory interview you know what you want, but the employer just doesn't know if the company can offer what you want or can use what you have to offer.

An exploratory interview is a good way to get your foot in the door at a target employer—and it's certainly better than no interview at all—so you should take the opportunity to go on them whenever possible. And, you should take this type of interview as seriously as a regular interview. When handled right, an exploratory interview can turn into an interview for a specific position, or you may even find that a place is made for you if no opening exists.

How do you do that? You use your asset statements to show the interviewer what you have to offer. You also turn the tables and convert what is likely to be a conversational interview into a behavioral one. In other words, you raise the issue of particular situations with which the employer may be dealing and talk about how you would handle them.

Based on research you conduct about the employer, you go in with a sense of the organization's needs and goals, and then you ask enough questions during the meeting to get a better idea. Each time you get an information gem about the employer's concerns, you let one of your asset statements kick in, showing them how you could address that concern.

By the time the interview is over, you will have made such an impression that the employer will do whatever it takes to bring you on board. Of course, the fact that you will be extremely appreciative of the chance to have the meeting in the first place will establish good rapport and strengthen your case. If the meeting does not eventually result in a job offer despite your efforts, you at least have made a good contact who can become a valuable member of your network over time.

Interviews with Headhunters

If you're using employment agencies or executive search firms for help in finding a job, you may wonder if any special strategies apply to interviews with them. Interviews at these firms are somewhat tricky because the headhunter is working on your behalf on the one hand, yet is someone you must impress as you would the actual employer.

While recruiters in agencies and search firms are not in the business of acting as career counselors, they do take on a career coaching sort of role in advising you about your resume, your interviewing style, and your attire. They also might need to discuss sticky issues with you, such as why you were fired from a job or how to negotiate for a higher salary. At the same time, their primary allegiance must be to their client—the employer—so they must be selective in who they meet with and work with.

As a result, job-seekers often don't know how candid they can be with a headhunter and how

Unofficially...
When an employer finds you through a search firm, they pay the recruiters an average of 30 percent of your first year's salary as a fee.

much they need to employ strategic interviewing with them. Unfortunately, no clear-cut answers exist for this dilemma. A rough rule of thumb is that your initial approach to a headhunter should be no different than your approach to an employer. You must make a case for why that recruiter should pay attention to you. Once you have your foot in the door and have lined up a preliminary interview, you should tread carefully until you're able to determine how candid you can be. Never should you lie to a headhunter, because his or her reputation is on the line every time you're sent out; if the employer catches you in a lie, the headhunter gets blamed. (You don't, however, have to tell your deepest secrets. You should use some of the strategies suggested in the "Overcoming Interviewers' Objections" section of Chapter 12. These will help you put a positive spin on some of the more negative matters you might have to discuss with your recruiter.)

Graduate and Professional School Interviews

If you find yourself returning to school to pursue a graduate or professional degree, you might have an interview as part of the application process. Many people who have been in the work world for a while find that they don't know how interviewing in the academic arena differs, if at all, from interviewing for jobs.

The fact is that almost all the interviewing strategies suggested throughout this book are effective for academic interviews. The only twist is that, instead of tailoring your asset statements, image, and communication style to fit a prospective employer's needs and organizational culture, you are doing so for a particular degree program. You are being judged on what you can contribute to the scholarly pursuits and student life in that university and that department, as well as to the academic discipline or profession you enter after completing the program.

An interview for graduate or professional school often takes place on-campus, where you are interviewed by some combination of admissions officers, faculty members, and current students, either together or individually. You might also find that you meet with only an admissions representative or a faculty member, while the student(s) leads you on a campus tour.

If distance and finances prevent you from visiting the school for an interview, you might be interviewed by an alumnus of the program in your geographic area or by an admissions rep who travels to you.

If given the opportunity to interview as part of the application process, always try to do so. If you're waiting to receive an acceptance or rejection, or if you're put on a waiting list, try to get an interview even if one is not required. If you live out of town and can be in the area, admissions officers will often give you an interview if you say you're going to be in the area.

Strategies for academic interviews include the following:

- Make sure you are clear on how the degree you're seeking fits with your long-term career goals. Too many applicants are short-sighted, focusing on convincing the admissions reps that they have the intellectual ability and academic record to do the coursework.

- Don't assume that any students you meet have little or no say in the admissions decisions. Be cordial and in a subtle self-promotion mode with everyone you meet, including students.

Unofficially... According to the U.S. Department of Labor, three out of the four fastest-growing occupational categories between now and the year 2006 are executive, administrative, and managerial; professional specialty; and technicians and related support. Jobs in these areas often require bachelor's or graduate degrees and/or highly specialized professional training.

Watch Out!
Many people go
to graduate
school because
they don't know
what else to do
or don't want to
go through the
hassles of a job
search. If you're
contemplating
going back to
school, be sure
you have better
reasons for
doing so.

▪ Cultivate contacts who are alumni of the program to which you're applying. See if any fellow alumni from your undergraduate institution attended, or currently attend, your target graduate schools. Or, if you can't find any fellow alumni, ask around among your network to see if anyone knows anyone affiliated with the schools you're approaching.

I once had a client who was applying to MBA programs and was wait-listed at her top-choice school. She had met an alumnus of that school briefly at an event, but was hesitant to contact him again. I suggested she do so, and she found that he was happy to speak on her behalf to the admissions committee. He did, and she ended up being accepted.

▪ Show how you fit with the particular program. Each graduate department in each school has a unique character. Some are research oriented, while others are more practical. A program in psychology might have a psychoanalytic bent, while another is cognitive-behavioral. An MBA program may be known for it's entrepreneurial specialties, while another has an international flavor.

Just the Facts

▪ The most popular style of interviewing is the behavioral approach, in which you have to describe what you have done in actual situations in the past or what you would do in a hypothetical situation.

▪ If your interview has a structured question-and-answer format, as in a directed interview, be sure to maintain an equal balance of power with the interviewer and work your asset statements into the conversation.

- Don't be lulled into complacency by a conversational interview.

- When faced with a stress interview, the most important thing to do is stay relaxed and mentally sharp.

- The setting of an interview has an impact on the way you should communicate and comport yourself.

GET THE SCOOP ON...
The rationale behind tough questions ▪
Strategies for acing any question ▪
How not to be misled by the wording of
a question ▪ Sample responses that work

The Fifteen Trickiest Interview Questions

Chapter 9

This is a dangerous chapter. Anytime typical interview questions and sample responses hit the page, they have the potential to negate all strategies advocated up to this point—strategies such as viewing the interview as a consulting arrangement or conversation between two peers, maintaining the balance of power, and letting the real you come through instead of being robotic. When a discussion of questions and answers enters the picture, there's a danger that you might revert to the traditional—and counterproductive—role of lowly job-seeker sitting back being grilled by the mighty Prospective Employer, and responding with memorized key words and phrases.

It doesn't have to be that way, though. As long as you realize that these are just examples of questions and replies—not a script—there's no harm in planning for them. In fact, anticipating the questions you may be asked—particularly the toughest ones, as you'll find in this chapter—is vital to your success in the interview. Many questions require some advance preparation, so it is important to plan for the ones that are likely to trip you up. You also need to prepare for the ones that seem easy enough in the abstract but that can stump you once you're on the spot in an interview. (Many such questions are discussed in Chapter 10, "Some More Questions You Might Be Asked.")

On the pages that follow you'll find 15 questions that are often cited by job-seekers as the ones most likely to cause problems. These also happen to be the ones that interviewers rely on to get some of their best information. Of course, there's no sure way to predict which of these questions, if any, will be asked in your interviews. It's a good idea, however, to be prepared for any and all of them just in case.

Also keep in mind that these 15 questions can be worded in an infinite variety of ways, so even if you're not asked one of these exact questions, you may be asked something comparable—and you'll still be prepared with an effective reply. If you have any idea which type of interview you might have (whether directed, stress, or conversational), then you can have some idea of what to expect, because the questions—or ways that questions are worded— usually reflect the style of the interview.

For example, the interview request "Tell me three adjectives that describe you" is an old-fashioned, textbook-type question that is typical of a directed interview, while "Tell me about a time when you distinguished yourself from your peers and felt successful" would be the comparable request in a behavioral interview. At the root of both is the interviewer's desire to know about your professional assets and to see how you distinguish yourself from the competition. You would answer both by stating those assets and by giving an example of how you have demonstrated them; in other words, you would use one or more of your asset statements. (At this point you may want to review Chapter 4, "Making Yourself the Top Candidate," and Chapter 8, "Variations on the Interviewing Theme," for asset statements and interviewing styles.) Remember that it's the rationale behind the question that is more important than the actual wording of the question.

Obviously, you have no way of knowing exactly what you will be asked or how it will be asked, so it's best to have some strategies in mind that will help you ace just about any question fired at you. Let's look at those first, then get to the 15 tough questions later in this chapter.

Watch Out!
Non-specific questions such as "Tell me about yourself..." may be the sign of an inexperienced or unprepared interviewer who hasn't planned more precise lines of inquiry. If you suspect that's the case, take charge of the interview as much as possible to get your points across.

Strategies for Fielding Any Question that Comes Your Way

As mentioned before, you shouldn't go into an interview with a script of exactly what you're going to say, or with so much rehearsal under your belt that you sound like an automaton. What you do need to take with you are tactics that are versatile enough to navigate any twist and turn the interview might take. So, let these general rules be your guide:

- **Do** answer the question. As obvious as that sounds, it has to be the first tactic listed here because not answering the question asked is a common—and disastrous—pitfall. Listen carefully to what is being asked, and answer that question—nothing less, nothing more. (There's nothing wrong with adding a little extra information that wasn't directly asked for, as long as it is central to making your case and doesn't take you off on a tangent. But, you still have to answer the core question.)

- **Do** be candid—but do so strategically. Remember that employers want to get to know you. If they feel they're getting canned responses, they'll be turned off. For example, if you're asked about something negative —like "What is your biggest weakness?" or "Tell me about a time when you made a mistake"—you have to be candid enough to answer the actual question asked but not so much as to shoot yourself in the foot. (More detailed advice on this point is offered in the "Questions That Look for Flaws" section of this chapter.)

- **Don't** ever give a yes or no answer. When copywriters compose an advertisement, they know they have a very limited space in which to convey information and elicit a desired response. Every word is critical. You must have the same attitude when responding to interviewers' questions. Realize that every chance you have to respond to a question is a chance to convince the employer of your value. While you should never be long-winded, make sure that at every turn you have to speak packs a lot of punch.

- **Do** review your asset statements before every interview, and adapt them as needed for each prospective employer.

- **Don't** get hung up on the actual wording of a question. Focus instead on what qualities and experiences are being sought. For the toughest questions, such as those in this chapter, pay extra attention to the objective behind the question. What might sound like an off-the-wall question may simply be an original or creative way to ask for fairly mundane information.

- **Don't** be thrown by questions off the subject of the job. As long as they are legal (see Chapter 12, "Interview Curve Balls," for a discussion of how to know if a question can be asked legally), every question is worth answering and relates to the job in some way. Asking about your thoughts on current events or about hobbies you enjoy can yield valuable information for the interviewer and add a human dimension to the interview.

- **Do** be direct. Never be evasive or hesitant. If a question makes you squirm, don't let on that you are uncomfortable. Answer it directly while presenting yourself in the best light possible. (See strategies offered throughout this chapter as well as the discussion of overcoming obstacles and objections in Chapter 12.)

- **Do** be patient. No matter how tedious the interview may be, try to stay fresh, enthusiastic, and cooperative. Don't say things like "I think I already addressed that" or "You can find that on my resume." In the case of multiple interviews at the same company, never say "I already discussed that earlier today with Mr. Jones." Always provide the information requested, even if doing so seems redundant to you.

- **Do** collect your thoughts before speaking rather than blurting out a response. A pause of a few seconds may seem like an eternity to you, but it's usually a natural, brief pause to the observer.

Unofficially...
If you aren't sure of the meaning of a question, it's okay to ask for clarification.

- **Don't** ever be negative. Unless you are specifically asked about such topics, never bring up heavy subjects such as death, illness, accident, or failure. Also, don't speak ill of any person, place, or thing.

For more strategies to guide you in answering questions, review Chapter 2, "The Biggest Mistakes Interviewees Make," for mishaps to avoid, and read over Chapter 7, "Strategic Communication for Interviews," for a framework for effective oral communication.

An Introduction to the Fifteen Trickiest Questions

In some respects, no one interview question is any more or less difficult than the next. If you follow the previous guidelines and go into an interview equipped with versatile asset statements, you should be able to handle any question with aplomb. So why single out 15 questions as the toughest? It's all in the wording, the scope, and the "squirm factor"—how uncomfortable the questions make you feel—that qualifies them as trickier than the rest.

In some cases, the way a question is worded can throw you. Most people find it easier to respond to "Give me an example of a creative project you've worked on" or "Tell me what kind of person you are" than to answer "If you were a tree, which kind would you be?" Yet, the tree question is seeking the same information as the others: How creative are you, and who are you?

Similarly, the scope of a question can be intimidating. Remarks like "Tell me about yourself" and "Why should we hire you?" give the interviewee few parameters with which to structure a reply. But the rationale behind the questions is not much different from that of more specific requests, such as "Name three skills you possess" or "Tell me how you would solve this problem we have." The broader questions call for the same information as the more specific ones; they just require that you choose which information to provide.

Finally, some of the questions discussed in this chapter are particularly difficult because they make you squirm. They ask you to discuss negative personal qualities, failures, or controversial topics: matters most job-seekers would prefer not to bring into the conversation.

In this chapter, you'll find examples of 15 questions that may give you pause due to their wording, scope, or the "squirm factor." For each one, I provide strategies to guide your responses; in some cases, I offer actual sample answers. Keep in mind that the issue of how to reply to these questions is highly debatable.

If you surveyed 20 people who know anything about interviewing, you'd get 20 different takes on how these questions should be handled. What you will find on these pages are the approaches that have been found to be most effective by the many successful job-seekers I've worked with, recruiters I've spoken to, and research I have conducted to bring you the inside scoop. Where relevant, I've also given you more than one option from which to choose when structuring your replies. How to deal with tricky questions is a matter of personal choice. You can use your own judgment to decide what works best for your circumstances, personal style, and desired level of risk taking.

As for the sample answers given here, I'm sure I don't have to tell you not to use them verbatim in your interviews. The examples in this chapter (and in Chapter 10) are written in one person's voice and with one person's choice of language. You might—and should—choose to answer in a completely different style. In addition, keep in mind also that the answers are written as someone would speak them, so they will sound less formal than the surrounding text.

The "Tell Me About..." Questions

Watch Out!
When the interviewer says "Tell me about ..." you might be tempted to ask "What would you like to know?" While asking for clarification is usually acceptable, doing so can backfire on you when it comes to this question. Many interviewers use this lead-in as a test to see how you structure your reply, so they don't want to define parameters for you.

These first questions are not so much questions as they are conversation starters or lead-ins. They're open-ended requests that can be tricky because they provide few clues to the interviewer's motives. Fortunately, the rationale behind the "Tell me about..." questions is somewhat predictable, as you'll see in the description of these first three.

1. **Tell me about yourself.** "Tell me about yourself" occupies a place of honor in the Hall of Fame of difficult interview questions. Because it provides no parameters to guide a response, job-seekers usually find this interview opener bewildering. Sometimes that reaction is unwarranted, as this is often an innocuous icebreaker, a simple conversation starter not meant to challenge you but intended to let you say a few words of your choosing. More often, however, "Tell me about yourself" is a calculated way of finding out how you organize your thoughts, how you articulate them, and on which information you choose to focus. When planning how you'll respond, consider the following strategies:

   ■ Prepare sufficiently. This question requires much more preparation than any other because there is a danger of not knowing where to begin—or of knowing where to start but not knowing when to stop talking.

■ Weave your story tightly. Limit it to the high-lights of your current situation and past experi-ence, as well as a brief mention of what you have to offer. While you can never know exactly what any one interviewer has in mind when asking "Tell me about yourself," you usually won't go wrong if your response includes the following points:

> Your current situation (such as where you work and what you do, or where you are in school and what you're studying)

> An expression of your enthusiasm for being in the interview (if not already mentioned when you first met the interviewer)

> A brief overview of three to four of your best assets

■ Focus on professional topics more than per-sonal ones. It is sometimes appropriate to mention a couple of brief facts about your per-sonal situation (such as the mention of reloca-tion and having a family in the sample answer below), but this is not a time to tell your life story. Do not begin with "I was born in..." or "I'm a single parent...." Stick to the facts related to your professional situation or assets. If you feel that personal information is relevant or to your advantage to present, you may choose to include it, but just don't let it be the focus of your statement.

■ Be concise. Don't let yourself ramble on to the point of being boring or incoherent. If you bab-ble, you'll not only lose the interviewer's inter-est and sound like you can't organize your thoughts well, but you give yourself more opportunity to put your foot in your mouth.

Moneysaver
During a job search, never make more than about 25 copies of your resume at a time (unless you're doing a large mailing) because you will most likely make changes to it as you go along. You don't want to get stuck with hundreds of unusable versions.

Remember, too, that you don't have to tell everything there is to tell in this opening statement. You'll have the chance to build your case completely as the interview progresses.

An effective reply to "Tell me about yourself" might go something like this: "Well, first I'd like you to know that I'm really pleased to be here talking with you today because I think I have what you're looking for and I've long admired the work you do here at XYZ Company. My family and I just moved here last month from Raleigh, North Carolina, where I had worked for 12 years in quality control and as a production supervisor for two furniture manufacturers. I'm an effective manager, a good trouble-shooter and expediter, and a hard worker. And, I'd be happy to elaborate on any of those points if you'd like."

2. **Tell me a story.** As with "Tell me about yourself," a request that you tell a story may be used as a conversation starter meant to elicit a brief overview of who you are and why you're there in the interview. In fact, "Tell me a story" often simply means "Tell me *your* story." In that case, you would reply in the same way as you would for "Tell me about yourself."

Other times, "Tell me a story" means literally tell a story—perhaps an amusing anecdote from an activity outside of work or an account of one particular incident from your professional life. (The latter could be one of your examples from your asset statements, as described in Chapter 4.) If you choose to tell a story from your personal life, make it one that demonstrates your skills, personality, or values in some way.

For example, I know of one man who wanted to make a career change from advertising account management to management in a social service agency. When I asked him what had been the catalyst for this transition, he said that it was the day his six-year old daughter asked him if his work "made his heart feel good." He realized that he would be lying to her if he said "yes." This incident, coupled with the fact that he had been contemplating a career change for over a year, led him to make some changes. When he went on interviews in the not-for-profit sector, he found that this story was a powerful statement that proved his commitment to their work.

"Tell me a story" may also be a way to find out how creative or entertaining you are. If you'll be interviewing for creative positions or ones requiring a certain amount of charisma (such as sales), be sure you have a good story or two at the tip of your tongue.

Questions That Look for Flaws

On the flip-side of the open-ended questions are those that are a little too specific for comfort. Questions that require you to discuss negative aspects of your character or experiences go against the grain of every job-seeker who wants to make a positive impression in interviews. The three examples that follow typify this perplexing line of questioning.

3. **What is your greatest weakness?** Next to "Tell me about yourself," the question about weaknesses has got to be one of the most dreaded in the history of employment interviewing. You go into an interview wanting to discuss your assets,

Bright Idea
Always have a "grab bag" of conversation topics on hand to show interviewers that you are a well-rounded—even entertaining—person. Include a tasteful joke, an interesting tale from traveling or a sports pursuit, the name and author of your favorite book and last book read, and the name of your favorite movie or last movie seen.

so the last thing you want to do is talk about your deficits. The key to being comfortable with this question is to remember that you'll be more successful in an interview that lets the prospective employer get to know you fully than in one in which you come across as too good to be true. Once that realization sinks in, you then need to craft a reply that is at once candid and positive.

The most important thing to keep in mind when answering this question is to avoid a canned response. There's a long-standing myth in the world of job hunting that says you should answer this question by choosing a positive quality and making it sound negative. Don't even think about it! Saying that your weakness is that you're a perfectionist to a fault, or too detail oriented, or a workaholic is a thinly veiled attempt to dodge the question. Everyone has weak areas, and employers want to know about them. They wouldn't ask the question if they didn't. Your best bet is to give an honest answer involving a genuine deficit—but to do so strategically. Here's how:

Watch Out!
When choosing a weakness to talk about, don't choose one that has absolutely nothing to do with the job you're going for. Your answer will sound phony and like an obvious attempt to dodge the question.

- Choose a weakness that is not critical to success on the job in question. Obviously, you shouldn't talk about your poor math skills if you're going for a job as a bookkeeper. Select an area that would be a minimal part of the job.

- Discuss a weakness that relates to content knowledge as opposed to an innate personal quality or a transferable skill. Saying that your weakness is lack of knowledge of a particular computer application is preferable to saying that your problem is in managing people or following-through on a task (even if those are minimal parts of the job). Content knowledge can be learned and is less connected to your basic character and aptitudes.

■ Select a weakness that the interviewer is already aware of—or is likely to discover—so that you're not raising a negative that wouldn't have been noticed in the first place. With this strategy, the question "What is your greatest weakness?" can actually work in your favor because it gives you a chance to address a concern before it festers in the interviewer's mind.

■ Always talk about how you are working on the problem. Give tangible evidence of your efforts to improve in that area, such as courses you've taken, books you're reading to teach yourself something, or mentoring you've sought to help with your professional development. If you've already shown improvement, give an example of it.

■ Ask a question as soon as you give your answer. Say, "How important is X for success on this job?" If your deficit is a major concern, then you have the chance to address that concern right then and there.

4. **Tell me about a time when you had a personality clash with a coworker or boss.** This request is particularly difficult because the issue of personality clashes is a topic you want to avoid like the plague in interviews. Personality conflicts between bosses and subordinates, between coworkers, and between employees and clients or customers are rampant in the world of work, but they are a taboo topic for interviews almost 100 percent of the time. The reason for this is that it is nearly impossible to discuss a

Bright Idea
Whenever you're asked to discuss something negative about yourself or your background, begin your reply with a statement like, "I've given this considerable thought because I'm always trying to work on my professional development." You'll sound like the question doesn't make you uncomfortable because you have nothing to hide and that you strive for self-improvement.

personality clash without having yourself end up looking like a bad person. If you own up to your role in the conflict, you come across as someone who is difficult to work with. If you place the blame for the clash on the other person, you look like you are not only difficult but, at minimum, are just not a team player; at worst, you look like a back-stabber.

In asking this question, the interviewers are getting at that issue of fit. They want to know if you have problems getting along with other people. They are also trying to find out how tactful you are—do you say negative things about others, or are you diplomatic in how you describe a situation? This question also serves as an indirect way of asking what you look for in a boss or coworkers, to see if your work style and preferred way of managing or being managed is congruent with the prospective employer's workplace.

Your best bet here is to say as little as possible. You basically have three options for answering this question, presented here in order from safest (but most evasive) to riskiest (but most direct):

1. Say that you have been very fortunate in that you've gotten along well with everyone you've ever worked with and that no personality clashes come to mind. In other words, evade the question.

2. Answer the question in a seemingly direct way, but interpret the wording of the question to your advantage. Define "personality clash" (or "conflict") as a clash of values or work ethic rather than one of personality. Talk about how a boss wanted you to do something illegal or unethical, or how a coworker never held up his or her end

of the workload and that the problem led to a conflict.

3. Be more candid, and talk openly (but tactfully) about the lunatic boss or psychotic coworker you've had to deal with. You would usually choose this option only if you know the interviewer is familiar with your situation enough to know about this person. This actually happens more often than you might think, particularly in tightly knit industries where everyone knows everyone else and knows who the notorious bosses are.

A word of caution is in order if you choose the second or third option, however. Whenever you even venture near candor when discussing a personality conflict, do so very diplomatically. Be brief and matter-of-fact. Don't sound emotional—not angry, bitter, or whiny. Don't sensationalize the issue or sound gossipy. Always bear some of the blame for the problem, and talk about what you did to resolve it and how it has never happened since then. Also, mention that you were not the only person to have a problem with this boss or coworker. If you can site turnover rates or formal complaints other employees filed, you objectify the situation and make it sound less like your problem and more like fact.

5. **What mistakes have you made in the past?** This question is similar to "What are your weaknesses?" in that it forces you to make yourself look less than positive. You have similar choices here in that you can be evasive and say you've never made a mistake, or you can admit to a mistake—remember that everyone on this planet has made at least one—but do so in a way that doesn't damage your credibility. You can

choose one that does not reflect a serious error of judgment or a character flaw and that is not central to the work you would be doing for the prospective employer.

As before, use your own judgment to decide how direct you want to be. Keep in mind, though, that as long as your answer is carefully crafted, you will usually come across as more sincere if you do admit to a mistake or two in your past.

If you opt for the direct approach, choose a mistake that is somewhat related to your professional life but unrelated enough to your day-to-day work, one that's not a critical error. For example, the sample answer below uses relocation as a mistake:

"Fortunately, I've had a pretty good track record, but, of course, everyone makes mistakes on occasion. I guess the one that has been on my mind lately is the decision I made to leave Boston two years ago. I uprooted my family and left all the family and friends I had here to go to the West Coast, where the economy was stronger at the time. While we adjusted pretty well considering the culture shock we faced, and while I thrived in my work with California Capital, I knew soon after the move that we all belonged back in New England. I had made the decision on purely objective data, overlooking the more subjective aspect of a decision like that—would we feel like fish out of water? So, I'm eager to get back here in my old stomping ground. I even miss shoveling snow! And, as with all mistakes we make in life, I learned a great deal. This incident reminded me not to make a decision based solely on how something looks on paper, so I think in an ironic way, this mistake has made me a better manager."

Timesaver
If you have a copy of the organizational and/or departmental chart for your current or most recent job, bring it along to the interview. It will help the prospective employer get a quick, clear sense of where you might fit in.

Questions to Reveal Your Character and Uniqueness

Questions that ask you to describe yourself or particular types of situations you have been in are often difficult because they test your self-awareness and self-confidence. These are the questions that really put the interview on the line and force you to distinguish yourself from other candidates.

6. **What are three words that describe you?** This question might also be asked as "How would your friends describe you?", "How would your boss describe you?", or "Name three adjectives that describe you." If you have done the self-assessment recommended in Chapter 4 and the research suggested in Chapter 3, "Research: The Root of All Strategy," you should have no difficulty answering this question. You know what your assets are and which ones are relevant to the prospective employer.

Nevertheless, this is often seen as a difficult question for two reasons. First, it requires that you sing your own praises in a blatant way, something many people are not comfortable doing. Second, it is easy to become overwhelmed when you have to choose just three words to convey who you are out of all the possible words you could use. It's a little like going into a video store to rent a film and not being able to decide among the thousands of titles available, so you opt for seeing a film in the theater where you have a more limited number of choices.

To deal with the first concern, remember that your asset statements objictify the claims you are making about yourself. When you say that you possess certain positive qualities, you are not just boasting, but are stating a fact.

To tackle the second problem, plan in advance which three words you'll use instead of trying to come up with them on the spot—and make sure you choose ones that represent three different aspects of yourself. For example, you might pull one personal quality, one transferable skill, and one area of expertise (that is, content knowledge). Also, make sure that the three words you choose do not relate to the same functional area. For example, saying you are organized, detail-oriented, and a good planner is a poor use of this question because all three speak to the same general category of qualities. Make sure that the three terms each represent a distinct area.

7. **How do you define success?** This question is sometimes difficult because it is one of those borderline-philosophical queries that few people pause to consider in the course of their day-to-day lives. The rationale behind it—and the strategy for answering it—however, are fairly straightforward, so it need not be a question that stumps you.

Most interviewers use this question to determine whether your values are in line with those of the job in question or the organization as a whole. This gets to the issue of what motivates you, how you'll fit in, and how committed you will be. Some definitions of success are obvious and almost stereotypical. In brokerage firms, for example, entry-level brokers need to show that they are motivated by making money, whereas someone interviewing for acceptance into a graduate school of social work has to define success as helping others.

Most situations—and even those two, to some extent—are not quite as obvious. In determining how you will answer a question about your definition of success, start by simply thinking about it.

What does motivate you to work hard? When have you felt successful, and what were the circumstances? Then compare your findings with what you think would be valued in the organizations where you are interviewing. If there is a match, then you have nothing to worry about. But if you suspect a conflict, then you must decide how much you are willing to modify your true feelings to tell the interviewers what they want to hear, or how much you would prefer to look elsewhere for an employer whose values would jibe with yours.

> The secret of success is constancy to purpose.
> —Benjamin Disraeli

8. **Why should we hire you?** Here's another broad question that can easily throw you off track, but it need not be nearly as intimidating as it sounds. This question begs for you to use your asset statements, so it is really quite simple to address. What the interviewer is saying with this question is, "Please do my work for me. Tell me how you are different from the last five people I interviewed and the next five candidates I will meet."

What you have to do to ace this question is to be aware of the employer's needs, to assess what you have to offer related to those needs, and to give an example of how you have met similar needs in the past. Sound familiar? That is the process recommended in Chapter 3, on conducting research, and in Chapter 4's "Building Your Case" section.

The worst answer you can give to this question is one that is completely undistinguished, such as "You should hire me because I'm a hard worker with excellent skills and experience." So what? Anyone can say that. You have to zero in on the two or three qualifications the employer cares most about, and the one or two problems that need to be solved, then deliver a powerful punch of a reply, such as this:

"From what we've discussed this afternoon, it sounds like your department needs someone who can hit the ground running to get your operations streamlined, reduce your production costs, and boost the staff's morale. I've done that before, and I can do it for you." (At this point, the interviewee would continue with one or two asset statements as examples to back up that last claim, or would cue into the listener's signals to pause before continuing.)

9. **Tell me about an ethical dilemma you've faced.** This request is typical of behavioral interviews in which your integrity and work ethic are assessed through real-life examples you provide. The interviewer wants to know what sorts of ethical issues you've had to deal with, how you handled them, and what you learned from them. In describing an ethical dilemma you've faced, consider the following:

- Choose one in which you were involved only as an observer or secondary participant. You might describe witnessing someone violating a company policy, cheating, or stealing. This is preferable to choosing one that involved your own behavior. (An interviewer might press, however, for you to discuss one in which you were directly involved. In that case, you have to respond to that request.)

- Be tactful and diplomatic in the way you describe the situation. Speak of it in neutral terms instead of sounding self-righteous or like a snitch.

- Don't reveal confidential information that violates the civil rights of past coworkers or the proprietary rights of your employer. Obviously, you should not identify anyone by name and should provide only as many details of the incident as are needed to tell the story.

- Say that you first defined the problem to make sure that there was indeed a breach of ethics taking place before jumping to conclusions.

- Show that you dealt directly with the parties involved to let them know of your concern and to give them a chance to explain their position before reporting them to any relevant authorities.

- Conclude your account with a discussion of what you learned from the incident.

10. **Where do you see yourself 5/10/15 years from now?** This question is less common than it used to be because companies no longer offer an implicit guarantee of lifelong employment. In fact, some job-seekers assume that it is not asked anymore at all, but it is. With complex reorganizations and strict belt tightening the norm in many organizations, employers want to know that the efforts they'll make to position you within their ranks are worth the trouble. They do want to know that you will be with them long enough to make their investment in hiring and training you pay off.

The best way to answer this question is to balance specific information with broad brush strokes. Employers' eyes will roll if you are too broad, giving a canned response such as "I hope to grow and advance with a company that can offer challenges and opportunity." That means nothing. Talk

Unofficially...
Some interview-
ers ask about
your future plans
not just to see if
you will work for
them for a rea-
sonable period
of time, but
also because
they want to
know if your
interests and
goals fit with
typical career
paths in their
organization.
Some com-
panies, for
example, expect
you to go to
graduate school
at a certain
point and then
return to work
for them. Others
might expect you
to relocate or
move into a new
functional area.

instead in terms of function, level, and areas of contribution.

You might say, "Well, of course I can't say exactly where I want to be five years from now, but I know that I will still be involved in desktop publishing and will be continually learning and applying cutting edge technologies. I also know that I would like to move into more of a supervisory role while still having my hands in actual production. And, I'd like to be able to say that I have contributed to a dramatic revamping and revitalization of a company's image through its print and online materials. I'd like to do those things here with [company name], if that sounds like someone you're looking for."

Nosy Questions

Some lines of inquiry make you want to snap back at the interviewer with "That's none of your business!" Before making that assumption, however, think about what the rationale might be behind the question. You'll see that each of the questions has an intent that goes deeper than the superficial information sought. The interviewer is not trying to be nosy but is looking for clues to such matters as your integrity, work-related skills, level of interest and commitment, and professionalism in general.

11. **Where else are you interviewing?** This question often throws job-seekers for a loop because they assume that they have to keep other prospective employers a secret. It's no coincidence that the term "courting" is sometimes used to describe the mating ritual in which employers and prospective employees engage. You might feel that if you mention other organizations, you will sound less interested in the one where you are interviewing. On the contrary, interviewers

know that a smart job-seeker is going to investigate every possibility and will rarely approach only one place at a time.

A direct approach to this question is usually the best approach. It will also have the added benefit of getting the employer's competitive juices flowing when you sound like you are in demand, being "courted" by others.

One decision you have to make when replying is whether to mention specific company names or just to speak of them in generic terms. If you do mention the actual name of another organization, do so only if you have a definite interview scheduled or have already been there. The person you're speaking to might know someone at the other organization and can catch you in a lie—or at least a stretching of the truth—if you say you're being considered somewhere you're not.

If you have no other interviews scheduled—or likely to be scheduled—but don't want to sound like you're not in demand, you can speak euphemistically. "I'm in the early stages of discussing opportunities at two other firms" is a handy euphemism for saying that you have placed preliminary calls to a human resources representative who told you that some opening might exist and that you should send in your resume and they'll call you—maybe. Of course, if you are not interviewing anywhere else because you are not in an active search, you can simply say so.

12. **How are you finding the time to interview?** This question (asked of job-seekers who are currently employed, obviously) may be used to determine if you are the type of person who takes unfair advantage of your employer. Are you the sort who lies and abuses company time

Watch Out!
Be sure you don't confuse seemingly nosy questions with illegal ones. Illegal questions (as described in Chapter 12) ask for personal information that can be used to discriminate against you. The "nosy" questions are ones that try to shatter the illusion of the effortless job-seeker to uncover the real you.

for your own gain? Do you say you're going on a client call when you're really heading for an interview?

Timesaver
If you're currently employed and having trouble finding the time to interview, ask your target employers if they can schedule your interviews over breakfast or after work.

It is also asked to find out how you manage your time. Never let down your guard when answering this question, saying something to the effect of, "Oh, what a time I've had trying to fit appointments into my work week—it's been a nightmare!" The best approach is to say that you're using vacation time and personal days, also called "floating holidays," to go on interviews and to conduct other job-search activities. You can also say that you are interviewing at breakfast, lunch, and after work whenever possible. Of course, if you haven't been managing your time that way and have been sneaking around, calling in sick, or using your employer's time for your search, then you'll have to limit your reply to something short-and-sweet like, "It hasn't been too difficult to interview and still do my current job effectively. I tend to manage my time well."

13. **How did you prepare for this interview?** Here's another question that forces you to shatter the illusion of the effortless interviewee. There's no need to be cagey here. The interviewer expects that you did some preparation and will value the professionalism you demonstrate in doing so. Remember, conducting pre-interview research is not cheating.

When describing how you prepared, focus on the research you conducted about the organization and the industry or profession as a whole rather than on your own mental preparation or rehearsal. There's no need to tell them that you prepared asset statements, participated in a mock interview, worked on your communication style, and the like.

You want to come across as someone who is always self-aware, self-assured, and a good communicator, not someone who needed a major overhaul to get up to speed in those areas.

Discussing the research you conducted is also the preferable focus because it serves as a springboard for another direction in the conversation. Bringing up something you read on the company Web site or in the organization's newsletter will invariably lead toward a discussion of that content and away from the question of how you prepared for the interview.

14. **How much money are you looking for?** You probably know not to bring up the issue of salary in a first interview, and also not in subsequent interviews until an offer is on the table (or nearly there). Interviewers don't always live by the same rules, however, so you might find yourself asked point blank what salary you are seeking. Chapter 14, "Evaluating and Negotiating Offers," deals with salary negotiation in detail, offering strategies to use when you are actively involved in negotiating the terms of an offer. For now, just keep a few strategies in mind for answering this question when it is asked prematurely—that is, when the issue of money is raised before an offer is being extended.

Avoid stating any precise dollar amounts, but don't avoid the question entirely. Say something like, "I know that my salary needs are in line with typical compensation for [type of position] in an organization this size. And, I'm confident we'll be able to come to an agreement on an appropriate compensation package, but I'd rather not discuss specifics until I have a chance to know more about

Unofficially...
Headhunters will almost always expect you to discuss salary in a first interview with them, so be prepared to disclose your current and previous earnings and your salary requirements. Otherwise, they won't be able to work with you effectively.

Watch Out!
Employers want to find out if your salary requirements are in line with what they can pay, so they may not let you brush off the question "How much money are you looking for?" Be prepared to discuss at least general salary ranges. (See Chapter 14 for more advice on salary negotiation.)

the position and until you know more about what I have to offer."

Most employers will expect a fairly pat answer like this, but they ask the question anyway on the off chance that you'll give a reply that actually mentions specific figures. If that were to happen, they'd then have the upper hand in subsequent negotiations. They also ask the question to avoid wasting their time and yours. They need to know that your salary requirements are not completely out of line with what they can offer.

15. **What do you think about [controversial topic] ...?** You might come across an interviewer who would rather discuss the day's headline news than your skills and experience. He or she may want to know what you think about the latest government scandal, a recent Supreme Court decision, an international conflict, or some other major issue. While such a discussion can be a welcome change from the relentless focus on you and your qualifications, it inevitably raises some tricky issues. It is difficult to discuss politics or social issues without stating personal opinions, and any time you give an opinion on a controversial topic in an interview, you risk alienating the interviewer.

To handle these situations diplomatically, use the following strategies:

- Consider the nature of the organization in which you're interviewing. If it is related to journalism or other media, public policy, religion, or any other pursuit directly related to events in the news, then you will be expected to discuss those issues in some detail. For any other type of organization or position, give a brief reply that doesn't encourage further discussion.

- Similarly, take into account the style and philosophy of the organization. Is it conservative or liberal, traditional or progressive? Then decide how much of a maverick you can be. If you feel strongly about being able to voice your own opinions, then go ahead and do so. But if you want to play it safe, make sure that any opinions you express are likely to be shared by the interviewer.

- If you want to take the safest course of action, express no opinion at all or one that is entirely neutral. If the interviewer asks, "What did you make of that mandate the Pope announced this morning?" reply with something innocuous like "That was really something, wasn't it? I'm interested in seeing how the world reacts." With this tactic, you deflect the query and put the dialogue ball back into the interviewer's court. A downside to this approach is that you might come across as someone without convictions or sharp analytical skills.

- Subtly change the subject. If, for example, the question is about a matter being hotly debated in Congress, compare the issue to a debate that went on at your last company and discuss how you helped to resolve the disagreement.

Just the Facts

- While it is important to be prepared for specific questions, you shouldn't expect an interview to conform to a textbook-style format.

- You can't predict exactly which questions will be asked or how they'll be worded, so arm yourself with versatile strategies rather than detailed scripts.

Unofficially...
Interviewers want to get to know you as a person, so asking for your opinion on a controversial topic may not be a trick question. It might simply be a way of finding out how you think and who you are.

- Focus more on the rationale and objective behind a question than on its wording.

- Prepare concise, but powerful statements for the open-ended "Tell me about…" requests.

- When answering questions that ask you to discuss something negative about yourself, don't give a canned reply that tries to make a positive sound negative.

- Deflect questions about your salary requirements until after an offer is extended or is imminent.

GET THE SCOOP ON...
Questions asked in behavior-based and directed
interviews ▪ Meaningful questions you can ask

Some More Questions You Might Be Asked

This chapter deals with the heart of the interview: the questions you are asked to determine how strong a candidate you are. Even if your interview is predominantly conversational in nature, you are likely to come across at least a few of these questions. If you find yourself in a directed or behavior-based interview, you will probably encounter many of these.

On the surface, most typical interview questions explore your work experience, education, activities, skills, career goals and job objectives. Beneath the surface, though, a good interview question probes your psyche. It uncovers your personality traits, values, work style, and thought process—and might even identify character flaws, failures, and any other Achilles' heel you were hoping to hide. The questions discussed in this chapter represent a sampling of the most common interview questions, ranging from easy to challenging. After each question, you'll find a discussion of the rationale behind it and suggested tactics for your response.

In addition to the tactics specific to each question, keep in mind the guiding principles recommended in Chapter 9, "The Fifteen Trickiest Interview Questions," and throughout this book; these bear particular significance at this stage:

- Remember that you are interviewing to join an organization, not just to do a job, so your replies to interview questions must go beyond demonstrating that you meet the basic job requirements.

- Balance being genuine and sincere with a strategic approach that, in some respects, lets employers hear what they want to hear.

- Don't memorize answers to anticipated questions, but do plan the words and phrases you will use to answer them to ensure a smooth delivery and effective content.

- Focus on the rationale behind a question, not the surface meaning.

- Keep in mind that rarely is there one right answer to a question. The interviewer is often more interested in how you structure your thoughts and whether you have opinions than in what that opinion actually is.

- Use your asset statements as often as possible to give strength to your responses.

The questions that follow are sorted into three categories, which mirror the hiring criteria outlined in Chapter 1, "How Hiring Decisions Are Made": Can you do the job? Will you fit in? Do you want the job? Of course, some questions fit into more than one category, but each question is listed in the category of which it is most representative. You will find that questions worded as they would be in a behavior-based interview—such as, "Tell me about a time when you were under pressure"—are inter-spersed with more traditional ones, such as "How do you handle criticism?" As you read all the questions, keep in mind that each can be worded differently, depending on the interviewer's style. For example, the previous questions could be asked as, "How do you handle pressure?" and "Tell me about a time you faced harsh criticism." Despite the wording, the strategy for answering them would remain the same.

Also note that, for the sake of brevity, some questions refer to "your last job," as in, "Tell me about your responsibilities on your last job." That same question could, of course, be asked about any of your prior jobs—not just the last one—and if you are currently employed, an interviewer might ask those same questions about your current job. So, when reading these questions, adapt them as needed to fit your own situation.

Questions to Find Out if You Can Do the Job

As discussed in Chapter 1, employers want to know that you not only can handle the basic responsibilities of a position, but also that you can add some value—both to the immediate job at hand and to any future needs of the organization. The sample questions in this first section are ones that are typically used to assess your skills, content knowledge, and personal qualities, as well as your potential to be instrumental in reaching organizational goals.

1. **Tell me about your responsibilities on your last job.** This request is tailor-made for your asset statements, so it should be easy to answer. Start by providing a brief overview of your responsibilities, then describe in more detail two or three aspects of the job that are most

Moneysaver
Ask your accountant which, if any, of your job-hunting expenses are tax-deductible. Many may be.

relevant to the prospective employer. And, of course, talk about the skills you acquired or demonstrated while doing the job and how they might relate to the needs of the prospective employer. In other words, use your asset statements rather than simply reciting the job description off your resume.

2. **What percentage of your time was spent in which activities on a typical day in your last job?** This is a smart question. The interviewer is probing for more detail to get a complete and accurate picture of exactly what you did on a job. Don't reply by saying, "There was no typical day." That's obvious (unless your job is unusually routine). Give a more descriptive answer, even if you have to describe a few different types of typical days, such as the day a week that you were in the field, the days you were in the office in meetings and making calls, and the day you allotted for paperwork and long-range planning. By breaking down your week for the interviewer, you are not only telling what you did and the skills you demonstrated, but you're also showing how you managed your time. In other words, answer this question thoroughly.

The only exception to this rule is if you are trying to obtain a job that involves responsibilities you have not held in the past or that you have dealt with only minimally. In that case, do not cite actual numerical percentages, but talk instead in more general terms.

3. **How did your responsibilities evolve or progress during your tenure with your last company?** This question is a boon for job-seekers who do not have a clear picture of advancement on their

resumes (through progressively responsible titles) or on their salary histories through pay increases. It gives them the chance to describe ways that they were charged with additional responsibilities which might not be reflected in their titles or earnings. Whatever your situation, when answering this question, be sure to talk about the qualities and accomplishments for which you were being rewarded rather than the perks and prestige that came with the moves.

4. **Describe the process you go through to plan and implement a project.** This is a straightforward question aimed at seeing how you do your work (for jobs involving some sort of project management, which is just about every job). When answering it, keep a few pointers in mind:

- Avoid giving painstaking details; just walk the interviewer quickly through the steps you take.

- Talk in terms of a specific project you completed successfully to make the discussion more real rather than speaking hypothetically.

- Try to choose a project that relates to the same sort of work you would be doing on the job for which you're interviewing.

- Mention the assets you demonstrated in accomplishing the task so that you spell out your transferable skills, knowledge, and personal qualities for the interviewer.

5. **On average, how many hours does it take per week to get your work done?** Interviewers usually have multiple objectives in asking this question. First, they want to see how effective you are. If you begin to rant and rave about how

Timesaver
If you have a tendency to be rather talkative, keep your mouth in check during interviews. Be thorough but concise with your replies. Being long-winded wastes your time and the interviewer's.

Watch Out!
If you're trying to get a job that would involve long hours but your past jobs have been more 9-to-5ish, many interviewers will doubt your ability to adjust to their schedule. So, don't just say, "Oh, I wouldn't mind working lots of overtime." Give examples of times when you have had to do that—even if they are from academic or personal experiences.

many hours you work—thinking that you are making yourself sound very industrious—you may actually sound like you don't use your time efficiently during your regular business hours. If you do say that you work considerable overtime, make it clear that you do so because the workload calls for it—not because you're using the time to catch up.

Second, interviewers want to know if you will fit into the collective work ethic at their organization. Do you seem willing and able to work long hours if they are required, or do you sound like you would do so only grudgingly?

6. **What qualifies you to do this job?** As with "Why should we hire you?" and "Tell me three words that describe you," this question is a clear request for you to prove your value and distinguish yourself from other candidates. All you need to do is to identify the most salient job requirements and employer's needs and use a couple of asset statements to show how you qualify.

7. **How long would it take you to start making a contribution to our organization/ department?** This is yet another way to ask what you bring to the table. One difference, however, is that this particular wording might signal a special need the employer has for new hires who will make a contribution above and beyond normal job duties. From your pre-interview research, you should know if the organization is grappling with certain problems, facing challenges down the road, or attempting to reach some major goals. If so, your response to this question should address those needs directly,

using your asset statements to prove that you
have a track record of similar accomplishments.

8. **What can you do for us that someone else can't
   do?** As with the last two questions, this one calls
   for skillful use of your asset statements as relevant to the employer's needs. The difference
   here is that this wording might clue you into the
   size and quality of the applicant pool from
   which the employer can choose. Though this
   may simply be a standard question that a particular interviewer always asks, it might also mean
   that you are having to distinguish yourself from
   a large number of equally qualified candidates.
   Or, if asked in a follow-up interview, it may indicate that the applicant pool has been narrowed
   to just a few people. In that case, you not only
   need to reply with your asset statements, but
   you also need to pay close attention to the rapport you establish with the interviewer(s) to get
   the edge over the competition—competitors
   who may answer all the questions well but not
   really connect with the interviewer(s).

9. **Give me an example of a time when you've
   taken the initiative on something.** This is a classic request in a behavior-based interview. The
   phrase "taken the initiative on something"
   could just as easily be "solved a problem," "followed through on a complex task," "demonstrated skillful management," or any similar
   accomplishment. As with previous questions in
   this category, this one calls for choosing an asset
   statement that reflects the needs of the prospective employer and that best showcases your abilities. Remember, too, to share credit for your
   accomplishment with any colleagues involved.

10. **In past performance reviews, which areas of your work have been singled out as needing improvement?** Like some of the questions in Chapter 9, here's one that forces you to say something negative about yourself. Some interviewers will ask to see your past reviews, though this is not a common practice. You might also include particularly favorable ones in your portfolio. If you are asked to discuss problem areas, keep two tactics in mind: Choose only one problem, and speak in the past tense. Even if the interviewer words the question with problem "areas" in the plural, there's no need to offer more than one. When you do speak about a problem, choose one that was not central to successful performance on that job, and speak about it as a former issue, not a current weakness.

You might say, for example, "My performance reviews have always been generally excellent, but a few years ago one supervisor pointed out my tendency to be somewhat disorganized with the papers and files in my office. It never caused any major problems, but I sometimes got slowed down having to look for a particular file or phone number. Well, I set out to make some changes in that part of my life. I took some very helpful seminars and, at my own expense, hired a professional organizer to come in and help me get on track. People now comment on how organized I am, and I always laugh to myself and think 'If only they'd known me back then!'"

11. **Assorted questions related to the specifics of your functional area.** An interview will usually include at least a few technical questions designed to test your knowledge of

the principles and procedures involved in doing your job. You may be given a hypothetical problem to solve and be expected to walk the interviewer through the steps you would take to solve it and give an accurate answer. If you're rusty in any aspects of your work, you need to review them before interviewing.

Questions to Find Out if You'll Fit In

In some respects, employers can determine if you will fit with the position, your coworkers, and the organizational culture by simply watching you. Are your attire, demeanor, and body language in sync with those of the place where you'd like to work? Remember, though, that as discussed in Chapter 1, the issue of fit is more than appearance. Fit also consists of values, preferred style of working, and personality. The issue of fit in a more literal way is important as well: "Do we have a place for you?" and "Can we afford you?" are questions employers ask before hiring. The questions in this section are samples of ways interviewers chase down that elusive quality of fit.

Bright Idea
When you're researching the companies at which you plan to interview, find out what you can about the workplace style and work ethic you'll encounter in each. You'll have a better idea not only about if you'll fit in with *them*, but also how they will fit with *you*.

12. **Tell me about a time when you had to work under much more pressure than usual.** This request gets at your character and work style. It is a behavior-based one that doesn't merely ask how you deal with pressure in a hypothetical sense; it also asks how you have handled it in an actual situation. Be sure to choose an example that mirrors situations you might face on the job for which you are interviewing. In describing it, be sure to sound balanced and fair, not placing the blame on any one person for causing the problem that led to the pressure. Also, don't sound overly negative as you describe the

situation. Make the description brief, giving just enough facts to set the stage. Then move onto an account of how you handled it, citing assets you used to remain calm and clear-headed. Conclude by describing the outcome of your efforts. Did you prevent something catastrophic from happening? Did you protect your boss's reputation? Did you keep morale up in the people working around you? Did you set a good example by remaining on an even keel in the face of adversity?

13. **Do you think you have done the best work you are capable of doing?** This is an interesting question because it presents a damned-if-you-do, damned-if-you-don't dilemma. If you say that you have done your best work, you'll certainly be saying something positive about your past performance but will be implying that you have nothing left to offer. If you say you haven't, then you are indicating that you have a lot to contribute but that your past work has been less than stellar. This is one of the few interview questions which has only one satisfactory answer: "I have always tried to perform to the best of my ability and have done some excellent work, but I also strive for continual improvement, so I know I can do even better." It's a bit corny, but it works. (And, remember, you'll be putting this in your own words, so you can make it sound natural for you.)

14. **What do you consider to be your biggest accomplishment?** This question is one of the easiest you'll come across. You simply consider what the employer's biggest need is in a new employee and use the asset statement that best

demonstrates how you can meet that need. To give an even more powerful reply, consider the organization's values and philosophy, and select an example that best fits those. Because this question gets at the issue of success (as discussed in question seven of Chapter 9), you need to consider how the employer might define success—what they would consider to be a big accomplishment, that is.

15. **Describe your energy level.** Of course, most employers want to hire people with high energy levels who will work hard, put in extra hours as needed, and keep up with a fast pace. Be careful, though, that you don't go to extremes in describing your energy level. Present a balanced picture, saying that you are a high-energy person but that you don't overwhelm people with enthusiasm and energy when a situation calls for a more low-key, composed approach.

16. **Where did your last job fit in its departmental structure or the organization as a whole?** This question relates to the issue of fit in a literal sense: Do we have a place for you? It also lets the employer know that you have worked at the level at which you claim to have worked. Rather than relying only on your title to discern your level of responsibility—because the meaning of titles varies from place to place—the interviewer asks you to specify your role in a department or organization. If your role clearly matches that of the job you're seeking or the organization's needs, then you have no problem.

If, however, you're attempting to work in a different functional area or at a higher level (or even

Watch Out!
Your current title can hold you back if you try to seek a job at a higher level or in a different functional area than those of your current position. To prevent this, try to take on special projects with a more senior person or in another department. That way you can discuss them in interviews and the interviewer won't get hung up on your actual title.

at a lower level) than you have in the past, then you might run into some stumbling blocks. Be prepared to make a case for how your official position on a company chart does not reflect the actual work you did. Use your asset statements to demonstrate your potential and to distract the interviewer from the original question.

17. **To whom did you report on your last job?** Like the last question, this one shatters any illusions about your level of responsibility and functional area on your last job. It enables the interviewer to determine whether you have been consorting with the upper echelons or just answering to someone who barely outranks you. Use the strategies described above for this question as well.

Bright Idea
If your first interview is with a human resources rep—or anyone else who would not be your boss on the job for which you're interviewing— use that opportunity to ask about the prospective boss to find out what she or he is like. Then, in any subsequent interviews at the same company, you will know what to say when asked "What kind of boss do you want to work for?"

18. **What will your references say about you when I speak to them?** This is often a pointless question because it rarely elicits any meaningful information for the interviewer. Presumably, you provide names of people who will give you good recommendations, so there's not much to tell here. Being asked point-blank about what those references will say, however, does force you to give some descriptive information about yourself. You might describe how your references view your character, work style, or personality, making this something like the question "Tell me three words that describe you," as discussed in Chapter 9. A clever interviewer realizes that, in answering this question, you are projecting your own self-concept onto the referees. You are more likely to be describing how you see yourself than how you believe they see you.

Some interviewers might also ask this question because there is a chance it will trip you up. If you become visibly agitated when the subject of references is raised, and if you hesitate when replying, a red flag is raised about how well you have performed your jobs and how well you have gotten along with coworkers and bosses in the past.

19. **Tell me about a difficult decision you've had to make.** On the surface, your reply to this statement tells the interviewer what kinds of decisions you've dealt with in the past—and, thus, whether you are used to handling the kinds of issues that the job in question would entail. And, it lets the interviewer know how skilled you are at making decisions.

On a deeper level, it says something about your values and work style. You might describe a decision-making process that is autocratic or one that involves others. You might talk about the pressure and stress that accompanied a decision or a tug-of-war between head and heart.

To answer this question effectively, choose a decision that is similar to ones you would have to make on the target job. And, be conscious of the values and work style that you are exemplifying when describing your decision-making process.

20. **What kind of boss do you want to work for?** Tread very carefully with this one, especially if you are speaking directly to the person who would be your boss! If you have done sufficient research and networking prior to the interview and have uncovered inside information about the nature of your prospective boss, then you will have no problem with this question. If you're going in cold, however, and don't know

what makes the prospective boss tick, you need to play it safe. Your best bet is to say something innocuous, such as, "I like working for someone who is fair and who shows me respect as long as I'm deserving of that respect." If the interviewer does not accept that off-the-shelf answer and presses for more detail, just be sure that you don't sound demanding or picky when describing what you look for in a good boss.

21. **How did you get along with your last boss?** The rationale behind this question is two-fold. First, it may simply be another way of finding out what kind of boss you're looking for. If you praise certain qualities in your last boss, the interviewer can infer that you hope to find those same qualities in the next boss. It's best to keep your reply simple and say that you got along well. If the interview asks you to elaborate, speak in positive terms about the relationship you had with your boss.

Unofficially...
You don't have to be a scholar to keep up with management theory and cutting-edge business practices. You can easily follow such trends in books found in your local bookstore or library, including those by Gellerman et al, Pinchot, Reichheld, and Rosen & Berger as listed in Appendix C, "Recommended Reading."

The second rationale behind this question is that your response may hint at a personality clash, which could signal a difficulty you have getting along with colleagues. As always, leave the battle scars out of the interview, and talk about anything positive you can possibly come up with to describe the relationship. Discussing what you learned from your boss is usually a good option, since we often learn valuable lessons from even the most unpleasant bosses.

22. **What is your management style?** Obviously, this question will be asked only if you are applying for a supervisory or managerial position. If you're aiming for such a job, you must have a management philosophy in mind—even if you are more inclined to wing it in reality. Your

management style does not have to be a formal doctrine off the pages of an M.B.A. course textbook (unless you're interviewing in the type of organization or with a type of person who would appreciate your citing formal theories). Just be able to describe the thought process underlying your behavior, and also make sure that the approach you describe fits with the organizational culture.

23. **What kind of boss are you?** This question is essentially the same as the last one, but this one gets more at the issue of how you deal interpersonally with subordinates as opposed to your formal management philosophies. As with other matters, it is in your best interest to sound balanced: fair but firm, democratic and egalitarian but able to take charge, empathetic but objective, or collaborative but self-directed. Your pre-interview research comes into play here, as well as your active listening during the interview. Both skills enable you to pick up on clues the interviewer may give as to what is needed in a boss. Listen for words and phrases used to describe what is needed in the new hire, and adapt your own style to fit those needs.

24. **What kinds of people do you get along best with?** The best way to answer this question is to cover all bases and say that you get along with all types of people. Try to get away with a short answer and move onto another topic so that you don't have to get into a discussion of the personalities of people you've worked with. Such a discussion invariably requires that you voice judgments about various temperaments and work styles, thus opening the door to offending

the interviewer. If the interviewer does press you for more specific definitions of types of people you have worked with or would like to work with, never mention race, ethnicity, gender, or sexual orientation when describing with whom you do or don't get along well. Cite characteristics that you know reflect the organizational culture, such as being hard-working, creative, motivated, intelligent, and the like.

25. **Do you prefer working alone or in groups?** While being a willing and able team player is an almost universally desired trait in job candidates, there are positions that require you to be considerably self-sufficient and comfortable with autonomy. If you know something about the job and organization as a whole, then you should have no difficulty answering this question. Give a balanced answer that makes you sound versatile and able to work well alone or in groups, but put the emphasis on the one aspect that best describes the job in question. Also, be sure to give an example of how you have done both, along with one showing how you have performed well either alone or in groups, depending on which aspect you need to emphasize.

26. **When working on a team, which role do you usually take?** As discussed in the "Assessment Through Observation" section of Chapter 11, "Passing Muster: Tests, Observation, and Other Ways You'll Be Assessed," employers concerned with how you function in a team setting might have you participate in a group exercise that simulates a workplace task. Not every organization has the time or resources to set up such observation sessions, however, so you are more

66

The fact is each of us has his own style, his own preferences, and his own ways of facing life's challenges. One person's laid-back style is another person's lack of motivation ... someone's need to keep up with change is someone else's conviction to not fix what ain't broken. Those differences in style can lead to a great deal of misunderstanding, miscommunication, and resentment.
—Otto Kroeger and Janet Thuesen, *Type Talk at Work: How the 16 Personality Types Determine Your Success on the Job* (New York: Dell, 1992)

99

likely to be asked about your teamwork style during a conventional interview.

Answering this question involves two steps: The first is to determine which role(s) the employer is most concerned with. If the job you are going for requires leadership qualities, then obviously you need to talk about how you usually emerge as the natural leader of a team (but a democratic one, of course). If you aren't sure which roles would be most valued, your safest course of action is to describe how you can play two or three different roles, depending on what the situation calls for. The second step in preparing an answer to this question is to identify an example of a team effort in which you have taken part and describe your role(s) in that function, as well as its successful outcome.

27. **Are you a leader or a follower?** This question is similar to the one about teamwork in that it seeks information about roles you naturally take on. You might be tempted to look at this question as a particular easy one, with no right answer except "I am a leader." Don't make that assumption. Of course, leadership is usually viewed as the more admirable quality of the two, but there is a place for being a follower in every job and every organization. Plans have to be implemented, projects completed, and rules and procedures followed. If you emphasize your leadership skills too much, you might sound like you are not willing to be a team-player, so try to paint a balanced picture.

28. **In which kind of atmosphere do you work best?** This question gets at your work style and directly relates to the issue of fit. Interviewers not only want to know if the kind of

environment you seek is the one they have to offer, but they also want to identify any character flaws you might inadvertently reveal in answering the question. Be careful that you don't sound like you require any extremes, such as too much structure or too much autonomy. And don't slip up and contrast your desired work environment with that of your past or current job. There's no need to volunteer negative information about other workplaces.

29. **What aspects of your job do you like best?** This question may also be posed as. "What are you looking for in your next job?" Regardless of the wording, it is one of the most straightforward and easiest to handle. Obviously, you should speak about the aspects of your last job that relate most to the job in question. Be sure to answer only this question. Resist the temptation to be overly candid and volunteer information about what you liked least on that job. Finally, when describing what you liked best, don't just tick off the responsibilities in a detached way as if someone else had carried them out. Talk about the skills and character you demonstrated while doing them.

30. **What were the most repetitive or tedious tasks of your last job?** This question might also be asked as, "What did you like least about your last job?" or "What would you have changed about your last job if you could have?" This question is often intended as a way to trip you up and get you to describe something that is an important part of the job for which you are interviewing. Don't be afraid, however, to give a genuine answer here.

Every job involves some degree of tedium, so it is best to be candid and name something you didn't like rather than pretending that you loved every moment of the work. To soften the blow, however, couch your candor within a positive statement and an example of how you got the tedious task done despite the boredom. For example, you might say something like, "Fortunately, I genuinely enjoyed just about every aspect of my work, but if I had to single out one thing I wouldn't mind doing less of, I suppose it would be the monthly sales reports. But, I developed a system for doing them that made the process go more smoothly and painlessly.

31. What do you enjoy doing in your spare time?
This question is usually asked when you have not listed any hobbies or interests on your resume. It is often merely an innocuous conversation starter, but it can be a way of finding out about your values, personality style, and skills. It is important that you not launch into a lecture on the wonders of bee-keeping or recite the 200 ingredients in your favorite paella recipe. Just say a little something about one of your more interesting pursuits, then pause and ask if the interviewer knows anything about that pursuit. Getting a read on his or her experience with the topic and interest level keeps you from being boring or from preaching to the converted.

Bright Idea
If you discover that your interviewer shares a hobby or personal interest of yours, mention it in your follow-up letter (thank-you letter) to further clinch the relationship. (See Chapter 13, "Following Up to Get to 'Yes'" for more advice on such letters.)

You should be aware, however, of the legalities involved when the interviewer inquires about your personal activities. You do not have to discuss any interests or activities that are not related to the job for which you are being interviewed. If you would prefer not to discuss any aspects of your personal life, you can reply to the question with a tactful brush-off, such as, "I manage to rest and relax during my spare time so that I have a balanced life and am fresh for the next day of work." If you do choose to speak about anything more specific, be aware that the prospective employer has no legal right to know about your personal beliefs, such as religion, sexual orientation, or political leanings. This issue is discussed in more detail in Chapter 12, "Interview Curve Balls."

32. **What would you like your obituary to say?** Your response to this rather morbid question tells the interviewer what you value, how you define success, and which accomplishments you are most proud of. It is also an indirect way of getting at your career goals. If you say that your obituary will mention a particular career that is not part of your current target career path, your reply may call into question your commitment to that current career direction.

This question can also be a sneaky way of finding out about your personal life. For example, a nosy interviewer who suspects you're gay might be looking to see if you include "devoted family man" or "loving wife" in your obituary. Similarly, if someone wants to know whether you have children, your obituary might mention that fact.

To answer this question effectively, be sure to give it some thought in advance, as it is not an easy one to deal with off the top of your head. As always, balance being yourself and reflecting your true values with emphasizing the qualities and accomplishments that would fit with the prospective employer's values and needs. And, reveal only as much personal information as you are comfortable doing.

Note: A related question you might be asked is, "What would you want the epitaph on your tombstone to say?" This, too, can be a tough one to answer because you must come up with a pithy statement that captures the essence of you. That can be particularly difficult to do on the spot, so it's a good idea to prepare for it in advance.

33. How quickly would you expect to advance here? Most employers are looking for three types of information here:

- Is your projected career path in line with what the job and organization in question can offer?

- Are you willing to take the initiative in determining your own course rather than expecting the employer to coddle you?

- Are you too eager to move up? Are you going to get impatient if you don't advance quickly?

In responding to this question, be sure that your expectations for advancement are realistic and fit with the structure of the prospective employer. Also express your willingness to be responsible for your own success and patience to move when the opportunity is right for the organization as a whole, not just for yourself.

Questions to Find Out if You Want the Job

As discussed in Chapter 1, employers will extend an offer when they are confident that you know what you're getting into. They want to hire people who have taken charge of their own career development—and who will continue to do so—by assessing their own strengths and needs, setting clear but flexible goals, and thoroughly investigating their employment options. The questions in this section are examples of ways employers try to find out if you

> ❝
> Employees are expected to look after their own self-improvement. This is compared to several years ago, when the manager was more responsible for the development of his employees. Now, it is a mutual role with more emphasis on the employee.
> —From *The Career is Dead: Long Live the Career,* Douglas T. Hall and Associates (San Francisco: Jossey-Bass, 1996)
> ❞

really know what you're getting into and, thus, if you do indeed want the job you claim you want.

34. **What did you like most (or least) about your last job?** The obvious rationale behind this question is to find out if the elements of your work that you find most interesting and motivating are in line with the position for which you are inter-viewing. This question is an example of why you need to find out as much as possible in advance about what a position would entail, or to ask questions early in the interview if you weren't able to learn much beforehand. You can then choose one or two aspects of a past job that are relevant to the target job (or irrelevant, in the case of things you did not like about your last position). Also, be sure you choose aspects that reflect a strong work ethic and other admirable qualities, as opposed to saying that what you liked most was the short workday or ample vaca-tion time.

Watch Out!
Some interview-
ers are more
intrigued by
what you have
left off your
resume than by
what is on it.

35. **Tell me about any jobs you've held that are not on your resume.** An employer does have a right to know about your complete employment record. In fact, you might have to complete an employment application that asks for a detailed work history. Employers know that your resume—when done right—is really a market-ing tool which presents your background in the most favorable light. They also know that space limitations may prevent you from listing all your jobs and activities.

If you choose not to include certain jobs on your resume simply because they are from more than several years back or from a previous career field not relevant to your current target, then you have nothing to worry about. You can give the employer a brief run-down of that part of your work history and then shift the focus back to your more recent employment or educational experiences.

If, however, you omitted jobs because you were in them only for a short time—usually a few months or less—or because you left on bad terms and don't want to have a reference checked, this question is trickier to answer. If you are interviewing in companies that do comprehensive background checks, you must reveal all prior employment because it will probably be discovered anyway. Also, if interviewing for jobs in tight-knit industries in which everyone seems to know everyone else, it is usually wise to disclose everything. For other situations, you have the option of committing a sin of omission by simply forgetting to mention the firm that fired you after only 30 days. The choice is yours to make, but do keep in mind that any lies you tell or information you conveniently forget can come back to haunt you.

36. **What do you know about this organization? what appeals to you about us?** Here's an example of why conducting research prior to an interview is so critical. When interviewers ask outright "Why do you like us?" you must have credible, thoughtful reasons for doing so. If you have done sufficient research, this should be a welcome question—one that really lets you shine. You get to show how well prepared you are and can state your case for why the employer is the right place for you. Just be sure you don't overwhelm the interviewer with a dull recitation of facts and figures gleaned from your research. A common pitfall is to focus only on the first of these two questions and overlook the second

one. Interviewers don't want to hear about every detail you picked up in your research. The question "What do you know about this organization?" is really asking "What appeals to you about us, and do you know what you're getting into?"

37. **Why do you want this job?** This question is essentially no different from the last one. You cannot simply state all the perks and enticements of the job—things like the salary, hours, opportunity for advancement, or prestige of the employer. You must give reasons that are not so self-serving, ones that benefit the employer, such as the chance to apply your skills and knowledge or to make a contribution to a particular effort. Also mention something specific about the nature of the organization and the position itself (based on your pre-interview research) that makes the job appealing to you.

38. **What are you looking for in your next job?** Here's another way of finding out whether your needs and goals are in line with those of the target employer. The answer to this question is fairly simple: State responsibilities and opportunities that you know the job offers. In doing so, focus not on what your employer can do for you, but on what you can do for your employer. Come across as someone who is looking for the chance to use what he or she has to offer—whether that's creativity, the ability to cut costs, or strong management skills. Don't sound like someone looking for perks and prestige.

39. **What are your career goals?** You would be surprised at how often this question elicits such candid information for the interviewer that it

Unofficially...
Employers differ radically when it comes to their need to be flattered by prospective employees. Some are so hungry for good workers that they aren't too concerned about whether you have singled them out as your employer of choice. Others want to know that they are your top choice. Through networking and research you can find out where your prospective employer stands.

changes the course of the interview. One employer I know was interviewing a man for a sales management position in the office supply industry. The candidate was coming across as well qualified and interested in the work until he was asked about his career goals. Without skipping a beat, the applicant replied that he hoped to become a chef and was currently taking courses in a culinary institute. In a friendly and interested manner, the interviewer subtly pressed for more information, asking what the courses were like and how the culinary program was structured. Unwittingly, the candidate talked about how he was nearing the end of his course requirements and that the school required a three-month apprenticeship for the degree. As he spoke, the applicant realized that he had let the proverbial cat out of the bag and that there was no way he would get the job. The interviewer spoke about her need to hire someone who would stay at least a couple of years and politely brought the meeting to a close.

You may not be concerned that you will be so candid about career goals that don't mesh with the employer's needs, but be aware nonetheless of how a seemingly friendly conversation can close doors for you. If you do plan to go in an entirely different direction, you have two choices: (1) lie about it and face the potential consequences when your true goals are revealed later on; or (2) seek only jobs that do fit into your career plan so you don't have to lie.

40. **How did you choose this career?** This is another way that employers can test your level of commitment to a particular field. If you describe a thought process that is thorough, logical, and based on accurate data, then you will prove to

the interviewer that you belong in the field you're in—or hope to transition into. If, however, you describe "falling into" a career, your credibility will be called into question unless you can show convincingly that the career has turned out to be right for you even though you did not consciously choose it.

41. **Why do you want to leave your current job? (or, why did you leave your last job?)** Good reasons for leaving a job include these:

- Factors beyond your control, such as a company's closing, a departmental phase-out, a massive lay-off, or your need to move for a relocating spouse.

- Reasons that demonstrate your positive personal qualities, such as desire for growth and challenge, or desire to use your skills and talents more directly.

If you do use any of those latter excuses for leaving an employer, just be sure that you describe any efforts you made to make things work with that employer. In other words, you shouldn't just say, "I left because they couldn't offer me what I was looking for." You need to show that you took the initiative to analyze your job and speak to your bosses about how your responsibilities might be altered, or added to, so that you could find the growth and challenge you were seeking.

If you left your job for less than admirable reasons, such as being fired, refer to the suggestions for dealing with that issue in Chapter 12.

42. **What do you think about [current event/recent development in the industry or profession]?** This question demonstrates the importance of

keeping up with developments in your industry or profession—and not just limiting your research to information about the organization itself, as advocated in Chapter 3, "Research: the Root of All Strategy." The specific content of your answer to this question is not as critical as the fact that you demonstrate some awareness, knowledge, and opinions in discussing that content.

43. **Would you be willing to relocate?** Answering this question is fairly simple if you are indeed willing to relocate. You simply say "yes." You can make your case stronger by giving an example of how you have been flexible with past employers, relocating as needed. If you don't want to relocate, or if you're not sure how you feel about it but you don't want to miss out on a job offer, answering this question becomes a little more complicated. If you say "yes" but don't mean it, then you will face problems down the road when your employer expects you to pull up stakes and move. If you say "no," then you might not get the offer. Because this question is sometimes asked despite the fact there is little or no chance relocation would be required, it is unfortunate to miss out on an offer because you said "no."

To take a safe middle ground, you can say that you are open to the possibility but would prefer to discuss that matter in more detail if and when an offer is extended. Of course, if your pre-interview research shows that relocation is a standard part of a particular job, then you have no choice but to say "yes" if you want an offer.

Watch Out!
If an interviewer pulls you into a discussion of current events or developments in your industry or profession, steer clear of gossipy topics. Stick to neutral—but thoughtful—observations and analysis of what's going on rather than the "dirt" about specific people or organizations.

44. How long do you think you would stay with us?
This can be a tricky question because you have to know how long the employer would want you to stay. As discussed throughout this book, most employers these days do not expect you to stay with them until you retire and get the proverbial gold watch. It is something of a myth, however, that they don't care at all about how long you stay. As mentioned in Chapter 1, hiring and training of a new employee can be an expensive endeavor. Add to that cost the effort that goes into analyzing staffing needs and carefully plotting where personnel are needed, and you find that employers invest a great deal in a new hire. So, when answering a question about how long you'll stick around, take these factors into account and don't sound like you'll be out the door when the next great opportunity comes around. Also rely on your research about the company—particularly the networking you will have done to get the inside scoop on what's happening at a given organization. Your research findings should give you some indication of what the norm is for tenure in various positions, as well as how much job-hopping is the norm for a given industry.

If your research does not turn up any clear signals, or if you simply want to hedge your bets, a safe answer is something along the lines of: "I'd want to be with [company name] as long as I'm making a valuable contribution."

Do You Have Any Questions for Us?
You are probably already aware that in addition to anticipating certain questions to be asked of you, you need to prepare questions you will ask. Many

Questions Typically Asked of Undergraduates, Graduate Students, and Recent Grads

How did you choose your college/graduate school?

Why did you choose to major in?…

Tell me about your senior project/thesis/other major project.

How has your college experience prepared you for a career?

Why did you decide to attend graduate school?

Describe your most rewarding extracurricular experience in college/graduate school.

If you had to do it over again, how would you plan your education differently?

Are your grades representative of your abilities?

What was your worst grade, and how did it happen?

What were your standardized test scores? (SAT, GRE, LSAT, and so on)

Who was your favorite professor, and why?

Which teaching styles do you learn from best?

Tell me about your internships and part-time jobs.

Why didn't you work during college/graduate school?

Why didn't you hold any leadership roles in college/graduate school?

How did you pay for school?

How much did you study during college/graduate school?

How would your classmates describe you?

As an alum, how do you plan to be involved in your school?

job-seekers dread getting to that point of the interview when they hear, "So, do you have any questions
for us?" It can be difficult to come up with questions
to ask because many will have already been
answered by your pre-interview research or throughout the interview. This is particularly true in a
conversational interview in which the interviewer is
likely to have told you everything you need to know
about the position and the organization—and then
some.

So how do you ask intelligent questions when
you don't really have any in mind? Or, how do you
know if questions that you do have in mind are
appropriate? Consider the following tactics:

- Avoid the problem altogether by asking questions throughout the interview rather than waiting until the end of the meeting.

- Don't ask anything that you should know
  already, such as information easily available in
  an organization's online or print publications.

- Ask questions that a consultant would ask, such
  as questions about the organization's needs,
  problems, plans, and goals.

- Don't ask about money and perks, such as
  salary, health benefits, vacation time, sick leave
  policy, and the like. You'll have time to find out
  about those things when an offer is on the table.

- Ask questions that help you get a clear picture
  of what the job would really be like day-to-day
  instead of the glossed-over image the interviewer might portray.

- Similarly, ask probing questions about the organization's future plans so that you can assess its
  stability and strength and can see whether the

direction it is heading matches your own career goals.

Questions you should ask fit into three basic categories: the position, the organization, and next steps in the hiring process. Questions about the next steps in the hiring process are discussed in Chapter 13. Questions to ask about the position for which you're interviewing and the organization you're seeking employment with are listed in this next section:

Questions About the Position

You might ask these questions that address the specific position and its intricacies:

Bright Idea
If you ask questions about an organization's problems, plans, and goals early in an interview, you'll be able to structure the rest of the conversation around how you can meet those needs.

> Where does this position fit into your organizational chart?
>
> To whom would I report?
>
> With which other groups or departments would I interact?
>
> What are the future plans for this department?
>
> What are the biggest challenges facing this department?
>
> What is a typical career path for this position or is there one?
>
> Why is this position open?
>
> What qualities are needed for success on this job?
>
> What are you really looking for in a candidate?
>
> What percentage of my time would be spent in the various duties?

Questions About the Organization

Or ask these questions about the organization itself:

> What are the organization's plans for the future?

> What are the biggest challenges facing this organization?

> Which of your competitors pose the biggest threat these days?

> How would you describe the working environment here?

> What do you most like about working here?

Just the Facts

- Always consider the meaning behind a question rather than taking it at face value.

- Don't memorize answers to each anticipated question; just have flexible strategies in mind to use with any question.

- When answering questions about your skills and abilities, always show how you could add value above and beyond the basic job duties and the organization's immediate needs.

- When faced with questions about your work style, work ethic, and values, give a response that fits the organization's culture.

- Don't wait until the end of the interview to ask questions yourself. The more questions you ask early in the interview, the more easily you can build a case for why you're the best candidate.

GET THE SCOOP ON...
Skill and aptitude tests ▪ Why you might
have to do homework ▪ Psyching out the
psychological tests ▪ The debate over
drug testing

Passing Muster: Tests, Observation, and Other Ways You'll be Assessed

Just when you've weathered the storm of tough interview questions, you might find yourself having to take a test, be observed interacting in a group, or be sent off with homework to complete. Employers have all sorts of tools at their disposal with which to judge you. Exercises that simulate a day-in-the-life of the job for which you've applied, tests that prove you really can do what you say you can do, and questionnaires that probe your psyche are some of the most common measures that add to the set of data an interviewer needs to collect on you.

While it is possible that you can get through an entire job search without having to face any assessment technique other than the traditional interview, jobs involving specialized expertise and knowledge almost always require skills tests. High-level management or technical positions often require the

Bright Idea
To get a sneak peak at some of the group exercises in which interviewers might have you participate, read *Games Trainers Play or More Games Trainers Play* (both by Scannell & Newstrom), or *101 Great Games & Activities* by VanGundy (all published by Jossey-Bass, San Francisco).

measurement of your personality characteristics and aptitudes to make sure you're cut out for the job. And positions that depend on platform skills—such as training, teaching, sales, and consulting—may not be yours until you successfully make a presentation to the hiring decision-makers.

This chapter describes these types of assessments, as well as other bumps in the road you may encounter, including drug testing, medical examinations, and background checks. These forays into your psyche, your body, and your bank account are often the most nerve-wracking parts of a job search, but they need not be. Knowing what to expect, how to handle them, and what your rights are can make the process much less intimidating.

Assessment Through Observation

The best way for an interviewer to find out whether you can do something is to watch you do it, not to ask how you think you do it. Assessment through observation involves having you complete tasks or take skills tests, either at the employer's office, at your home, or in an assessment center.

Simulation Exercises

Some tasks you might have to complete include exercises that simulate job-related situations. You complete these exercises alone or in a group, while your ability to do the job well—along with the character you demonstrate when doing it—is observed by the prospective employer.

The classic among simulation exercises is the in-basket test, which has been around for decades. This measures your organizational and time-management abilities by presenting you with phone calls, e-mails to answer, papers to process or file, projects to attend to, correspondence to write, and other administrative or operational responsibilities. You will be bombarded with more than any person could handle during the time allotted, but you are not expected to complete everything. Showing that you know how to prioritize is the most important part of this test. Sort the papers according to urgency and importance, remembering that what seems urgent is not always of the highest importance. (That's the whole idea behind prioritizing.) Also make out a mock to-do list and schedule to show when you would address the matters you don't get to right away.

Other simulation exercises involve staging a mock meeting, discussion, or collaboration session with a group of fellow candidates. The group might be charged with solving a problem, discussing an issue, completing a task, or coming to consensus on a matter. You might also find yourself in a team-building exercise that has the group pretending to be lost at sea, trying to survive in the wilderness, or stranded in a snowstorm.

Whatever the task, the observers are watching for roles to emerge as participants fall into their natural patterns of leading, managing, organizing, selling, empathizing, or being a resource. They're also looking to see who's a team player, who is confrontational or conciliatory, who is authoritarian or a consensus-builder, and who causes or calms disputes.

You can ace these exercises by determining which traits and roles the job in question entails and the organization as a whole values. Then strike a balance between being yourself and giving them what they want. Don't try to be someone you're not; it

Bright Idea
When you've completed a test of your prioritizing skills such as the in-basket exercise, go one step further and talk about organizational systems you would put in place if you were actually on the job. This idea of long-range planning that takes the place of "putting out fires" daily is addressed in Steven Covey's *The Seven Habits of Highly Effective People* (Fireside, 1990).

does you no good to fake certain qualities just to get an offer.

It is also to your advantage to appear versatile, particularly if you don't know exactly what qualities are sought for the position. For example, you might show that you are committed to building a consensus in a democratic fashion but can be assertive, too. Or, you might play up the team-player bit, but demonstrate that you can think for yourself as well. Don't take this balancing act so far that you come across as a chameleon, but do keep in mind that most employers these days want to hire people who can wear many hats.

Presentations

You may be asked to make a presentation to a small or large group as part of a first screening interview or as a follow-up to a first interview. This method of evaluating candidates is common for jobs that would require you to make presentations on the job, such as in training, teaching, sales, and consulting.

You will either be assigned a topic or be asked to choose one, and then be expected to prepare a talk, workshop, or training session. The presentation is usually about one hour in length but may be longer or shorter. The obvious advantage to the employer is that this activity enables a much more accurate assessment of your skills and style than even a behavior-based interview can. From the candidate's perspective, this approach really lets you shine—assuming you do have the qualities needed to do the job. It catapults you into that important role of doer, not just talker.

Watch Out!
Employers often plant difficult participants in a group when you're in a simulation exercise or making a presentation. They are put there to see how you deal with people who challenge you or are belligerent, slow to understand, or otherwise disruptive.

Of course, such an assignment is not without its intimidating side. Even if you are an accomplished public speaker, trainer, or teacher, you might get a bit rattled when thinking about a job offer that's contingent upon one presentation. If that's the case—or even if you're not particularly nervous—consider these tactics for success:

- Try to get the inside scoop on the department and organization where you'll be presenting. What is their philosophy toward training/sales/consulting and so on? What style do they prefer?

- Be sure to ask (in a preliminary interview or by phone prior to the presentation) what problems or goals they are trying to address. I once had a client who worked in insurance sales and was applying for a position that would entail making presentations on insurance products to employee benefits administrators at various companies. He learned that the company was in the midst of redefining their sales approach, encouraging their sales reps to make more of an effort to educate prospective customers than to push products on them. Because he had a background in teaching prior to working in the insurance industry, he was able to call upon that experience and conduct a presentation that had an educational flavor. The hiring managers liked what they saw and offered him the job.

- If you've not had much public speaking or training experience but are trying to get a job that would involve making presentations, don't try to wing it. Read some of the books on public speaking listed in the "Oral Communication"

Unofficially...
To put candidates' platform skills to a more stringent test, some employers ask them to make a presentation on a topic completely unrelated to the job or profession, perhaps on the subject of a personal interest or knowledge area, such as how to select a wine or buy a car.

section of Appendix C, and practice by giving a mock presentation to a group of friends, family, or professional colleagues.

Bright Idea
If you want to improve your platform skills, take every opportunity to observe others. Attend lectures or seminars sponsored by professional and trade associations, adult education centers, and other venues for ideas on what to do—or not to do.

- If you are an experienced presenter, don't try to change your approach drastically for your interview presentation. If you have a good thing going, now is not the time to mess with it. Make any minor adjustments necessary to fit the needs of the employer, but don't completely revamp your style.

- Remember that the presentation is just one aspect of your overall candidacy. If you give a less than stellar performance but have exceptional credentials and references, then the decision-makers might cut you a little slack and forgive a presentation with a few minor flaws.

Homework

Some job-seekers are surprised to find that they leave an interview with homework to do. This is particularly common with entry-level positions, where you do not have a substantial track record or portfolio on which a hiring decision can be based. You may be directed to complete some task at home after a first interview and then will be called back for a follow-up interview if your work is satisfactory.

Homework is often given for jobs that would involve writing or editing. I have seen job-seekers copyedit a manuscript for a job in publishing, write a synopsis of a manuscript for work with a literary agent, and write an article on an assigned topic for a newspaper.

If you are assigned homework, the best thing you can do for yourself is to get it done quickly and completely. Half the reason—if not more—that homework is assigned is to see if you are truly committed to getting the job and if you can be relied upon to follow through. You should also make an effort to complete the task on your own. Ask questions when it is assigned so that you know how to proceed, but then do your best to be self-directed and not pester the employer with questions once you're underway. (If you really need to ask something that comes up after you get started and that is critical to the quality of your finished product, then there's no harm in calling or e-mailing with a couple of questions.)

You can usually assume that at least half the applicants given a homework assignment will not complete it, so if you simply turn something in, you are likely to make the first cut. Of course, you should submit your best work, but don't agonize over the task so much that you procrastinate and miss the boat.

Skills Tests

As with homework assignments, you might be asked to complete a task that demonstrates your skills and knowledge, but this time, you do so at the interview site or at an outside assessment center. Skills tests have traditionally been most common for clerical and administrative positions. Typing (or keyboarding), word processing, filing, grammar, spelling, and punctuation are just some of the tangible skills that may be tested. Other positions that require specialized knowledge such as computer programming, using computer spreadsheet programs, and undertaking some types of research or analysis may require testing as well.

Some of the written communication fields assign tasks such as those described in the previous section

Bright Idea
If you don't do well on a skills test, ask if you can brush up on the skill on your own and come back to take the test. If your other qualifications are strong and you've established good rapport, many employers will give you a second chance.

in the form of an on-the-spot test instead of as homework. You might be asked to edit a written document, write a press release, or come up with an idea for an advertising campaign. A paralegal or legal secretary may have to proofread a legal document or conduct some research.

Whatever the task is, pay close attention to the instructions, asking for clarification as needed. Take the test cooperatively, even if you are annoyed that you have to do so. For tests such as typing and keyboarding, make use of the practice time that is usually allowed so that you can warm up before the clock starts ticking.

If you find that you don't perform very well on any particular test, address the problem directly. Now is a good time to use some of the tactics suggested in the "Making Up for Deficits" section of Chapter 4, "Making Yourself the Top Candidate." You might say, for example, "I guess I'm rustier on Filemaker Pro than I thought. I've been using another database program for so long that I'm a bit out of practice with Filemaker. When I was using it, though, I was the person in the office that everyone turned to when they got stuck with some of the more complex procedures, so if I brush up on it, I'm sure you'll be pleased with my skills." In this statement, the job-seeker isn't just making excuses and empty claims but is attesting to her past success with that task.

Psychological Tests

In addition to testing for skills, employers might want to have a formal measure of your character and personality traits. A gut-feel impression in an interview goes only so far toward helping the interviewer predict how you will act in various situations.

The tests you might take would be administered and interpreted by a psychologist or expert in psychometrics, either in a private practice or at an assessment center. Assessment centers are set up to test multiple candidates simultaneously. You might also talk one-on-one with a psychologist in lieu of, or in addition to, taking tests.

Some tests are created specifically to aid employers in making hiring decisions and are therefore generally reliable in giving some clues to (though not an outright prediction of) your future behavior and success in a given job. However, many—if not most—of the personality and psychological assessment tools commonly used were not originally designed for selection purposes. Their intended use is in counseling and clinical settings, but because they provide valuable information about the test-taker's patterns of behavior, they are sometimes used as part of pre-employment screening. In that case, reputable employers will be cautious in relying on the findings as a predictor of how you'll act on the job and will simply factor them into the larger set of data they collect on you.

Some degree of overlap occurs between tests designed to measure your personality traits or style and those that diagnose your emotional stability or detect mental disorders. Most, however, are developed for one purpose, so I am presenting them to you here in two separate categories: personality and mental health.

Personality

Most measures of personality traits (often called "personality inventories") are designed for counseling and clinical settings. Career counselors such as

Unofficially...
Most psychological "tests" are not actually tests, in that there are no right are wrong answers to questions. Most measure your own impressions of your personality and your preferred methods of communicating and behaving. The more accurate term is "assessment instrument," but the word "test" is used customarily as a convenient shorthand that is often more meaningful to the lay person.

Unofficially...
You might find
that your per-
sonality or psy-
chological tests
are administered
and interpreted
by someone who
has a degree in
psychology but
is not a licensed
psychologist.
This is legal and
normal. The pub-
lishers of each
test dictate the
credentials and
experience nec-
essary to work
with their tests,
so as long as
those require-
ments are met, a
license is usually
not required.

myself use them to help individuals make career choices or understand how their personality type affects their job performance.

Personality inventories measure traits and characteristics not unlike the personal qualities listed in Chapter 4. They reveal your preferences and tendencies regarding communicating, managing, learning, and interacting with people. They tell us how you take in information, how you process that information, and how you make decisions. They help predict how people will act in various situations.

It is important to realize that personality tests do not measure serious mental disorders but simply describe normal adult personality. As a result, you need not be threatened by a personality inventory. It does not delve into the deep recesses of your psyche but instead takes stock of the traits you exhibit in everyday life.

Because personality tests are not measures of psychopathology—and because it is human nature to be fascinated by the measurement of our personality traits, as evidenced in the popularity of quizzes in magazines—personality inventories are widely used in a variety of settings. In addition to their use as a career-development tool, they are used in relationship and marriage counseling and in organizational settings to help people understand how they communicate and work with each other.

Some of the traits typically measured by these inventories include (but are by no means limited to) the following:

Aggression	Leadership
Ambitiousness	Need for achievement
Assertiveness	Need for autonomy
Comfort with change	Need for affiliation with others
Conformity	Need for control
Deference	Need for order
Dominance	Nurturance
Endurance	Objectivity
Exhibitionism	Planfulness
Extroversion	Restraint
Independence	Sensitivity
Introversion	Sociability

Personality tests that you might encounter include:

Birkman Method (Houston, TX: Birkman International)

California Psychological Inventory (Palo Alto, CA: Consulting Psychologists Press)

Edwards Personal Preference Schedule (San Antonio, TX: The Psychological Corporation)

Guilford-Zimmerman Personality Survey (Orange, CA: Sheridan Psychological Services)

Myers-Briggs Type Indicator (Palo Alto, CA: Consulting Psychologists Press)

NEO Personality Inventory (Odessa, FL: Psychological Assessment Resources, Inc.)

16 Personality Factor (usually referred to as the 16PF) (Champaign, IL: Institute for Personality and Ability Testing)

Because personality inventories are not tests with right or wrong answers, you do not pass or fail them. Nevertheless, your results can exhibit traits and characteristics that may be more or less valued by the prospective employer. I do not recommend that you falsify your answers on these tests to appear as someone you're not just to please the employer, however. Doing so is not in your best interest because you don't want to be hired for a job because some test says you have "Personality A"—the personality type required for the job—when, in fact, you have "Personality Z."

While you should be honest and give responses that reflect your true self, you can improve your chances by being strategic with candor. What I mean is that you can distinguish between the personality traits you exhibit in your personal life and those in your professional life. You might, for example, be an orderly, organized person at work but take a much more go-with-the-flow approach to your affairs at home. Obviously, when answering questions on a personality inventory that might have to do with this trait, you'll want to answer as you would in the professional arena.

As a career counselor, I have administered personality tests to thousands of clients over the years, and also have taught fellow career consultants and human resource professionals how to administer them. I have found that when people respond to these tests with their work lives in mind, the results often differ markedly from those obtained when they put the questions in the context of their personal lives. As you take a personality test, try to figure out what type of quality each question or item is measuring, and then consider how important that trait is in the workplace and respond accordingly.

Bright Idea
Every organization has an aggregate "personality" that evolves out of its mission, philosophy, and culture. The organization might be extroverted or introverted, cautious or cavalier. When thinking about which personality traits will be valued on any test you take, don't just consider those needed to do the job, but take into account the personality of the organization as a whole.

Some additional tips for taking a personality test strategically are listed here:

- Keep in mind that you have considerable control over the outcome because these tests are based on your self-expressed observations as opposed to tapping into unconscious motives.

- Don't answer off the top of your head. There is usually no time limit on these tests, but you will probably be encouraged to answer each question quickly. Don't. Take some time to consider the rationale behind each question, and relate it to the traits needed to do the job you're going after or those valued in the organization as a whole.

- As you take a personality test, you may have the sensation that you are being asked the same thing over and over. Well, you are. Personality inventories look for patterns. For example, a 300-item questionnaire might measure 15 traits by asking 20 questions per trait. If you want to appear balanced on a particular trait—perhaps neither extremely introverted or extroverted— then you can manipulate the results by responding slightly differently to each of those 20 questions.

- Mark your answers carefully. Some inventories have hundreds of questions, so they can become tedious. It is easy to start inadvertently filling in the wrong boxes on the answer form, which will obviously render your results inaccurate. Some tests have a built-in mechanism to check for this error (often called the "infrequency scale"), and your test will not be scored if you seem to have marked your answer sheet incorrectly. Nevertheless, you should mark your responses carefully, as it is obviously not in your best interest to have your test sent back unscored because you were careless.

Mental Health

As with most personality inventories, assessment tools that measure your emotional stability or diagnose serious mental disorders are not designed as personnel selection measures. While it is unlikely that you will have to take a true psychological test, you may come across such tests when interviewing for extremely high-level positions or for jobs in which your mental stability and integrity are especially critical, such as positions with the F.B.I., law enforcement or public safety.

Most of these are projective tests—tests that tap into your unconscious motives to reveal your true nature and behavioral tendencies. The infamous Rorschach inkblot test is typical of this genre, as are similar exercises that ask you to tell a story about a picture you see or to complete a sentence that has been started for you. A qualified psychologist then analyzes your statements to determine where you stand on a number of characteristics and to identify any indication of psychiatric disorder or mental instability.

Intelligence and Aptitude

Some employers will want to collect objective data on your ability to learn, to master tasks, and to think in the way that the job or the organization requires. Measures of intellectual aptitude (a.k.a. IQ tests)—along with tests that measure such areas as mathematical, creative, and verbal abilities—are controversial in that their ability to predict success on the job has not been proven unequivocally. Nevertheless, when used conscientiously and

Unofficially...
Some employers these days measure emotional maturity using a tool called the EQ Map Questionnaire from Executive EQ, by Robert Cooper and Ayman Sawaf (Putnam, 1998).

factored into the overall equation of who you are, they can provide employers with useful information.

Some aptitude tests are actually batteries of several individual tests that measure multiple aptitudes, while others focus on a single area, such as sales ability. Some of the most widely used aptitude and intelligence tests include the following:

Differential Aptitude Tests (San Antonio, TX: The Psychological Corporation)

GATB—General Aptitude Test Battery (Washington, D.C.: U.S. Department of Labor) *Note:* The GATB is used primarily in government offices and schools)

Multidimensional Aptitude Battery (Odessa, FL: Psychological Assessment Resources)

WAIS—Weschler Adult Intelligence Scale-Revised (New York: Harcourt Brace Jovanovich)

Watson-Glaser Critical Thinking Appraisal (San Antonio, TX: The Psychological Corporation)

Bright Idea
For a comprehensive list of psychological and vocational assessment instruments, visit the Web site of the Division of Psychology, at Australian National University: http://psy. anu.edu.au/ testlib.htm.

While there is not much you can do to alter your basic nature when it comes to innate talents and intelligence, you can employ tried-and-true test-taking strategies to improve your scores. Many of these are techniques you may have used when taking standardized tests for college or graduate school, or for a professional credential or license.

■ Get plenty of rest and eat healthy, well-balanced meals the day or two before the test.

■ If you have a choice, schedule your assessment appointment at a time of day when you are typically most alert mentally.

- Realize that the best thing you can do for yourself is to stay relaxed and avoid getting nervous. (See Chapter 5, "Developing the Right Attitude," for a review of ways to combat nervousness.)

- Read all instructions carefully. Far too many errors occur due to misreading directions rather than to lack of ability.

- Answer each question in the way that seems the most socially desirable. You want to come across as someone who seems sociable, honest, and cooperative. Now is not the time to reveal your rebellious, independent streak. You're better off looking like a conformist (unless you're up for a job that requires creativity and independent thinking above all else).

Drug Tests

Before you assume that you don't need to read this section because you don't do drugs, please reconsider. Understanding the who, what, when, where, and why of drug testing as a pre-employment screening tool is relevant for even the most chaste job-seeker. Drug testing, particularly the most common method of urinalysis, is an inexact science that often leads to test results that are false-positives, so you need to be knowledgeable of the process and aware of your rights. Drug testing is also a process that is seen by many as an invasion of privacy, so if you are particularly fond of your civil liberties, you might want to know which companies test for drugs and why they do it before agreeing to work for a company whose practices conflict with your values.

Bright Idea
If you are opposed to the idea of drug testing on grounds that it is an invasion of privacy, or if you are worried about being the victim of a false-positive, you'll find about 200 companies on the *Non-Testers List: A Consumer Guide to Companies That Do Not Drug Test* at www.geocities.com/CapitolHill/6443/ntl.html.

Though subject to state legal restrictions, drug testing by employers (or prospective employers who have extended you a job offer) has become more common in the past decade. Most large companies these days test for drug use before finalizing a job offer, and it is required for just about all federal government positions. If you will be doing a job in which safety is a major concern—such as work with heavy equipment, law enforcement, transportation, and care-giving—then you can be certain you'll be tested. A drug test is usually not given until after an offer has been extended and you have accepted it. Your employment is then contingent upon a negative result from your drug test. If both the initial test and back-up tests turn out positive, you will most likely not be hired.

Unofficially...
In most cases, it is against the law for private employers to give you a polygraph test.

Urinalysis

The most common method of testing is urinalysis, also called enzyme multiplied immunoassay. This method tests for traces of amphetamines, cocaine, marijuana, opiates, and PCP in your system. This test is limited in that it can detect only drugs that have been in the system for a short period of time, usually a few days or a week or so. Opiates and cocaine are water-soluble, so they typically leave your system in 48 to 72 hours. Marijuana, on the other hand, has a slower urine excretion rate, so regular users can test positive for several weeks. Despite its limitations, urinalysis is a relatively inexpensive test with hundreds of testing labs that provide prompt and convenient service, so this is the method of choice for most employers.

Unofficially...
Some people are skeptical of hair analysis because scientists do not yet fully understand how drugs are actually absorbed into hair. They believe that drug metabolites (the traces of drug consumption) could be introduced into hair from external sources, such as sharing a sweaty cap with a drug user. (Source: *Using Hair Samples To Test Employees For Drugs,* by Stephen Thomas Davenport, Jr. at www.laborcounsel.com)

Hair Analysis for Drugs

The analysis of hair follicles, or RIAH (radioimmunoassay of hair), is growing in popularity as a way to detect drug use, and experts in employment law say its use should continue to rise. Hair follicle analysis is a more precise and reliable test than urinalysis and is much less prone to false-positives. This method can detect drugs that have been in one's system for several months, depending on the length of the hair. It also reveals when drugs were used and if use has increased or declined.

Brief periods of abstinence from drugs will not significantly affect the outcome of hair analysis, and contaminating or altering a sample to manipulate the test results is much more difficult with hair than with urine. Research has shown that even treating hair with strong chemicals to strip it will not completely remove traces of illegal drugs. Also, hair samples are easier to handle than urine ones, they require no special storage conditions, and they carry less risk of disease transmission. Hair analysis is more expensive than urinalysis, however, so employers have been reluctant to convert fully to this method.

Controversy Over Drug Testing

Drug testing in the workplace—not just for pre-employment screening, but also after you're on the job—is the source of much debate. Many question its constitutionality, seeing drug testing as intrusive and an invasion of privacy. They argue that what you do in your personal life should not be of any concern to your employer, as long as the use of controlled substances does not impair your functioning on the job. They also object to the fact that drug tests may reveal personal information, such as health problems and pregnancy.

Numerous Web sites have been created by people who object to the idea of testing on constitutional grounds, as well as, of course, by those who advocate the use of controlled substances and want to help job-seekers outsmart the tests. They offer tips such as flushing your system with water, taking certain vitamins and herbs, altering your diet, calculating how your rate of metabolism will affect the longevity of drug traces in your body, adulterating urine by adding chemicals to it, and other ways to cheat.

From the perspective of most employers, drug testing is an important and necessary part of the hiring process. Every year, businesses lose billions of dollars in drug-related insurance claims, accidents, lawsuits, turnover, absenteeism, tardiness, and theft. Research has shown that as much as 70 percent of drug users in the United States are actively employed—and a single drug user can cost a company more than $7,000 a year.

The Risk of False-Positives

False-positive results occur for a number of reasons. You might be taking legal drugs prescribed by a physician, which in certain combinations cross-react in a way that makes them appear like controlled substances. Some over-the-counter medicines can be problematic as well, particularly diet pills, cold medications, and Ibuprofen, which can yield a positive result for narcotics. Something you've eaten can also skew the results. Tales of poppy seeds jeopardizing employment because they show up as opiates are legendary and have led many job-seekers to forego poppy-seed bagels before interviews. The chances of your looking like a heavy drug user just because you consume one innocent poppy-seed

Timesaver
Before taking a drug test, you can save time and confusion down the road by bringing the prescriptions for any medications you are currently taking or have recently taken (or the actual medication with the pharmacy label) to the test.

bagel are slim, but why not play it safe and have a plain bagel that morning?

False-positives also result from mishandling and mislabeling of samples, as well as faulty analysis. Laboratory errors should be decreasing now that the U.S. Department of Health and Human Services accredits testing labs. Most reputable employers use only accredited labs, but the risk of human error will always be present.

If your results are positive on the first go-round, reputable labs follow up immediately with a more precise test called a GCMS (gas chromatography/mass spectrometry assay). If that test turns out positive, you do have the right to demand another one, though you may be hard-pressed to convince the prospective employer to try again. In that case, you have a decision to make about how far you want to push the matter. When they agree to allow you to undergo another test with a new sample, you will most likely have to pay the cost yourself.

As with any job search issue critical to your livelihood and reputation, you should consult an employment law specialist rather than relying solely on advice given here, as the legalities of drug testing fluctuate from state to state and change over time.

Physical Exams

Very few employers require that you undergo a medical exam as a part of the pre-employment screening process. Exceptions to this rule are those jobs that are physical in nature or that involve public safety, such as for airline pilots and emergency medical technicians. If you are asked to undergo a medical exam, the human resources department of the hiring company will usually instruct you to complete the exam at a medical office or clinic of their

Watch Out!
Don't be surprised if a same-sex observer accompanies you to the rest room to verify that you are the source of your urine sample. While more testing labs now have other methods of verification, many still use observers.

choosing. In some states, the law requires employers to allow that you submit a report from your personal physician rather than an appointed one.

You should be aware that The Americans with Disabilities Act prohibits employment discrimination on the basis of a physical or mental handicap, so if you are concerned about any health problems that might be discovered, you should find out whether they are legally classified as disabilities.

Credit and Criminal Record Checks

Some companies will run credit and criminal checks on you as additional assurance that you are a responsible person. This is most typically done by large corporations and government employers. Any companies monitored by federal regulatory agencies such as the SEC and FDIC—including brokerage firms and investment banks—also require credit and criminal checks before employment.

If employers find any negative information in your credit report, they will usually give you a chance to explain yourself in a written statement. You can also provide any supportive documentation from attorneys, accountants, creditors, or the IRS to show how you have resolved any problems. If matters are unresolved, you will not, in most cases, be denied employment simply because you have some unpaid bills or have racked up large credit card debt. Employers are usually more interested in serious matters such as bankruptcies you have filed, as well as liens or judgments against you. Even then, however, they cannot discriminate against you without further investigation of court disposition papers and without allowing you to explain your situation. The best thing you can do is to be up-front from the beginning and to disclose to the employer any

Unofficially...
To find out how any physical or mental disabilities you may have affect your employment rights, contact the Americans with Disabilities Act (ADA) Information Line at: 1-800-514-0301 (voice) or 1-800-514-0383 (TDD). Or, visit the Department of Justice's ADA home page at http://www.usdoj.gov/crt/ada/adahom1.htm.

adverse information likely to be uncovered so that you don't look like you're trying to hide anything.

Similar laws are at work with criminal checks. Employers cannot discriminate against you for being arrested, but they do have the right to question your employability if you have been convicted of a crime. Employers are allowed by law to check with superior courts for any criminal convictions you may have had and to check with civil courts for any civil judgments. If you are being hired for a job in the securities or banking industry or other fields in which you must be bonded, your offer will be withdrawn if a background check uncovers that you are not bondable.

Often, the employment application will clue you in that credit or criminal checks will be conducted; you might be asked to sign a statement indicating that you grant permission to have them run one. Or, you might be asked to sign a consent form separate from the application. In most cases, you will be told at the time an offer is extended that your credit history and criminal record, if any, will be investigated. The letter you may receive as written confirmation of your offer will usually include the caveat that the offer may be withdrawn if the results of those reports are not satisfactory.

While the impact of these investigations on your candidacy is pretty much out of your hands—you either have skeletons in the closet or you don't—you should be aware of your rights and the possible consequences of any negative reports.

With credit checks, the employer is obligated to provide you with only a description of the nature and scope of the report received, according to the Federal Fair Credit Report Act. This can be problematic if you wish to dispute the outcome and salvage your job offer. So, if the employer says there's a problem with your credit and you ask for details, you might be given only a summary of the report, since that's all the law requires. However, no law says they can't provide you with more than that minimum amount of information, so you should ask for the full report.

It's a good idea to get an up-to-date credit report for yourself early in a job search so that you won't have any unpleasant surprises down the road. People commonly pay back a debt that had gone to a collection agency or resolve some other credit problem, only to find that the new status of that account is not reflected on their report. You can request your credit report through any of the following companies:

CBI/Equifax
Atlanta, GA
800-685-1111

CSC Credit Services
Houston, TX
713-878-4840

TransUnion Credit Information
Chicago, IL
312-408-1050

TRW Consumer Assistance
Cleveland, OH
800-682-7654

Just the Facts

■ Employers use formal assessment methods (such as observation, homework, or tests) to supplement interviews and obtain more objective data on you.

- Exercises such as the in-basket test are designed to gauge your ability to prioritize.

- When being observed in a group exercise, keep in mind which kinds of roles the employer values and demonstrate your ability to perform those roles well.

- If asked to make a presentation, try to find out the preferred style and approach for presenters in that organization, but don't stray too far from your natural style.

- If you leave an interview with homework to do, the most important aspect of the assignment is that you get it done in a timely manner.

- Don't be intimidated by personality or aptitude tests. Remember that understanding how the test is constructed helps you affect the outcome.

- Due to the risk of false-positive results, you should be knowledgeable about how, why, where, and when drug tests are done.

Interview Curve Balls

Besides anticipating the usual suspects when it comes to questions you might be asked in interviews (as discussed in Chapter 9, "The Fifteen Trickiest Interview Questions," and Chapter 10, "Some More Questions You Might Be Asked"), you also need to prepare for some curve balls interviewers may throw your way. All kinds of barriers can come between you and the job you want, including concerns that prospective employers may have about your qualifications or background, as well as interviewer biases that test the boundaries of discrimination laws.

To push these barriers aside and clear a path to the job you want, you must be aware of common obstacles so that you're not caught off guard. You also need to prepare strategies for finessing these sticky situations. This chapter will help you identify possible objections to your candidacy, understand your legal rights, and craft a plan for not only dodging the curve balls, but tossing them back with confidence.

Overcoming Interviewers' Objections

You're overqualified. You're underqualified. We think you'll leave us within the year. These declarations on the part of interviewers leave job-seekers frustrated and often unsure of whether they should fight back with a counter argument. And if so, how hard and for how long should they fight?

Some objections are legitimate. If you've held 10 jobs in the last nine years—assuming you're not a freelancer, a professional temp, or a consultant—a prospective employer might have just cause for concern that you won't stick around for too long. Other objections are not so justified. Some are based simply on ignorance, bias, or paranoia. The interviewer creates a problem where there really doesn't need to be one and assumes you shouldn't be hired when, in fact, you'd make a top-notch employee.

Let's look at some general strategies that can help you get around any barrier thrown in your path to a job. Then we'll explore some of the specific objections job-seekers often face.

Strategies for Dealing with Interviewers' Objections

Whether the interviewer is concerned about gaps in your employment history, why you were fired from your last job, or anything else, the following tactics can help you talk your way out of a sticky situation:

- Anticipate objections in advance. If you know that something about your background or qualifications is likely to be problematic, don't wait until you're in the interview to think of how you're going to explain it. Discussing negatives about yourself—and building a case for why those negatives shouldn't knock you out of the running—is hard to do off the top of your head. So, take an objective look at what might concern interviewers—or ask someone else to help you identify the potential objections—and be prepared to address them.

- Understand the root of an objection. To build an effective counter argument, you must know why something is a problem in the first place. For example, let's say someone left the corporate world to open and run a restaurant, but he couldn't make a go of it and is now back in the job hunt. You might assume that when an employer says, with raised eyebrow, "I see you had a restaurant for 18 months ..." that she is concerned that the business failed. In fact, that interviewer probably doesn't care that it didn't succeed—everyone knows how tough it is to make a restaurant successful! and that lots of businesses fail. What might be of concern to her, however, is that the candidate's entrepreneurial leanings could make him antsy and unable to settle back into a 9-to-5 job. So, don't make assumptions about what the objection is or where it's coming from until you find out what is really at the heart of the objection.

- Ask questions. Before launching into a major counter argument, ask what specific concerns the interviewer has. If that former restaurant owner started making a case for why he's still a good businessman despite the fact that his restaurant didn't succeed, he'd be missing the boat. He should instead be talking about his desire to make a commitment to a particular employer and how he has done so in the past.

- Don't be defensive. The worst thing you can do for your case is to act agitated, aggressive, or overly apologetic.

■ State your case succinctly. This is one time when it's not such a bad idea to have a script in mind to guide what you are going to say. Explaining something that has the potential to do major damage to your candidacy (such as having been fired from a job) must be done with finesse. You need to know exactly which words and phrases you will use, and you need to have your story straight. Hemming and hawing will only make matters worse.

■ Keep it in perspective. Many objections you expect an employer to have may never surface at all—or, if they do, they're not the big deal you assumed they would be. I've worked with countless job-seekers who think that they are virtually unemployable because they were fired from a job, left their last job after only a few months, or got a bad reference. As you'll see in the sections that follow, there's almost always a way to break down seemingly impenetrable barriers to employment.

You've Been Fired

This is one of the toughest situations to deal with in a job search. No one trying to make a good impression in an interview wants to get bogged down in a discussion of having been fired.

Inevitably the issue will come up, however, so you need to have a well-crafted plan of how you will address it. Consider the following strategies and options:

■ Don't blow the issue out of proportion. People get fired every day. You may feel like the only person on earth who has suffered this degradation, and the emotions you are experiencing may be painfully raw, but try to remember that it is quite common and that it does not spell the end of your career.

- If you left your bosses on terms even the least bit cordial, speak to them about how you might discuss the termination with future prospective employers. You'd be surprised how many are willing to let their former employees say that they resigned.

- Don't overlook honesty as possibly the best policy. Rather than weaving a tangled web of lies and deceit, consider stating the facts of your termination concisely and matter-of-factly. Many employers will appreciate the candor and understand that these things happen. As long as you describe the firing in a tactful way, citing a difference of opinion and a willingness to acknowledge your role in the problem, you may be pleasantly surprised to find that the matter is not such a big deal.

- Consider not mentioning the job at all if you were employed there for a short period of time, perhaps less than six months. As long as you are not applying for a job with the type of organization that does an "FBI-style" background check, and as long as you are not interviewing in a tight-knit industry where everyone knows everybody else's business, you have the option of not listing the job on your resume or on an employment application. Remember, however, that lying in a job search is usually not a good idea for many reasons. So, I'm not advocating this strategy but just letting you know it's one that many people resort to when more honest alternatives just don't seem to exist.

Bright Idea
If you're worried about what your former employer will say about you to future employers, see the later section "Your References are Bad" to know how to get good references even though you've been terminated.

PART IV ■ THE INTERVIEW ITSELF

You Have Gaps in Your Work History

If you have been out of work for a period of more than several months at some point since your career began, employers will most likely want to know why. You have nothing to worry about if the gap in your work history is due to valid reasons such as being a full-time student, being a full-time parent, recovering from an accident or illness, caring for a critically ill family member, or taking time off to travel.

If, however, you were not working because you couldn't find a job, you need to prepare a defense for objections the employer might have. If your unemployment was due to a recession or wide-scale job shortage in your field, most employers will understand that the problem is no reflection on your character or qualifications. Also, if you have made a major career change, prospective employers understand that it can take time to define your new focus, get the necessary training, establish new contacts, and make the transition.

But if the reality is that you left a job, spent a few months lying on the couch before getting motivated to look for a new job, then spent several months or more trying to find one, the gap may be more difficult to explain. If you have been employed since the gap occurred, then the problem is not as pronounced, but if you are currently job hunting after having been unemployed for the past several months, you have some explaining to do.

People don't like to hire people who have been rejected by lots of other potential employers. So, if you say that you have been actively searching for several months, or even a year or more, the prospective employer may assume that something is wrong with you. You'll need to account for your time. Exactly how you do that is a bit controversial.

Unofficially...
If you have been out of work for a significant period of time in the past due to psychiatric problems or incarceration, you are protected by laws that prohibit employers from rejecting you on those grounds (with some exceptions, such as for jobs in financial institutions or those that involve public safety). That doesn't mean, of course, that they won't find some objection to your candidacy that is a legally justifiable reason for rejecting you.

The reality is—and I'm not advocating this—that people lie. They may talk someone at their former job into stretching the end date of their employment out by a month or a few months to buy them some time. Then they say that they traveled for a month or so to take a break before starting a job search. Then, they took time off to re-evaluate where they wanted to move next in their career. (Actually, that last excuse might very likely be true and is certainly acceptable and plausible.) By the time all those activities are factored in, the active job-searching process gets reduced to just a few months, which is a reasonable period of time to be looking. In addition to—or besides—those excuses, some people go so far as to concoct stories about caring for sick relatives or other seemingly noble deeds to account for their time.

Others who did have some sort of professional activity going on while job hunting get creative about how they describe it. Someone might spend a couple of weeks helping out a friend start a business by doing a little public relations, but in an interview this person calls it a six-month consulting job. Someone who volunteers for a few charities might list the title "fund-raising consultant" on a resume.

Whether you tell a bald-faced lie or merely stretch the truth to your advantage is your call. As I've said throughout this book, lying in interviews is usually a bad idea. The embarrassment and damage to your reputation that you might suffer if caught rarely justifies the advantages the lies bring.

You Look Like a Job-Hopper

As changing jobs and career fields has become more the norm over the past several years, job-hopping is less common a concern among prospective

Bright Idea
If your search looks like it's going to drag on for a while, find some way to make productive use of your time in addition to job hunting. Volunteer, take classes, find freelance work, be a temp—anything to account for your time and to build your resume.

employers than it used to be. The massive downsizings and reorganizations of the '90s forced many well-qualified professionals to move from job to job more frequently than was customary in previous generations. This movement created a climate of tolerance in which short tenures at jobs are now more acceptable, even if they are due to the employee's own desire to make a move. Added to this phenomenon is the fact that some industries—such as the media, advertising, public relations, and high-tech, among others—are characterized by revolving-door employment patterns.

Nevertheless, if your resume lists so many jobs that it sends up a red flag, be prepared to explain the movement. The key to doing so is to be brief and to the point when explaining why you left each job. It's best if the reasons for leaving have little to do with you and as much as possible to do with problems on the employer's side: a company that went out of business, a not-for-profit group that lost funding, an organization that downsized, or an organizational structure that offered little room for advancement. In describing your work history, don't sound bitter, negative, or passive. Show how you took charge of situations, such as leaving before a business failed or cutting your losses if a job just wasn't the right fit.

To put an additional positive spin on the situation, think of something you have stuck with for a considerable period of time. If your resume says you've had five jobs in five years but you've served meals at a soup kitchen every Saturday morning for those five years, tell the employer about it. Any example you can give of your ability to make a commitment and stick with it will help your case.

You Started a Business That Failed

As mentioned with the restaurant example earlier, this problem is more likely to be a concern in your own mind than an objection the employer will voice. As long as you don't give evidence of poor judgment or management skills when describing the failure, you don't have much to worry about. Focus on how you showed initiative, ambition, and a tolerance for risk-taking by striking out on your own. Also, talk about what you learned from the experience and any successes that you did have. Make it clear that you have now sewn your entrepreneurial oats and are more than ready to commit to working for someone else.

Your References Are Bad

There is a pervasive, and potentially dangerous, myth in the world of job-hunting. Most people assume that their former employers won't say anything bad about them when a future prospective employer calls to check their references for fear of being sued. That's often not true. The laws in most states actually protect employers in these cases. As long as the former employer gives a reference that is truthful and without malice, and that is job-related (as opposed to being a personal attack), they are protected by statutes that minimize or deny litigation the former employee might attempt. This law is based on the idea that employers should be free from civil liability if they have information to reveal that could protect the well-being of a future employer or of society in general.

A famous example of this is the case of a Boston hospital that terminated a doctor who was convicted of sexual assault. When the doctor's prospective new employer in another state called to check his refer-

Unofficially...
Keep in mind that we are living in the Age of the Comeback and a culture of forgiveness. We excuse major transgressions on the part of prominent figures such as celebrities and politicians, so that little skeleton in your professional closet is unlikely to keep you from getting hired.

ence, the hospital chose not to disclose that information, and the new employer hired the doctor based upon an overall good reference. After he was hired, the doctor assaulted a patient in the new hospital, and the patient sued the hospital for negligent hiring. The hospital produced a record of its efforts to conduct a reference check on the doctor prior to the offer. The new employer sued the Boston hospital for withholding the information, and the case was settled for a seven-figure sum.

You are most likely not dealing with such an extreme situation, but you may just be concerned that a former boss might give you a less than glowing report. If that's the case, you have a few options:

- Find someone else at the same organization to serve as a reference. If you had a better relationship with your boss' boss or with a manager in a different department, that person may be a better choice for your reference list. You don't have to use your immediate supervisor as long as the person you do use had enough opportunity to observe your performance closely.

- Use a client or external colleague as your reference. If you were in the sort of job that involved maintaining relations with clients or customers, or that involved collaborating with colleagues for other organizations (such as lawyers and bankers working on the same deals), you can use one or more of these people as your references. Be aware, though, that a prospective employer will probably ask why you aren't listing your boss as a reference, so you may still have to confront the issue of a bad relationship with that boss.

■ Be candid and explain tactfully, concisely, and unapologetically that you and your boss did not always see eye to eye and that you would prefer that someone else at your organization (or someone externally, as in the previous point) be used as a reference. If you take this approach, refer to Question 4, "Tell me about a time when you had a personality clash with a coworker or boss," in Chapter 9 for suggestions on how you can describe a difficult relationship without doing damage to your image and professionalism.

You're Overqualified

When employers say that you are overqualified for a position, 99 percent of the time they're really saying that they assume you want more money than they can pay. The way to know whether that's the case is, of course, to ask.

If salary is the issue—and if you don't mind earning whatever they can pay, even if it's less than what you've been making—then deal with it by building a strong case for why you don't mind taking a salary cut. Discuss how you are making a career transition and that you are well aware that you have to make some sacrifices to get where you want to be. Don't just sound like you're making empty claims. Let them know you have given this careful thought—perhaps even worked out a new personal budget. Also let them know what motivates you besides money so they'll see that you would find other rewards from the work and thus not leave the new job after a few months in search of a bigger paycheck.

Unofficially...
Among human resources specialists, there is a code question of sorts that enables someone checking a reference to get a true picture of a prospective employee. They ask the former employer, "Would you hire this person again?"

Watch Out!
If you are willing to take a pay cut and plan to supplement the lower salary by moonlighting, keep that plan to yourself. Prospective employers don't want to hear about the business you plan to operate from home, the weekend job you'll be taking, or any other distractions.

If you aren't willing to take a pay cut but want them to see that you are worth the money you deserve, talk about how you can save them money, and give examples of how you have done so in the past.

In addition to the money issue, claiming that you are overqualified might also mean that the employer is worried that you'll be bored and will leave, or that you'll get antsy to be promoted sooner than is convenient for them. This is particularly common when you are making a major career change and are willing to start at the bottom—or at least on a low floor—in the new field. You have to alleviate employers' concerns by conveying the amount of thought that has gone into choosing the new target job. Also try to think of tasks on your past jobs that correspond to those of the prospective lower-level job. Explaining that you not only know what you're getting into, but that you have performed similar duties in the past with no complaint may be a way to deflect their objections.

You're Underqualified

Often, labeling you as underqualified is a legitimate call. You may not have the experience, skills, credentials, or content knowledge needed for success in a position. If this is true, your best recourse is to discuss the assets that you do bring to the table. These may balance out the deficits. Also, don't just say, "I'm a quick learner" when talking about how you would boost your qualifications. Give examples of how you've gotten up to speed quickly in the past when a situation called for doing so.

Another option is to offer to work on a trial basis for no pay for a period of weeks or months to prove yourself. Or, you might ask to work as an intern or apprentice of sorts while simultaneously getting the necessary skills through courses or other means (and while working in another full-time or part-time job just to pay the bills). Sometimes, getting from where you are to where you want to be in your career requires having a "patchwork" life for a while. The point is to be creative and persistent and not give up.

However, if there is just no chance of working in any capacity for the employer who has labeled you as underqualified, you can at least take from the experience new insight into how you might improve your candidacy elsewhere. Ask the employer to be specific in describing your deficits and to suggest ways you might overcome them. And, who knows, if you accept the rejection gracefully and show a willingness to work on your professional development, you might be successful in applying with that same employer in the future after you boost your qualifications.

You're Just Not the Right Fit

This may be a legitimate objection if it is based on concern about the nature of your experience, your tangible qualifications (such as your skills and expertise), or your education and training. If that is the case, you need to find out which aspects of your qualifications are seen as deficits and discuss how you can make up for those deficits, as discussed in the section "Making Up for Deficits" in Chapter 4, "Making Yourself the Top Candidate." Talk about how you can take classes, attend seminars, teach yourself on your own time, or speed up your on-the-job learning by putting in extra hours. As with the problem of being underqualified, you should also reiterate your asset statements to remind the

Bright Idea
If an interviewer is concerned that you lack direct experience required for the job, point out the benefits of the fresh perspective you would bring coming from a different industry or sector.

interviewer how your transferable skills might make you a good fit.

Be aware, however, that saying you just aren't the right fit can be a euphemism for saying they want someone more attractive, older or younger, of a different race, or some other discriminatory criterion. The discussion of illegal questions later in this chapter will help you identify lines of questioning that might clue you in to some bias.

Anticipating Objections

To ensure that you won't be caught off guard when an employer raises an objection, consider completing a form like the one that follows to help you prepare.

Unofficially...
Objections often aren't raised until well after the first round of interviews, when an offer is close to being extended. In a sense, employers start to get "cold feet." To keep this from tripping you up, be sure to ask about any concerns early on—as directed in Chapter 13, "Following Up to Get to 'Yes'"— so you can get them out of the way.

As you can see, there is usually a way around even the most seemingly immutable barriers. With some careful advance planning, a well-crafted counter argument, and a positive, confident attitude, you can overcome most interviewers' objections. As long as you have other assets that would be of value, most employers will forgive a few hiccups in your past. If they won't, then you have a decision to make. You can keep beating your head against a brick wall trying to reason with an unreasonable hiring manager or recruiter, or you can cut your losses and move on. Throwing in the towel after you've done everything in your power to alleviate their concerns is often the best thing you can do for your search.

Sticky Situations: Discrimination and Harassment

Sticky situations of a discriminatory nature make you uncomfortable and likely to squirm in your seat, just like some of the situations described in Chapter

ANTICIPATED OBJECTIONS WORKSHEET

Potential objection:

Likelihood of it being a concern:

Possible reasons for concern:

—

—

—

—

—

How I will explain the situation (list key words and phrases you can use):

—

—

—

—

—

What I learned from the situation (if applicable):

—

Timesaver
Employment laws
are complex, so
trying to know
everything about
them can be
time-consuming.
Keep this simple
guideline in
mind: Everything
asked must be
job-related.

9, but the two are not the same. Tough interview questions merely test your metal, challenging you to think on your feet and to prove why you should be hired. The sticky situations described in this chapter, on the other hand, are an invasion of your privacy, are insulting, and may be illegal.

To deal with them, it is essential that you know what is legal and what's not when it comes to questions interviewers can ask and behavior they can exhibit.

Why Illegal Questions Make You Squirm

Deflecting or confronting a question that asks for personal information completely unrelated to the job or for information that could be used to discriminate against you is a tricky business. You may not know whether you should stand your legal ground and refuse to answer an illegal question such as, "What kind of child care arrangement do you have?" or to simply answer the question because you don't find it particularly offensive—even though you know it's not related to your qualifications for the job.

Fielding illegal questions is also tricky because you are trying to build rapport with the interviewer and gain some power in the process without being overly aggressive. In an interview that has been going smoothly, refusing to answer a question on the grounds that it is illegal can be as jarring as standing up and throwing your chair out the window.

Illegal questions also cause discomfort because they lead you to question your own judgment and doubt your knowledge. You may not know whether you're merely being an alarmist—turning an innocuous line of inquiry into a federal case—or whether you are objectively and accurately reading the situation as discriminatory. The only way to trust your judgment is to become as knowledgeable of hiring law as can reasonably be expected—"reasonably," because it is a complex topic that you should not expect to master.

Knowing Your Rights

It is often said that information is power, and that is particularly true when it comes to dealing with illegal questioning in interviews. The more you know about your rights under the law—as well as about the potential consequences of your approach to answering or deflecting a question—the better off you'll be.

The essence of the law as it pertains to hiring dictates that you cannot be discriminated against based on your race, gender, national origin or ancestry, religious beliefs, citizenship status, age, marital or family status (as in, asking the number and ages of your children, if any), appearance, or physical or mental disability. Some of the specific legislation driving these rules is presented in the "Job-Related Legislation" box included here.

More detailed information on these laws and other matters related to employment discrimination are available on the Equal Employment Opportunity Commission (EEOC) Web site, at www.eeoc.gov.

So, just what are the most common illegal questions, and how might they be worded? The "Questions a Prospective Employer Can and Cannot Ask in an Interview" chart shows off-limits subjects, ways an interviewer might try to obtain information on them, and related lines of questioning that are legal.

Unofficially...
To find out what human resources professionals and employment law experts are saying about legal issues in the workplace, visit the Government Affairs section of the International Personnel Management Association Web site at www.ipma-hr.org.

JOB-RELATED LEGISLATION

The Americans with Disabilities Act (1990)
Prohibits discrimination based on mental or physical disability, as long as those disabilities are not directly related to job performance (and even then, if reasonable accommodations can be made—such as special equipment—to enable you to perform particular tasks, then you cannot be discriminated against).

The Immigration Reform and Control Act (1986)
Prohibits the employment of illegal aliens, but also protects against discrimination of legal aliens based on national origin or citizenship status.

The Age Discrimination in Employment Act (1978)
Prohibits discrimination against applicants age 40 and older.

The Pregnancy Discrimination Act (1978)
Prohibits discrimination in hiring or employment of pregnant women or women with pregnancy-related medical conditions.

The Civil Rights Act (1964)
Prohibits discrimination in employment based on race, sex, national origin, ancestry, or religious beliefs.

QUESTIONS A PROSPECTIVE EMPLOYER CAN AND CANNOT ASK IN AN INTERVIEW

What They Can't Ask	What They Can Ask
Age	
What is your age?	Are you over 18?
How old are you?	
What is your birth date?	
When did you graduate from high school?	
When did you graduate from college?	
Citizenship	
Are you a U.S. citizen?	Are you legally allowed to work in this country?
Ethnicity	
Is English your native language?	Do you know (read, speak, or write) any foreign languages? (Can be asked only if relevant to the job for which you are applying.)
Where were you born?	
Where were your parents born?	
Marital/Family Status	
Are you married?	This job involves some travel. Would that be a problem?
What does your husband/wife do?	This job requires overtime. Would that be a problem?
Do you have any children?	Would you be willing to relocate?
How old are your children?	
What sort of child care do you have?	
Do you plan to start a family?	
Religious Affiliation	
What is your religion?	(No appropriate alternatives)
Do you believe in God?	
Do you go to church on Sundays, temple on Fridays, (or any similar question)?	
Where do you worship?	

continues

What They Can't Ask	What They Can Ask
Non-Professional Affiliations	
To which clubs or organizations of a non-professional nature do you belong?	Do you belong to any professional or trade associations related to this line of work? Which ones?
Appearance	
What is your height?	For jobs which require lifting and carrying heavy objects, it is legal to ask if you can lift specific amounts of weight and carry them specific distances
What is your weight?	For jobs which have minimum height and weight requirements for safety reasons, you can be asked your height and weight directly.
How would you describe/ rate your looks? (Might be asked in phone interviews.)	
Health and Disabilities	
How is your general health?	Are you able to perform this job? (If you need certain reasonable accommodations for a disability—such as special equipment—you may still answer "yes" to this question.)
How is your family's health?	
Have you had any operations or illnesses recently?	
Please list your medical history on this application.	
Do you have any disabilities?	
How did you develop this disability?	
Miltary	
Were you honorably discharged?	What training did you receive in the military?
In which branch of the military did you serve?	

Arrest Record	
Have you ever been arrested?	Have you ever been convicted of (a specified crime)? The type of crime specified must be related to the job for which you are applying. For example, a brokerage firm, might ask if you have ever been convicted of a Securities and Exchange Commission ethical violation.

Handling Illegal Questions

When faced with an illegal question—or an illegally worded question—like those listed in the previous figure, you have three choices:

1. *Answer the question.* You may come across some questions that are technically illegal but that do not offend you in any way. You might not mind if an employer knows that you are married or what your native language is. If so, there is nothing wrong with answering such questions, as long as you see no reason why the information you provide could work against you. Actually, in some cases, it can work in your favor. Because interviewers want to get to know you as a person, they will feel more comfortable knowing a little something about you personally and usually have no evil intentions.

   The reality is that seemingly illegal questions are asked all the time by employers who have no intention of discriminating against you but who are simply curious to know more about you than what's on your resume. If you feel completely comfortable with such questions, you can answer them. It is important, however, that you be attuned to the potential for bias and not

Watch Out!
Employment laws vary from state to state, so you can't fully understand a federal employment law until you know how it is affected by state statutes.

get too chatty. If you start talking about what a hassle it is to get your child to daycare on time and still be at work by 8 a.m., you might raise a concern that the interviewer hadn't even thought of.

Use your judgment to determine the spirit in which a question is being asked, and answer it only if you believe it is being asked out of genuine and harmless curiosity.

2. *Evade the question.* If you would prefer not to answer a question because you find it offensive or because you know that the information it elicits could be used against you, you do not have to answer it. You can choose to dodge it. Using humor is often one way of doing that. For example, if asked, "Do you have any children?" you can say, "Well, if you include my husband, my tank of fish, and our two cats, I suppose I have 17 children." (Of course, this reply presumes that you don't mind having the interviewer know you're married.) The interviewer is left not knowing if you have two children and 12 fish, or no children and 14 fish—and will probably be so taken aback and perplexed that he or she will move onto another question.

3. *Openly refuse to answer the question.* If a question is blatantly discriminatory, offensive, or just plain stupid, you might want to respond in a more direct manner. You can say, for example, "Does my religious affiliation have any bearing on this job?" However you reply, don't be defensive, and try not to make a major ordeal out of the situation. Keep in mind that some interviewers will ask illegal questions simply because they don't know any better, not because they are

Timesaver
For a one-stop source of legal information, log onto FindLaw at www.findlaw.com for a treasure trove of legal resources on the Internet.

biased. There's no need to alienate them unnecessarily.

Sexual Harassment

Of all the legal issues in the workplace, the matter of sexual harassment may be the one with which the general public is most familiar. Major legal battles in the public eye over the past several years have made all of us armchair employment attorneys. Yet, it often seems that the more we know, the less we know.

If the legal scholars on major networks and cable TV programs can't agree on how to interpret sexual harassment laws, then how can the average person be expected to do so? The answer is: Don't try.

If you're in an interview and think that the interviewer's behavior might constitute sexual harassment but you aren't sure (assuming it's a subtle verbal cue or action rather than an overt sexual advance), then keep your cool until you get out of there. Then consult with an employment law expert. Don't try to make the call yourself.

Of course, if the harassment is more overt—attempted physical contact or a statement or clear insinuation that you will not be hired unless you perform a certain act—then you don't have to sit tight. You should make a beeline straight for the door.

Protection against sexual harassment results from a 1980 Equal Employment Opportunity Commission interpretation of Title VII of the Civil Rights Act of 1964, an interpretation validated by two 1998 Supreme Court decisions. As a result, sexual harassment has become a major equal employment opportunity issue for employers. What this means for you is that, if you are at all uncomfortable

Unofficially...
You can keep tabs on Supreme Court rulings, including those related to sexual harassment, through the site of the Legal Information Institute and Project Hermes at Cornell University (http://supct.law.cornell.edu/supct).

with an interviewer's behavior or suspect that you are being evaluated on factors other than your professional merit, you may be able to find protection in the law.

Taking Legal Action

If you don't get a job offer and suspect that you were rejected on some sort of discriminatory basis—perhaps because you refused to give into a sexual harasser or you have the wrong skin color, gender, or religion—you have two choices: Accept the decision and move on, realizing that you wouldn't have wanted to work in an organization with that inhospitable climate or for that biased person anyway. Or, take legal action. Legal action may be warranted if the following conditions are met:

- An employment lawyer is confident that you have a strong case.

- You are so profoundly offended, angered, and/or hurt by the employer's actions that you want to sue based on principle.

- The course of your life has been dramatically altered—and your future career opportunities threatened—because you did not get a particular job or promotion for which you were well qualified.

- You are aware that you may be—probably will be—in for a long, expensive, and aggravating ordeal, and that the ongoing litigation could have a negative impact on the quality of your life.

If those factors are in place, legal action may be appropriate, particularly if you are determined to right a wrong. In my experience (and that of my colleagues), however, most people tend to put the

injustice behind them and move on to other opportunities. Whichever path you choose, seek the
advice of qualified legal and employment professionals—as well as the input of family, friends, and
other trusted advisors—before committing to one
direction or the other.

Just the Facts

- The best way to deal with interviewers' objections is to anticipate them before they come up
and to prepare a succinct, non-apologetic
counter-argument in advance.

- To overcome an interviewer's objection, keep a
level head, don't get defensive, understand the
root of the objection, and don't make it a bigger
issue than it needs to be.

- It is your responsibility to know your legal rights
in an interview so that you can recognize discrimination and know what information you are
required to divulge.

- Some interviewers ask illegal questions unwittingly simply because they aren't trained properly, so don't assume they are consciously trying
to break the law.

- If faced with a question that you know is illegal,
you don't have to answer it, but you should
dodge it tactfully to avoid alienating the interviewer and jeopardizing your candidacy.

Watch Out!
It is illegal in
the United States
for an employer
to ask that you
provide a photo
of yourself or to
take one of you
as part of an
application for
employment.

Closing the Deal

PART V

GET THE SCOOP ON...
How to close an interview ▪ Thank-you letters
that clinch the deal ▪ Knowing when and how
often to call ▪ How not to be a pest ▪ What to
do if the answer is no

Following Up to Get to "Yes"

Chapter 13

In Chapter 2, "The Biggest Mistakes Interviewees Make," you read that one of the most common errors is to sit back after an interview and wait for the phone to ring. Unfortunately, that practice can be fatal to a job search. Strategic interviewing doesn't stop at the parting handshake; the efforts you make after the interview are just as critical as those made before and during it—and are sometimes even more so.

If your encounter with an interviewer was less than magical, effective follow-up can turn the tables and salvage your candidacy. Or, if your interview went well but you face stiff competition, the contact you make afterward with the prospective employer can set you miles apart from other candidates.

You might already be aware of the importance of follow-up but simply don't know how best to carry it out. You may be all too familiar with those awkward moments when your hand is on the phone but you just aren't sure if you should leave the employer yet another message—even though it's been two weeks since your interview. You might have one voice inside of you saying, "Be aggressive, make the call," and another cautioning you not to be a pest. Or, you may consider faxing or e-mailing a note to be less obtrusive, but you aren't sure what to write. This chapter is devoted to getting you out of those dilemmas, as well as preventing them from occurring in the first place.

Starting Your Follow-Up Before the Interview Ends

Follow-up begins before you ever leave the interviewer's office. If you ask the right questions and cinch the rapport as the interview comes to a close, you will build a solid foundation on which to base your later follow-through efforts.

Imagine you had an interview three weeks ago and now you're sitting by the phone hoping to get a call. Let's say you mailed a thank-you note the day after the interview and left two phone messages the following week, but you have not received a call back. The three weeks since the appointment seem like an eternity, and you're so tired of waiting that at this point you wouldn't even mind receiving a rejection letter in the mail. You just want an answer, even if it's "no." You're left in the awkward position of not knowing whether you should call or write again.

Two simple things can prevent this scenario. The first is obtaining adequate information on the interview process. If you had found out how long the employer plans to be interviewing candidates, then you would know whether to be concerned about no contact for three weeks. If you had discussed the matter of follow-up with your interviewer before leaving the interview, then you would know whether you'd be seen as a nuisance or merely a diligent job-seeker if you placed another call.

The second thing to do is to leave the interview on a confident, positive note with good rapport established so that you will be received as something closer to a newfound friend than a pest when you make your follow-up calls or send notes.

Questions That Build a Foundation for Follow-Up

The questions you ask as an interview draws to a close should not be limited to inquiries about the position and the organization (such questions are described in the "Do You Have Any Questions for Us?" section of Chapter 10, "Some More Questions You Might Be Asked"). You also need to ask questions that help you know how and when to follow up and that also give you an idea of where you stand in the pool of applicants. Questions you might ask include these:

- *What is your time frame for making a decision?* You need to know whether the decision-makers are in a hurry to extend an offer and get someone on board or if they're in no rush. That way, if you find that a few weeks go by before you hear from them again, you'll know whether that passage of time is cause for concern.

- *How many more candidates do you expect to interview?* This question—if answered candidly—can elicit valuable information about the extent of your competition and how much more time the interviewing and decision-making processes might take. It can also provide an added bonus in that some employers reply by volunteering additional information about where your candidacy stands relative to the other applicants. For example, you might be so lucky as to hear, "I

Unofficially...
Don't be concerned if, during an interview, the interviewer gives you no indication of your chances of getting the job. Interviewers are often trained to keep a poker face and not to make promises they can't keep, so you might get only neutral verbal and non-verbal signals.

have two more people to interview, but I can't imagine they will be stronger candidates than you."

■ *When do you need someone to start in this position?* This is an indirect way of asking, "What is your time frame for making a decision?" Obviously, if the employer is desperate to have someone start as soon as possible, then a decision is going to be made quickly. If, on the other hand, there is no rush, then you may be in for a long wait. Whichever the case, it is essential for you to have this information so you'll know how long to stick it out for an answer.

■ *Do you have any concerns about my suitability for this position?* This question is controversial. Some job search experts advise against asking it, fearing that doing so makes you sound less than confident about your candidacy or that it unnecessarily raises a discussion of your deficits rather than keeping the focus on your assets. Many others—myself included—disagree. If the interviewer has concerns about your qualifications, you're better off addressing them head-on while you're still face-to-face, rather than letting them go uncontested. Rarely does an interviewer believe that you are 100 percent perfect for a position. There is always some nagging concern, whether minor or potentially devastating. By asking about those concerns, you get the upper hand because you can then lay them to rest on the spot or during your subsequent follow-up.

■ *Is there anything else you need from me to have a complete picture of my qualifications?* This question is similar to the last one, in that it enables you to leave the interview knowing that the employer has complete and accurate "data" on you. Some prospective employers will find two or three days after an interview that they'd like to see your college or graduate school transcript, or a sample of your writing, or any other documentation that will help them make up their minds. In the interest of time, however, an employer might decide to extend an offer to another candidate who has qualifications equal—or even slightly inferior—to yours but whose supporting materials are all there in the employer's file. Because getting your materials would require a phone call to you and then a waiting period to receive them, some interviewers may decide that it is simply easier to go with another applicant. By asking about such needs during the interview, you are able take action right away and thus avoid this problem.

Timesaver
Be sure you have the e-mail addresses, fax numbers, direct telephone lines, and complete mailing address of anyone who has interviewed you so that you can carry out your follow-up more efficiently. And, remember that all this information may not be on someone's business card, so check for missing data before you tuck the card in your pocket.

Establishing Rapport So You Can Maintain Rapport

Except those born with a gift for telemarketing, most people find it easier to call—or write a note to—a friend than a stranger. If you leave an interview without having connected with the prospective employer in any way other than an overly formal, superficial job-seeker/interviewer fashion, then your follow-up efforts will be with someone who still feels like a stranger.

As discussed in Chapter 7, "Strategic Communication for Interviews," establishing rapport does not mean becoming the interviewer's new best buddy; it simply means connecting in some meaningful way. The rapport you establish opens good lines of communication and helps you avoid awkwardness when you attempt to stay in touch with the employer. Also in Chapter 7, you were introduced to the idea of closing an interview with confidence and courtesy in the section "Leaving Good Feelings Behind After the Interview." Let's revisit that concept now as it applies to your follow-up efforts.

- A confident departure is one in which you spell out for the interviewer how you think you're right for the position. You restate your asset statements in a concise pitch to reinforce the case you've been building. This leaves the interviewer with the impression that you are indeed a strong candidate. When you close an interview in the typical, passive fashion—such as, "I'm very interested in the position and look forward to hearing from you"—you sabotage all your efforts up to that point and revert to the less powerful position of "job-hunter" (who merely needs something) rather than that of "consultant" or "problem-solver" (who has something to offer). By leaving in a more confident way, you clinch your case and leave a strong last impression, not just a good first impression. Then, when you call, e-mail, fax, or write during the days and weeks that follow the interview, you are more likely to be remembered as a candidate worth paying attention to.

- Departing with courtesy means that you thank interviewers for the opportunity to be considered and that you show your appreciation for their time. As with leaving with a confident air, closing the interview on a cordial, appreciative note leaves good will that may serve you well down the road. You'll see later in this chapter that one way not to be seen as a pest during your follow-up efforts is to be considerate of the employer's time and courteous at all times. So, departing interviews with an eye toward common courtesies establishes you in interviewers' minds as a considerate person and makes them more likely to be receptive of your follow-up efforts. Leaving an interview on a positive note can also come in handy even if you end up not getting the job. You may find yourself working with that person later, either on a common project or in some other capacity. After all, anyone you meet at a particular organization becomes a part of your network, and could resurface anywhere in the future.

What To Do Within 24 Hours After the Interview

You might think that all you need to do immediately after an interview is to write a thank-you note. That's a common misconception. Though the note is important, two steps must take precedence over it because they will help you write a more powerful thank-you note—or, as it is called in this book, "follow-up letter."

The two things you need to do first are to evaluate the interview experience and to seek feedback on it from key members of your network. This should be done within 24 hours after the interview. Then you can write the follow-up letter and make plans for further follow-up—two things that should also be taken care of within 24 hours, or at least within 48 hours.

The timing of these first follow-up efforts is critical. If you wait too long to get back in touch with the employer, you might lose the job to a candidate who acted more quickly but who was not necessarily any better qualified than you. You also need to be

Moneysaver
Job searches often involve frequent faxing, which can get expensive if you don't have your own machine and have to pay a dollar or more per page when sending from an office supply or print shop. Consider purchasing one of the many simple fax machines that are reasonably priced and that pay for themselves in no time, or get fax software for your computer.

prompt with your follow-up letter and other communication to perpetuate the professional image you conveyed during the interview. The employer may see you as disorganized or disinterested if you take too long to get back in touch.

Watch Out!
Be as objective as possible when assessing how you feel about a potential job and employer in the first hours or days after an interview. If the experience was pleasant on a social level, you might paint a rosier picture of the opportunity in your mind than is actually warranted. Objectivity now can help you better evaluate a job offer later.

Evaluating the Interview Experience

You may leave an interview feeling either like you're walking on air or trudging through quicksand—or something in between—but there's nothing like an objective, logical analysis of the experience to complement those gut feelings. While the encounter is fresh in your mind, it's important to jot down some thoughts on how you did, what the employer's main needs and interests were, and where you think (or know) your candidacy stands. You also should make note of any tidbits of information that can work to your advantage during the follow-through, such as pet concerns or hobbies of the individual interviewer, or interests you have in common.

These notes not only aid in the follow-up stage but can also serve as criteria on which to base a decision, should you end up receiving a job offer. Use the Interview Evaluation Form that appears in this chapter as a way to structure your notes. You may photocopy the form or create your own on your computer so that you can complete one for every interview.

How to Use the Interview Evaluation Form

The following commentary clarifies elements of the Interview Evaluation Form that appears in this chapter, and it's designed so that you'll know how best to respond to the questions and prompts it contains. (The letter and number of each guideline given below corresponds to the item of the same number and letter on the form.)

A1: This question is intended as an overall assessment of how you did during the interview. Are you pleased with your participation? Do you feel you built a strong case? Did you present a confident, professional image and establish good rapport? Or, did you feel like you could have done better—or even that you blew it? You might even want to rate yourself on a scale of 1–10 or 1–5, or give yourself a letter grade.

A2: Assess how equal the balance of power was between you and the interviewer. Were you able to have some control over the direction of the conversation? Did you get your agenda across and meet your objectives?

A3: Making note of the examples you used—ones from your past experience and examples of how you might contribute to the employer in the future—helps you remember what the employer already knows about you. That way, if you want to use any asset statements during follow-up phone calls or in letters, you won't use ones the interviewer has already heard. It's like knowing what tricks are still up your sleeve that the audience hasn't seen.

A4: It's very important that you make note of any particular qualifications in which the interviewer seemed to take particular interest. Doing so helps direct your follow-up efforts in that you can mention them again to reinforce their strength. This also prevents you from inadvertently "selling" the prospective employer on qualifications he or she doesn't particularly care about.

A5: Keep in mind that interviewing is a learning process. By reflecting on the questions you struggled to answer effectively, you can work on improving your interviewing technique.

Note! ➡
If you try to complete this form in painstaking detail for every interview, you may find the task too tedious and give it up altogether. To make yourself more likely to do it, just jot down the most pertinent information in each category and skip those categories that are not applicable.

INTERVIEW EVALUATION FORM

Interview date:

Interviewer name:

Company/organization name:

Address:

Tel: Fax:

E-mail:

A. My Performance

1.   How did I do? (generally)

2.   How was the balance of power?

3.   Asset statements I used:

4.   Aspects of my qualifications of most interest to the interviewer:

5.   Questions I had difficulty answering:

6.   Points I forgot to make:

7.   Things I said that might have been misunderstood:

B. What I Learned About the Employer

1.   The organization's most pressing needs or problems:

2.   Anticipated areas of growth for the organization:

3.   Other organizational goals:

4.   Which skills, content knowledge, and
     personal qualities are sought?

C. Do I Want the Job?

1.   How did the culture/work environment seem?

2.   What would the work schedule be?

3.   What would my responsibilities be?

4.   What did I learn about salary and benefits?

5.   How does this position/employer fit
     with my short-term goals?

6.   ...with my long-term goals?

7.   Does this position/employer seem
     right for me in general?

8.   What are my specific concerns about
     the suitability of this position/employer
     for me?

D. What Are My Chances of Getting an Offer?

1. Did I get a straight answer about my candidacy?

2. What were my strengths?

3. What concerns did the interviewer express about me?

E. Questions for Follow-up

1. What did I learn about the interviewer's personal and professional interests?

2. Over which work-related or non-work-related topics did we bond?

3. To which communication/personal style did the interviewer seem most receptive?

4. Is there some information or materials the interviewer expressed a need for or interest in that I can send?

5. When do they expect to make a decision?

---

6. How many more people are going to be interviewed?

7. When do they need someone to start?

8. How did the interviewer respond to my request to stay in touch after the interview?

9. Did the interviewer offer any guidelines for when and how he or she prefers that I follow up?

A6: It is inevitable that you will leave an interview without addressing at least one important point. In building your case, you might forget to talk about a particular accomplishment or skill, or how you would solve a certain problem the employer faces. After taking stock of what you left out, you can then decide whether that information is critical to your case. If it is, you can state it in a follow-up letter or phone call (or in any subsequent interviews you might have with that same employer).

A7: You might leave an interview concerned about something you said that was not clear to the interviewer. As discussed in Chapter 7, how a message is received is a critical element in the communication process. If you think that anything you said could have been misinterpreted or simply not fully understood, make note of it and consider clarifying it during your follow-up conversations or in written communication.

B1: It is often interesting to see how your pre-interview research concerning employers' needs stacks up against the reality you ascertain in an interview. If there was any discrepancy—and undoubtedly there will be—make note of it on your form.

B2: As with item B1, you need to compare what you knew going into the interview with what you know by the end of it in the area of the employer's growth.

B3: This portion of the Interview Evaluation Form is designed for any miscellaneous information you collected about how the company is growing. As you communicate with the employer after the interview, you should keep these goals in mind and continually talk about how you can help the organization meet them.

B4: If the interview went well, you probably found that the assets you had planned to discuss were indeed those that the employer was seeking in a candidate. If so, jot down those assets in this portion of the form to confirm that you were on track. If, however, you found that certain skills, knowledge, or personal qualities were needed that you either do not possess or were not prepared to discuss, then you should record those in this space on the form and plan how you will address them through your follow-up.

C1: Your observations of the actual work environment usually differ at least slightly from how you had imagined it to be based on your research or on hear-say. After the interview, listen to the gut feelings you have about how you would fit into the organizational culture, and make note of them on the form. Also record any more tangible data you gathered about the organization's values and preferred work style. (For a refresher on the issue of fit and organizational culture, you may want to refer to Chapter 3, "Research: The Root of All Strategy.")

C2: As with B2, you should make a note of anything you learned about a typical work day and work week: the hours you would keep, how much overtime is offered or required (if any), and how flexible or rigid the schedule seems to be. This information can help you evaluate an offer you might receive.

C3: By the time you receive a particular job offer, you might find that you have forgotten exactly what that position would entail. Record the responsibilities now while they are fresh in your mind, and you'll find that you have more accurate criteria on which to base a decision later.

C4: If salary and benefits were discussed, make note of any figures the employer quoted, as well as the results of any negotiations in which you engaged. Such records are critical for your final compensation negotiations.

C5: Consider where you'd like to be and what you'd like to be doing within the next year or few years. Does this position—or this employer, as a whole—offer employment that would meet your needs, match your interests, and utilize your skills?

C6: Do the same with your goals for several years or more from now.

C7: What were your overall impressions of how this would be as a place to work?

C8: If your reply to question C7 was not completely positive, what are your concerns?

D1: Make note of anything the interviewer was willing to share about how many more people are to be interviewed or about how your qualifications—and those of other applicants—match the organization's needs.

D2: In this space, make note of any skills, knowledge, personal qualities, or experience that seemed to particularly impress the interviewer. These are points you can reiterate in your follow-up communication to drive home the notion that you are the best person for the job.

D3: Making note of any concerns helps you build a stronger case for yourself during the follow-up phase.

E1: Make note of any professional and personal interests or hobbies the interviewer mentioned or that were evident through photographs or other clues in his or her office. If you come across anything related to these interests—perhaps an article, a Web site, or an upcoming event—it may be appropriate to send it along.

E2: If any of the interests you noted in E1 were ones you shared, make special note of those so that you can subtly remind the interviewer of that common interest.

E3: Were you able to be yourself completely during the interview, or did you have to alter your personal style somewhat to fit with that of the interviewer? If you had to be more or less reserved, casual, humorous, or anything else, make note of it so that you can continue to adapt your communication style during your follow-up.

E4: Occasionally, an interviewer will express interest in finding a particular professional resource, such as a book, an Internet newsgroup, the name of a person, and the like. If you come across something relevant and useful, then by all means, send it to the interviewer.

E5: If you learned anything about the time frame for making a decision, make note of it here.

Moneysaver
As often as possible—and when appropriate—follow-up with employers via e-mail rather than racking up big expenses from long-distance calls and faxes, or from postage and stationery.

E6: If you were lucky enough to get a straight answer to this question, record the number here.

E7: Make note of the start date, and indicate if it is required or preferred. If the interviewer expressed any flexibility on this point, make note of the conversation.

E8: Was the interviewer receptive and encouraging of your interest in staying in touch, or did you get a "Don't call us—we'll call you" brush-off?

E9: Does the interviewer prefer that you call, e-mail, or write—and, if so, on what approximate date?

Consulting with Your Network for Interview Feedback

Conducting the interview evaluation helps you lay a foundation for your follow-up letter and other post-interview communication, but it's just the first step. Next, you need to speak with people who can help you interpret things the employer said and take an accurate read on your assessment of the experience.

Some members of your network might even have access to the hiring authorities in question and can find out the inside scoop for you. When considering to whom you need to speak after an interview, determine if any of the following categories of people could be of help to you:

Headhunters. If your interview was arranged through an employment agency or search firm, the first place you should turn for feedback is to the recruiter you are working with there. In many cases, the prospective employer will let the recruiter know how you did on the interview and where your candidacy stands. The extent to which the employer is forthcoming with such information depends upon the nature of the relationship he or she has with the recruiter, so what you're able to learn will vary from place to place. Regardless of how much hard data you and the recruiter collect, you can work together to craft a follow-up strategy.

Other employees at the prospective employer. If you know anyone who works at the organization where you interviewed, don't hesitate to contact that person to get an insider's insight into your chances. Also ask for advice on what steps you should take next. If you had an initial screening interview followed by additional interviews with different people, you should consider contacting the person who conducted the first interview. If you got along well with that person, he or she may be willing to serve as an advocate of sorts for you with the other hiring authorities.

Your career counselor or job search coach. If you have been—or plan to start—working with a career development or employment professional, be sure to debrief your interview with that person. Career consultants know the right questions to ask to identify any red flags you might not have spotted. Though their assessment of the interview is based on your account of it—which, of course, is no substitute for being a fly on the wall—they often can help you pinpoint areas of concern if you describe the conversation and the atmosphere thoroughly.

Other members of your network. If you aren't working with a career counselor or job search coach, there may be other people—friends, family, or professional colleagues—who can give you the same kind of objective read on your description of the interview.

Sending a Follow-up Letter

After you have evaluated the interview—both on your own and with the help of objective third

Watch Out!
Never usurp the authority of an executive recruiter or employment agent by following up directly with the prospective employer when the interview was set up through the headhunter. With rare exceptions (and with permission from the headhunter), you have to let the recruiter or agent do the talking for you.

parties—you're ready to send your follow-up letter. This letter should be more than a thank-you note; it is a letter that either clinches the deal or encourages the employer to have you back for more interviews.

Most of your fellow candidates will send letters that do nothing more than express their appreciation for the interviewer's time and reinforce their interest in the position. To set yourself apart from the pack, you must do those two things but also use the letter as your chance to have the last word, to address any concerns the interviewer may have had with you and to further strengthen your case.

Your letter should include the following sections, roughly in this order:

1. An expression of your thanks for the opportunity to interview. If the interviewer expended any extra effort on your part—perhaps speaking to you at length, introducing you to others, or giving you a tour of the facility—be sure to note your appreciation for that effort.

2. A brief recap of your assets, focusing on those most relevant for the position or in which the interviewer expressed most interest.

3. A straightforward, non-apologetic counter-argument to any concerns the interviewer openly expressed about your qualifications. Remember, don't raise any worries that don't already exist!

4. A statement of your interest in the position and enthusiasm for the employer.

5. A subtle reminder of the next steps you agreed upon, such as, "As you suggested, I will call you next week to see where you are in the decision-making process."

Unofficially...
If two candidates are equally qualified for a position but only one sends a thank-you note, many employers will offer the job to the one who sent a note simply because that person made the effort to write it.

Bright Idea
When sending your follow-up note, you can encourage further communication by enclosing something the interviewer might feel obligated to thank you for: a magazine or newspaper article, a print-out of a Web site home page, or anything else relevant to the interviewer's personal or professional interests. But never send a gift or anything that looks like a bribe!

Keep the letter concise, but be sure to touch on each point described. A thank-you note that consists of only two or three lines is a waste of time, yet you'd be amazed how often I've seen such a thing. On the other hand, don't go overboard and send a letter that is longer than one page. You should be able to state your case succinctly in just three or four brief paragraphs.

If you had a panel interview or met with multiple people on the same day, be sure to send a personalized letter to each person you met. The letters need not be drastically different from each other (rarely do the recipients compare notes with each other), but they should vary slightly. Writing an original letter for each person is not only common courtesy, but it is also a wise strategy because you will need to gear the letters toward the interests and concerns of each individual.

When your letter is ready, you can send it through regular mail, express mail, e-mail, or fax—or you can hand-deliver it. Traditionally, follow-up letters are sent by regular mail to conform with proper business etiquette. These days, however, more follow-up letters are being sent by e-mail or fax because those have become such common means of transmission for business correspondence. These methods also come in handy if you are late with your letter (sending it more than 48 hours after the interview) or if you know that the time frame for a decision is short. Avoid hand-delivering or express-mailing the letter unless it is particularly urgent to get it to the hiring authorities before a decision is made. Sending a follow-up letter should look effortless, not like a major ordeal. You also want to keep up the image of having more important things to do with your time than to run around town dropping off letters.

Schedule Your Next Steps

When your follow-up letter is on its way, you need to plan the next steps in your follow-up. A typical scenario in a job search is that you have a first interview, send a letter within a day or so, then stay in touch with the employer (usually by phone or e-mail) until you are invited to return for a follow-up interview or are told that you are not in the running for a position.

You probably know that you can't be passive, but maybe aren't sure what exactly to do next. The section that follows, "Secrets of Persisting Without Pestering," offers some suggestions for what your next steps might be. For now, as we conclude this section on what to do in the first 24 hours after an interview, you just need to be aware that you should schedule your next steps as soon as that follow-up letter is out of your hands.

For example, if you say in the letter that you will call the following week, then you should decide on the day and approximate time that you will make the call and then record that in your appointment book. Scheduling not only ensures that you will actually carry out your plan, but it also relieves some of the pressure associated with a job search. When you schedule a task in writing on a calendar, you no longer have to clutter your mind with worries about how and when to follow up. You can focus on other things until the day comes when you see that appointment on the page.

Secrets of Persisting Without Pestering

When you're waiting to hear the results of a hiring decision, questions inevitably arise about how

Watch Out!
If you take longer than about 72 hours to get a follow-up note in the hands of your interviewers, they may forget that you exist, assume you have no interest in the position, label you as someone with bad manners, or—and this is the worst of all—let their concerns about your qualifications mushroom in their minds into insurmountable barriers to hiring you.

assertive—or even aggressive—you should be in chasing after those results. While you do need to do everything you can to produce a favorable out-come—to get an offer—there is a fine line between being persistent and being a pest. Follow-up that is done haphazardly or half-heartedly is worse than no follow-up at all. Staying in touch after an interview requires as much strategy as the interview itself. Let's look at the rationale behind your persis-tence—as well as some guidelines for it.

Why Your Follow-Up Efforts Are So Important

Getting employers to return your calls or reply to your e-mails can be an incredibly frustrating process. Sometimes matters are made even worse when you do finally get through to them and find that they are not forthcoming with information, are noncommittal, or—at worst—are downright rude. Despite these frustrations, following up is critical for the following reasons:

- Getting a job is your priority, but filling a vacant position may not be the employer's priority. When you're looking for a new job, it can seem at times that nothing else in the world matters. Your every waking—and even sleeping—moment is spent thinking about resumes you need to send out, interviews for which you're preparing, or an offer you're awaiting. For the employer, however, the position you seek might be one of many to be filled. And, there may be no big rush in hiring someone for it. Or per-haps, there's a fairly urgent need to bring some-one on board, but the hiring manager's time and thoughts must be divided among the hiring process and many other non-recruiting pur-suits. So, even if an interviewer was extremely impressed with you, picking up the phone to tell you that may not be at the top of that person's priority to-do list. By making the call yourself, you turn yourself into a priority.

- Some employers test candidates by seeing who follows up and concluding that the one who shows the most interest or makes the best case for his or her qualifications is the one who gets the job. This phenomenon is especially common with positions such as sales, in which you would need to be aggressive and persistent on the job. The follow-up phase then becomes a way of observing your behavior to supplement what was learned during the interview.

- Out of sight is out of mind. Sometimes jobs go to the person who happens to call on the day that the hiring authority feels like extending an offer—not to the one who is better qualified.

- Post-interview phone calls and written correspondence let you alleviate concerns the employer might have about you. Sometimes the follow-up letter sent immediately after the interview isn't sufficient; you may need to talk with the employer directly to address those concerns.

- Being persistent gives you a sense of power over the outcome. A job search can be stressful, so to keep your sanity during it, you need to retain as much control as possible. Even if you're not getting any immediate results from your efforts, at least you know that you're doing everything you can.

Guidelines for Considerate but Assertive Follow-Up

A typical follow-up effort involves sending a thank-you note—AKA a follow-up letter—within a day or two after the interview, then calling the employer anywhere from a few days to a week or more later (depending on the overall hiring time frame). If all goes well, you'll speak to the interviewer when you place that first call and will find out the status of your candidacy. More likely, however, you will have to place repeated calls to track down the employer, and you might need to send another letter or an e-mail until you get an answer. To be strategic in these efforts but not be seen as a pest, consider these guidelines:

- Let your follow-up efforts be guided by what, if anything, you found out during the interview. If you know the position might not be filled for two months, then there is no need to harass the employer with daily or even semi-weekly phone calls.

- Don't get hung up on exactly how frequently you should try to reach someone who's not returning your calls. There is no magic number. Use your common sense and imagine that you were the person receiving the voice mails or messages from your assistant. You probably wouldn't want to be called five times a day, but you might not mind two or three calls a week.

- Consider the nature of the position, the organization, and the industry as well as the style of the people there. Is aggressiveness likely to be not only valued but expected, or are you dealing with people who are more low-key?

- When you do reach someone on the phone, don't sound like you're just going through the motions of placing the requisite follow-up call. There's no point in making the call if you're merely going to say something like, "I'm just checking in to see if you've made any decisions." You'll sound passive, disinterested, and possibly like a nuisance. Instead, connect on a human level and also use the opportunity to build your case further. While exactly what you should say varies depending on the unique circumstances of your situation, you might say something along the lines of: "I wanted to let you know that I'm still very interested in the position, and to see if there's anything I can do to help with your decision."

- Remember how hiring decisions are made, as described in Chapter 1, "How Hiring Decisions are Made." You might be dealing with a process that is disorganized, or one in which multiple decision-makers must come to a consensus, or one that involves some wild card variables that are out of your control.

- Be sure you're following up with the right person. Don't waste your time chasing down someone who has little authority in the hiring decision.

- Know when to give up. If your follow-up reaches the point of absurdity (if it goes on for months and you're pushing the limits of common courtesy with the number of times you've called and written), then you may need to cut your losses and move on. Look at your candidacy objectively, and consult with trusted advisors to see whether you have little hope of getting an offer.

- If you have reached the end of your rope and need an answer, consider faxing a letter instead of leaving yet another phone message. Politely but firmly state that you need to have an answer so that you can pursue other opportunities, and

Watch Out!
Keep in mind that you'll be more successful in your job search if you be yourself. If being assertive is not in your nature, force yourself to be that way just enough to get the job done, but don't try to make a 180° switch to being an extremely aggressive person. Your actions will come across as contrived and phony.

Unofficially...
Asking an employer for feedback on your interviewing style and qualifications is a good idea, but be aware that many will be reluctant to offer any. The issue of giving feedback is an extremely controversial one among human resources professionals and hiring managers. Some feel they have no business acting as your career counselor, while others believe you deserve an honest critique.

you would appreciate a call or e-mail letting you know where your candidacy stands—even if the answer is "no."

- If you do find out that you're being turned down for a position, see if you can get any feedback on why you didn't get the job. Then accept the decision and begin pursuing other options. Don't take the rejection personally: Learn from it and move on.

Just the Facts

- Build a foundation for your follow-up efforts before you leave the interview. Ask questions about the decision-making time frame, what your chances are, and how you should follow up.

- Ensure that your follow-up calls, e-mails, and letters will be well received by establishing good rapport and being courteous during the interview.

- Don't waste your time sending a thank-you letter that does nothing but express your appreciation for the interviewer's time. Make it a true follow-up letter, in which you get the last word by restating your assets and addressing any concerns the employer might have.

- Make your follow-up efforts strategic, not haphazard.

- Consider the nature of the employer when determining how persistent to be.

- If the answer is no, try to get a straight answer as to why. Then accept it and move on without internalizing the rejection.

GET THE SCOOP ON...
Defining your priorities ▪ Identifying
an offer's pros and cons ▪
Negotiating compensation ▪ Foolproof decision-
making techniques ▪ Making the transition

Evaluating and Negotiating Offers

C h a p t e r 1 4

If you've ever tried to work one of those brain-teaser puzzles like a Rubik's Cube, you know how frustrating it is to move one piece of the puzzle into the right position, only to find that another one gets shifted out of place and sends you back to square one. Negotiating and evaluating job offers is a little like that. No job or employer is going to fit your interests and needs perfectly. One job might offer the money you want but would require an extra hour a day of commuting. Another may be just around the corner from home and offer a little more money, but would have a boss who seems like a loose cannon.

Accepting a job offer usually involves some degree of sacrifice and compromise. You might settle for less of a salary increase and more volatility in your boss in exchange for the convenience of walking to work. Or, you may say that the personality of the people you work with is of utmost importance, so you'll take the other job and find a way to live with the commute.

The way to feel comfortable with these trade-offs is to make a careful assessment of your priorities and to get a complete picture of exactly what the job will entail and what the employer has to offer. Of course, to avoid having to make many sacrifices or compromises in the first place, you need to negotiate favorable terms of the offer. The steps involved in negotiating and evaluating an offer are as follows:

1. Identify your priorities so that you have solid criteria on which to base a decision.

2. Scrutinize the offer so you know exactly what you're getting into and so you feel confident that you're getting a fair deal.

3. Determine whether the offer satisfies your priorities.

4. Negotiate more favorable terms, if necessary.

5. Decide whether to accept or decline the offer.

This chapter takes you through each of these steps and concludes with tips for making a smooth transition if you do decide to accept an offer, or for going back to the drawing board should you decline it. Let's first look at how to identify your priorities and scrutinize the specifics of the offer.

Identifying Your Priorities

One of the biggest mistakes people make when evaluating job offers is to do just that: evaluate the *offer*. They learn everything thing they can about the position's responsibilities, the stability of the employer, and the salary and benefits, but they neglect to evaluate their own priorities. Sure, they might assess what they'd like out of a job—more money, interesting new challenges, or opportunity for

Unofficially...
You'll be most satisfied with the decision to take a particular job if you consider not only how it will affect you professionally, but also personally. Consider its potential impact on your physical and mental health, daily routine, family or social life, and hobbies or other activities.

advancement, perhaps—but they don't define which of those desires take precedence over the others.

If you take this approach, you will be evaluating the offer in a vacuum. You'll know everything there is to know about the job, but you won't know how it satisfies your needs. This problem becomes particularly evident when you are evaluating more than one offer and must compare the advantages and disadvantages of each. The pros and cons may balance out to make the offers about equally attractive, so you don't know which to choose. In that case, you may find yourself in a situation of comparing apples and oranges, unable to make a decision because the nature of the pros and cons differs.

Avoiding the Apples and Oranges Dilemma

The following example illustrates the problem of trying to choose among offers whose pros and cons cancel each other out. I once worked with a management consultant who was trying to decide between two good job offers. Company A was offering a salary increase of almost 30 percent but would require significant amounts of travel; what's more, the company was notorious for its pressure-cooker work environment. It did, however, also offer excellent opportunities for advancement and partnership potential, and my client knew that some of the day-to-day pressure would be relieved if he reached the level of partner.

Company B offered about the same money as his current job but required less travel and would not be particularly stressful given the more relaxed corporate culture. The path to partnership was likely to be more circuitous at Company B, but the work itself would be extremely interesting and directly related to areas of business in which my client wanted to be involved. Added to the confusion was the fact that when he told his boss at his current job that he was going to be resigning (he and his boss were particularly close, so he did him the courtesy of letting him know he'd be leaving even before he knew where he was going), the boss made a counter-offer, saying he'd match the other salary offers.

This consultant found himself in quite a quandary. He was trying to leave his current job not only because he was tired of the constant travel and stressful environment, but also because he was bored with his area of consulting and wanted new challenges. He set about making his decision by carefully comparing the pros and cons of each opportunity, but he kept getting stuck when he found that none of the three options emerged as a clear best choice. He found that he was enticed by the 30 percent salary increase more than he had thought he would be, but he wasn't sure the money could make up for the sacrifices the job would require in his family life. And, he didn't know if delayed gratification of making partner was more important than doing satisfying work and being stimulated by new challenges in the short-term arena.

After going back and forth, unable to decide, he came to me to work out the problem. It was clear that his was a classic case of comparing apples and oranges and expecting an answer to emerge from the mix. I asked him to list all the variables—compensation, impact on personal life, advancement, stimulating job content, and work environment—and rank them in order of importance to him. The task wasn't easy—some variables ended up being tied—but it did help clarify the choices. He decided that having more time for his family and doing work that would be directly related to his professional interests were more important than the other factors. He chose "Company B" and felt confident that he'd made the right decision.

The First Step in Defining Your Priorities

To make the right choice when faced with one or more job offers, you have to take into account who you are, what you do well, what you enjoy, and what you need. One way to do that is to complete the Job Acceptance Criteria Worksheet that follows.

This worksheet lists 25 factors that may or may not be critical to your satisfaction on a job. The objective of this worksheet is to rate each factor on a scale of 1–10 according to how important it is that your next job satisfy that criterion. A high rating—such as 8, 9, or 10—would indicate that this factor is extremely important to you. Low ratings of 1, 2, or 3 reflect factors that you really don't care much about, while the middle ratings reflect criteria that you feel some degree of indifference toward or might like to have met but that aren't essential. The questions that follow each criterion can help you decide how important that factor is to you.

Making Tough Choices

If you ended up with just a few criteria rated at 8, 9, or 10 on the Job Acceptance Criteria Worksheet and the rest distributed fairly evenly across the scale from 1 to 7, then your priorities are in good shape. You have a clear picture of what you absolutely must have on your next job—and you're not asking for too much—and you know which factors would be nice to have but that aren't essential. You also know which ones you don't really care much about.

Then there's the other 99 percent of us. We either want it all—so almost every criterion has a

Note! ➜
In the space provided after each set of questions, you might find it helpful to jot down some specific thoughts to give your numeric ratings more meaning, particularly for those you rated as 6 or higher. For example, after the skills criterion, you might list some of the actual skills you would like to utilize or develop. After the perks criterion, you could list actual perks you care most about.

JOB ACCEPTANCE CRITERIA WORKSHEET

Read the questions that follow each criterion, and decide how essential that factor is to you. Write a number between 1 and 10 in the space next to each criterion, with 10 indicating utmost importance and 1 indicating little importance.

1. Interests met: the job
    Rating: _____
How important is it that the responsibilities of my next job fit my interests? Do I need to find the content of my work highly interesting?

_____

_____

_____

2. Interest factor: the employer
    Rating: _____
How important is it for me to be interested in the products and services of the next organization that employs me?

_____

_____

_____

3. Skills utilization
    Rating: _____
Which skills do I want to use on my next job?

_____

_____

_____

4. Skills development
    Rating: _____
Which skills would I like to develop on my next job?

_____

_____

_____

5. Learning opportunities
    Rating: _____

In which subjects, content areas, or topics—as opposed to tangible skills—would I like to gain more expertise or acquire more knowledge on my next job?

_____

_____

_____

6.   Personality fit
      Rating: _____

How necessary is it that my next job fit my personality? Am I willing to alter my natural, preferred way of acting to fit the job?

_____

_____

_____

7.   Work environment/organizational
      culture
      Rating: _____

How essential is it that the "culture" at my next job fit with my concept of an ideal work environment or style of employer?

_____

_____

_____

8.   Coworkers
      Rating: _____

How important is it that I work around the types of people I consider to be ideal coworkers?

_____

_____

_____

9.   Supervisor(s)
      Rating: _____

How important is it that my boss(es) have a management style, personality, and/or background that fits my ideal?

_____

_____

_____

10. Nature of the responsibilities
    Rating: _____

How much do I care about the content of my work?
Am I looking for new challenges or familiar tasks? Do
I want to deal with particular subject matters?

_____

_____

_____

11. Formal training
    Rating: _____

How important is it to me that I receive formal training on the job or through seminars or classes?

_____

_____

_____

12. Stability of the organization
    Rating: _____

Do I care if the prospective employer is financially
and structurally secure, or am I willing to tolerate
some volatility in exchange for exciting possibilities?

_____

_____

_____

13. Growth potential of the organization
    Rating: _____

Would I prefer to be with a well-established organization that might not experience much expansion
more than one that is rapidly growing?

_____

_____

_____

14. Advancement potential
    Rating: _____

How important is it that the employer offer clear
opportunities for promotions, increased responsibility, or lateral transfer into an area in which I hope to
work? (Remember that advancement doesn't always
have to mean moving up!)

_____

_____

_____

15. Schedule
    Rating: _____

How important is it that the schedule of my next job (hours, days, overtime) fit with my preferred way of working?

_____

_____

_____

16. Impact on personal/professional
    life balance

    Rating: _____

Do I need my next job to satisfy a desire for a balanced life, or does the job take precedence at this point in my life?

_____

_____

_____

17. The commute
    Rating: _____

Do I care how long it takes me to get to work and what modes of transportation I must take to do so?

_____

_____

_____

18. The location
    Rating: _____

How important is the geographic location of the job?

_____

_____

_____

19 The office itself
    Rating: _____

Do I care what the organization's overall facilities are like, as well as the size, style, and location of my actual workspace?

_____

_____

_____

20.   Travel involved
      Rating: _____

How important is it to me that my next job require the amount of travel I desire, whether that's no travel, a little, or extensive travel?

_____

_____

_____

21.   Salary and other monetary compensation
Rating: _____

How important is the salary and any bonuses, commissions, or other monetary rewards of my next job?

_____

_____

_____

22.   Benefits
      Rating: _____

How important are the benefits? Do I have specific needs regarding health insurance, amount of vacation, or other benefits?

_____

_____

_____

23.   Perks
      Rating: _____

How much do I care about perks? Is having a company car, an expense account, access to a VIP box at the sports stadium, or other perks a real plus to me?

_____

_____

_____

high rating—or we rated several criteria as 10s and can't make the tough choices among them. If you're part of that group, take heart. Defining priorities is one of the most difficult things you'll do in a job search. It is not an exact science, so you shouldn't expect to be able to define them precisely. The use of numeric ratings is just a way of defining them a little more precisely than the gut-feel approach that drives many people's decisions.

If you did rate too many items at 8 or higher, try to whittle the list down to just two or three criteria that get a 9 or 10 rating. Don't agonize over the task, but the more you can distinguish among the importance of the various criteria now, the easier your decisions will be later.

When you have adjusted your ratings as much as possible to have a reasonable distribution of rankings across the 1–10 scale, you should transfer your conclusions to one clear priorities list, as in the Job Evaluation Priorities form that follows. On this form, write the names of the criteria (from the list of 23 criteria on the Job Acceptance Criteria Worksheet) that reflect what you want or don't want on your next job. You can then refer to this priorities list when you have to evaluate any offers.

Watch Out!
When identifying your priorities, be sure they reflect what you really want out of a job or career, not ones that family or friends want you to consider important or that are socially desirable.

Scrutinizing an Offer

Have you ever made a careful career decision only to find that when you actually started the new job or ventured into the new profession, it reality didn't match your expectations? Part of the problem may have been that you had not adequately clarified those expectations in the first place. If you had not clearly identified your priorities before making the move, you might have taken a job that did not satisfy what you needed. The problem also might have

JOB EVALUATION PRIORITIES

On my next job...I must have these:

_____
_____
_____

I would really like to have these, but they are
not absolute requirements:

_____
_____
_____

It would be nice to have these, but I can do
without them:

_____
_____
_____

I am indifferent to these:

_____
_____
_____

I don't care about these:

_____
_____
_____

resulted from insufficient information about what the job would entail. The heading for this section of the chapter uses the term "scrutinize" for a reason: It's not enough to have a vague idea of what a job would entail or what an employer has to offer. You must read between the lines, second-guess, investigate, be suspicious, and leave no stone unturned. In other words, you have to find out what you're getting into.

Becoming a Job Offer Detective

Knowing what you're getting into requires some detective work. Just as you conducted research before your interview, you now need to combine print, electronic, and people resources for clues to the quality and suitability of an offer. The following are ways to find the information you need to scrutinize any offer:

- Refer to your pre-interview research. Take another look at the Information Gems form you completed (see Chapter 3, "Research—The Root of all Strategy") as well as any notes you took about the employer and the job in question.

- Refer to the Interview Evaluation Form you completed after interviewing for the job in question (see Chapter 13, "Following Up to Get to 'Yes'"). Look for observations you made about the position and the employer while the interviewing experience was still fresh in your mind.

- Talk to your network. Get input from anybody and everybody on the prospective employer. You may come across some inside scoop that could sway your decision significantly.

Watch Out!
In the excitement of getting a job offer, it's easy to be lax when it comes to scrutinizing an offer. Don't let the flattery that comes with receiving an offer cloud your good judgment. Get out the magnifying glass and see if it's really as great as it seems.

- Do a keyword search on the Internet using the employer's name to find the most recent information on the organization. You can also do searches related to the industry as a whole if you are deciding among job offers from employers in different industries.

- In addition to—or instead of—an Internet search, use a library's database of newspapers and magazines to search for recent press coverage of the employer.

- Ask to talk to the person who recently held the position you are being offered. (This is usually only possible if that person is still employed at the same organization, having been promoted or transferred, as opposed to leaving the company entirely.)

- Ask tough questions. Don't hesitate to ask the recruiters or hiring managers involved in the process any questions that will elicit the information you need. If they really want you, they'll be forthcoming.

As you're collecting information through the means described in this list, be on the look-out for red flags that could signal trouble. That management consultant discussed earlier in this chapter, for example, found that he had some regrets after he chose "Company B." It turned out that the job required more travel and was more stressful than he had anticipated. You'll recall that a major reason he decided to take the job was that it offered the chance to work in a specific content area that interested him. The interviewers had talked about how they would like him to be in charge of that particular area, given his interest in it and some familiarity with it. What he hadn't realized was that being in charge meant that from Day One, he was expected to build that area of the consulting business—and to do so in a way that would justify its existence. So, the "new challenges" that had drawn him to the position became "new headaches." He ended up sticking it out and finding satisfaction in the job because he truly did enjoy the work, but he learned that the next time around he would read between the lines more carefully when a job was described to him.

Some indicators that a job opportunity might not be all it's cracked up to be include these:

- The organization is in a major state of flux due to a reorganization, rapid expansion, staff cutbacks, lay-offs, mergers, or other significant activity.

- The changes described in the previous point are not yet happening at this organization but are rampant elsewhere in the industry as a whole, so they could strike this prospective employer any day.

- This position has had frequent turnover.

- The employer keeps emphasizing the need for someone who can hit the ground running. That phrase could be a euphemism for "We can't train or support you."

- Your prospective boss is very new and, therefore, an unknown, untested, quantity.

- Your prospective boss has been with the company since before time began and, therefore, might be burned-out or tuned-out.

- The job is with a small business that could go belly-up if not managed wisely or supported by adequate start-up capital.

- The position is in a not-for-profit organization that has a history of funding problems.

- The position is funded by a grant that could run out of money if mismanaged—or end sooner than you would want your job to end.

- You are not given the opportunity to meet—and talk privately with—your prospective coworkers.

- The interviewing and hiring process is disorganized and inefficient, which could signal a lack of professionalism in other areas of the organization.

- The offer was made before the hiring authorities had a chance to get to know you thoroughly.

- You have been subjected to a too-good-to-be-true sales pitch for the organization.

Matching an Offer to Your Priorities

When you're satisfied that you know as much as there is to know about a prospective job and employer, you're ready to see how the offer stacks up against your priorities. Go through each of the criteria you entered on the Job Evaluation Priorities form and see how the data you've collected holds up against those priorities. At this point, you might find that you want to readjust some of your ratings of those criteria. That's normal. When considering your priorities in the context of an actual offer, you might find that some are more or less important to you than you had thought. It's a matter of reality hitting and making you realize that you need something you thought you didn't need, or vice versa. That management consultant, for example, would have rated salary at about a 6 or 7 until he was faced with an offer of a 30 percent salary increase. He admitted to me that the money was very tempting and that he felt a little like a cartoon character with the pupils in his eyes turning into dollar signs. He ended up not making a choice based on money, but the money issue did factor more into his decision than he had thought it would.

If you find that the offer doesn't satisfy what you need, then you can negotiate for one that better matches your priorities. Strategies for negotiating are offered in the sections that follow.

Negotiating the Best Deal

Rarely do you have to accept the first offer you are given. Room almost always exists for negotiation—with some exceptions, such as union or government positions in which the compensation, job title, and responsibilities are fixed at a particular grade or level. (Even then, however, you might be able to propose that you come in at a slightly different grade than the one offered.)

A job offer will usually be extended verbally by telephone or in person. The hiring manager or human resources representative will—or should—state the position title and the salary being offered, and might recap what your responsibilities would be. You do not have to give an answer on the spot, but you should express enthusiasm and appreciation for the offer and tell them when you will give your response (or ask how long you can take to make your decision). You then use that time to evaluate the offer and prepare your negotiating strategy to make it a more attractive offer. In doing so, you need to remember one of the guiding principles of this book: You are not a desperate job-seeker. Employers need you as much as you need them. Coming from that position of strength can help you approach the negotiations with confidence and the decision making with a clear head.

Unofficially...
Most employers
expect you to
negotiate, and
some may even
lose respect for
you if you don't.

On the pages that follow, you will find tips for negotiating an offer effectively, as well as a section devoted to negotiating salary specifically. You can find more extensive and in-depth advice on these topics in *The Unofficial Guide to Earning What You Deserve* (Jason Rich, New York: Macmillan, 1999).

Principles of Savvy Negotiating

With the following guidelines, you'll be able to negotiate a favorable offer like a pro:

- Do your homework. As with an interview, a negotiation session involves building a case for yourself and your needs, as well as showing the employer what you bring to the table. To negotiate effectively, you need to prepare that case in advance by doing sufficient self-assessment and market research.

- Define your deal-points and breaking-points in advance. Know which issues are important to you (based on your priorities identification) and which ones are so critical that you would rather decline the offer than to have to concede them.

- Be yourself. Negotiating strategies usually fall somewhere on a spectrum from aggressive to cooperative in style. If you try to go to one extreme or the other in a way that doesn't fit your natural style, the negotiations will not only be difficult for you to pull off, but they are not as likely to work in your favor.

- Negotiate with a style that reflects the position, the employer, and the industry or profession. Adopt a more aggressive or more reserved approach as befitting the setting and the person with whom you are negotiating. In either case, however, never be rude or overbearing. Tact and consideration will take you far.

- Be fair. Skilled negotiators know that it's not about winning at the expense of the other parties involved but about coming to terms that are satisfying for both sides. So, don't play dirty or rough; doing so won't get you anywhere.

- Be truthful. Don't tell lies to win points. If you mislead the prospective employer about your salary history, qualifications, or anything else, you will most likely get caught in the lie and may have the offer retracted—or be fired if you're caught after being hired.

- Be flexible. Negotiations require that you give to get. You must be prepared to make concessions on some points to gain ground where it really matters to you.

- Negotiate more than salary. Keep in mind that you are discussing the terms of the offer as a whole. While the money factor may be important to you, the negotiation is a chance for you to shape an employment opportunity that will be satisfying to you in more ways than the impact on your bank account.

- Be resourceful in thinking of what you could get out of the negotiations. For example, if an employer cannot go up on your salary because the amount must be equal to that of your coworkers, think of ways you could be rewarded that would not be so obvious as to cause ill will among your colleagues. Could you get a couple extra days of vacation, a signing bonus, or some other perk?

- Don't let 'em see you sweat. Keep your cool, no matter how tough the negotiations get.

- Never be hesitant. The only way to make your case convincing is to do so in a persuasive, confident manner.

- If you receive another bonafide offer prior to— or while in negotiations with—one employer, play the offers off each other to see who can ultimately give you the best deal.

- As discussed in Chapter 12, "Interview Curve Balls," a useful way to overcome objections is to ask questions. This is particularly important in employment negotiations. For example, an employer might not want to let you work from home one day a week as a telecommuter because of a concern that the equipment you would need would cost the company too much money. If you didn't find out that reason, you might assume the objections are based on concerns about your ability to be productive at home or worries that too many other employees would want to do the same thing. By asking directly about the concern, you know how to address it and offer solutions rather than getting off on an irrelevant line of discussion.

- Be patient. Some employment negotiations take time. You might have to conclude a first conversation without agreement, then revisit the issue in a subsequent phone call or face-to-face meeting. Don't try to rush the process or you'll only do yourself a disservice.

- Be willing to hold out for what you deserve. While it is important to be flexible and let the other side save face occasionally, you do deserve to get an offer that is fair—or even more than fair. Walking away from an offer is a tried-and-true tactic that works. The employer realizes you mean business and sees that you must really think you deserve a better offer. Just be prepared, though, to lose out on the job if the terms you are refusing to accept actually are the employer's best and final offer.

Getting the Money and Benefits You Deserve

While all the negotiation tactics described previously apply to the issue of salary and other compensation, keep a few guidelines in mind when it comes to the money part of your negotiations:

- *Don't speak until spoken to.* Try not to speak first when it comes to discussing salary. Fortunately, most employers will tell you what the salary is at the time that they extend an offer. You are then expected to accept that salary or negotiate for more.

- *Redirect the conversation.* If an employer asks point blank what you are looking to make without stating a salary first, try to redirect the conversation by saying something like, "I think my salary requirements are in line with what is typical for positions like this. Why don't we look at the terms of the offer as a whole, then get into the specifics of the money?"

- *Talk in broad brush strokes.* If an employer won't let you brush off a question about salary and pushes for a specific figure, limit your reply to a general salary range with a statement like, "I'm looking for something in the 50s or 60s, but exactly where in that range depends on other aspects of the compensation, benefits, and nature of the position." Or, talk in terms of broad periods in your salary history, such as, "My annual compensation for the past few years

Watch Out!
If you get a signing bonus or relocation money, you may be liable for repayment of that sum if you leave the company soon after starting. While policies vary, a typical plan might be that you have to repay 100 percent if you leave before 3 months, 75 percent for 3–6 months, 50 percent for 6–9 months, and 25 percent after 9–12 months.

has ranged from $50,000 to $65,000." Doing so will keep you in the running with employers who can pay only $50,000, but it won't cut off your chances of getting $65,000 or more.

Unofficially...
If you're negotiating for a job in the private sector but your salary history looks low because you've worked in non-profit or government offices, make the discrepancy look less pronounced by explaining how the positions you held were comparable to higher-paying positions in the private sector but that they had lower salaries because of the type of organization in which you were employed.

■ *Know your figures.* Part of the homework you do for the negotiations must include a look into typical salaries for the type of position and employer in question. Through research and the input of knowledgeable people in your network, you should be able to get a sense of typical salary ranges and what amount you could command within that range. The salary data provided in Appendix D, "Important Statistics," may be helpful in this regard.

■ *Do the math.* Another important aspect of preparation is to determine in advance how various salaries play out in reality. For example, you might negotiate for $5,000 more per year only to find out that increment bumps you into a higher tax bracket. You also need to know how various incomes affect your daily life and personal budget. One job might offer $100 more of discretionary income a month than an offer with a lower salary, but it would require that you spend $75 more a month on gasoline, tolls, and parking because of the job's location. When you get into the thick of a negotiation, you may not have time to think through all the implications of various dollar amounts, so try to do so in advance.

■ *Look at the compensation holistically.* You must know how the entire pay plan works, not just what the annual salary or hourly wage is. Take into account any commissions, year-end bonuses, signing bonuses, relocation expenses, overtime policy, and schedule for performance reviews.

▪ *Don't leave the fringe benefits on the fringes.* Be aware of what a boon a good benefits package can be to your overall financial state. The money you save in medical bills or that you earn in pension plans and stock options can help you view that weekly or monthly paycheck in a new light. See the Benefits Checklist below for a thorough look at the extras a job might offer.

Bright Idea
If you're trying to get a higher salary than one you've ever earned, cite your previous salaries as aggregates of bonuses, commissions, and even the value of the benefits packages so that you're talking total annual income, not just base wages.

BENEFITS CHECKLIST

____ Medical insurance	____ Relocation expenses
____ Dental coverage	____ Tuition reimbursement
____ Optical coverage	
____ Life insurance	____ Company car
____ Short- and long-term disability insurance	____ Paid parking
	____ On-site daycare
____ Pension plan	____ Off-site child care subsidy
____ Paid vacation	
____ Federal or religious holiday closings	____ Health club membership
____ Floating holidays or personal days	____ Meals
____ Sick leave	____ Entertainment expense account
____ Maternity or parental leave policy	____ Corporate discounts (for sports events, theater, movies)
____ Profit sharing/ stock options	

Moneysaver
Look for hidden costs in an employer's benefits package. Some require that you contribute a portion of your pre-tax earnings to your health plan, life insurance, or other benefits, while others foot the entire bill for you.

Watch Out!
When negotiations come to a close and all parties make it clear that they accept the results, the case is closed. If you try to re-open negotiations after receiving written confirmation of your terms of employment, you will be seen as unprofessional and you could jeopardize the offer.

When your negotiations of compensation and other terms of the offer reach a satisfactory conclusion, you will most likely be ready to accept the job. Keep in mind, however, that you are still not obligated to accept the offer. If the terms are not favorable to you, or if you have simultaneously negotiated offers at more than one employer, then you may still have a tough decision ahead of you.

By the way, never mislead an employer by accepting an offer, then entering into negotiations, and then reneging on the offer because you were also in talks with another organization and received more favorable terms with that other employer. Before getting deep into negotiations, you should make it clear that you are not accepting the offer but are merely interested enough to try to work out a mutually satisfying agreement, and that your acceptance of the offer is contingent upon that successful conclusion to the negotiations.

Secrets of the Wisest Decision-Makers

Good decision-makers know that only they can make the right decision; no one else can do it for them. They also know, however, that they can't do it alone. A wise choice is based on input from others, through research and networking. They also know that the decision-making process must combine objective and subjective information. You collect all the data you need, but you also let your heart or your gut have a say in the matter. Good decision-makers also are methodical. They don't fly by the seat of their pants, but instead they follow a step-by-step process to get from indecision to decision. Let's look at those steps as well as some guiding principles for decision making.

Seven Steps to Making a Good Decision

1. Look for the magic answer. Yes, sometimes there really is one. Before you settle down for a long winter's night of decision making, prepared to agonize, hypothesize, and strategize, see if you already know the answer. Quickly but thoroughly run through what you know about the position and employer, then listen to your instincts and see if a clear answer emerges. In other words, don't make the process more difficult than it has to be.

2. Evaluate the quality of your information. Try to determine whether you have all the facts. Do you know everything you need to know about the offer? Can you go through that list of questions on the Job Acceptance Criteria Worksheet from earlier in this chapter and answer them all for the jobs you are considering? Is your data comprehensive and accurate?

3. Connect the dots. If there are gaps in your knowledge, as discovered in Step 2, do the necessary research to gather the information you need. Look to the Internet, the library, or the notes you took on research already conducted to find answers to your questions, or call the employer back to say that you need some more answers before you can make your decision.

4. Get outside opinions. Consult with advisors in your network—both formal ones such as mentors, career consultants, or headhunters, and informal ones such as friends and family—to put your choices in perspective and get input into your decision.

Moneysaver
If you want expert advice about your career but don't want to spend money on private sessions with a career counselor, visit some of the Web sites listed in Appendix C, "Recommended Reading." You can post questions on message boards and have the sites' resident experts offer solutions.

5. Do a systematic evaluation. Even if you're the type of person who prefers to listen to your heart rather than your head, you must do some sort of systematic—even quantitative—evaluation of your options. Get the pros and cons down on paper, and see what insights jump off the page at you. Read through your Job Evaluation Priorities form step by step, seeing how the job in questions holds up against your priorities. As long as you get the issues down on paper in some way, you'll make a better decision than if you try to make sense of the random thoughts floating around in your mind.

6. Adjust your priorities as needed. You'll recall from the earlier discussion of priorities that you might have to adjust the ratings or rankings of your priorities when considering them in the context of specific offers. Money may become more important when you're tempted with the big bucks, or location might become more important when you think about what a long commute would really mean to your daily life. At this step in the decision-making process, it is important to be flexible and to realize that your original take on your priorities might shift slightly now that reality is in the picture.

7. Listen to your instincts. Once you have completed a systematic evaluation of the options based on objective data, see how it all feels. Your heart or your gut—whichever way you prefer to label that subjective part of decision making—does deserve to have a say in the process. If an offer that looks good on paper doesn't feel right, you need to take a second look at the data and reconsider the job's suitability for you. As

long as you don't take the subjective approach too far and make a decision that is rash or haphazard, the heart and gut can be reliable sources for the right answer.

Principles to Guide You Through the Seven Steps

The steps listed previously describe the process, but every process has a set of dynamics that come with the package. These are the intangible aspects of the process—the things going on behind these scenes (usually in your mind)—that can trip you up if you're not aware of them. To ensure that you make a good decision, that the process is relatively painless, and that you can get past any barriers to a decision, keep the following guidelines in mind regarding decision-making dynamics:

- *Don't rush the process.* Good decisions take time. Don't expect yourself to come up with the perfect answer right away. Most people don't get to stop at the first step, but have to go on to Steps 2–7. Rarely must you give an employer an answer on the spot. On average, most employers will give you about a week to get back to them with your decision, though some might want an answer in a day or two. Occasionally, you can have a couple of weeks or more if there's no rush to fill the position. Just be sure to ask for as much time as you think you'll need—and as much as you can get without inconveniencing the prospective employer.

- *Do what you want to do, not what others want you to do.* Remember, this is your decision to make. You have to live with the consequences, so even though you should seek input from others, you must make a choice that you find comfortable, not one that is imposed upon you by someone else.

Timesaver
To avoid getting pressed for time when an employer expects an answer from you regarding a job offer, do as much advanced preparation as possible. Identify your priorities, ask a lot of questions, and get input from your network when you believe an offer is imminent.

- *Don't panic.* You can make a good decision only if you have a clear head. Even the most difficult choice has an answer. If you find yourself feeling overwhelmed or helpless, revisit the list of the seven steps to get you back on track, and seek emotional support from people who care about you.

- *Do be flexible.* Adjust your priorities as necessary, keeping in mind that you can't have them all satisfied. (If you do, then you really have found that proverbial perfect job!)

- *Do keep the big picture in mind.* You must consider how the decision will affect your life as a whole and the lives of people around you. Don't focus too narrowly on your immediate, short-term career goals.

- *Don't lose perspective.* No decision is permanent. Even though you want to make a careful one and obtain a job in which you can thrive for a reasonable period of time, you can reverse a bad job decision. While it may not be a particularly palatable thought, it is possible to quit a job you've taken in error. Cutting your losses is never anything to be ashamed of.

When the Best Decision is Not to Decide

One of the most overlooked aspects of evaluating a job offer is the issue of readiness to accept any offer, not just the one(s) you're considering. The focus is always on "Do I want Job A or Job B?", not on "Do I want any new job at all?" If you're unemployed and running out of money and patience, then, of course, you have to be ready to accept an offer and make the move. But, if you have the luxury of even a little bit of time and can wait until the right thing comes

Unofficially...
More often than you might think, employers are happy to welcome former employees back who resigned to take a new position only to find that the new job wasn't right for them. While you can't always count on it, your current employer might re-hire you if you discover that you should've stayed there after all.

along, then you might choose to decline all offers on the table if none feels right. What's going on when nothing feels right and all the decision-making techniques just don't get you any closer to an answer? Well, it may be the issue of readiness. Something that career counselors know but the general public doesn't is that readiness is a major issue in decision making. Donald Super, a major theorist and researcher throughout the latter half of the twentieth century, contributed much to our understanding of how people make career choices and how their careers develop. He introduced the concept of vocational maturity, which helps people understand whether they are in a position to make a good career decision.

Vocational maturity—AKA career maturity—has nothing to do with personal maturity or chronological age. It is a measure of how much you've done to prepare for a particular stage in your career. To be vocationally mature, you must know yourself and the world of work. You must thoroughly assess your talents, interests, values, preferred work environments, and goals. You need to conduct sufficient research to know what's out there in the world of jobs and employers. If you haven't done those things, you may need to stay where you are—as long as your job is reasonably tolerable—until you can take a step back to assess who you are, what you want, and where the best place is for you. Fortunately, that step need not take a long time, as career maturity can be acquired more quickly than personal maturity!

A second reason why the best decision may be to make no decision at all is that you might be experiencing too many changes in your life at once. In

Transitions: Making Sense of Life's Changes, William Bridges identifies several categories of changes that can have a profound impact on your life and mental state:

- Loss of relationships: the death of a loved one; the break-up of a relationship; divorce; children moving away from home; the loss of a friend over a disagreement or relocation.

- Changes in home life: getting married; having a child; experiencing changes in a spouse or companion (such as job change, retirement, or illness); moving into a new home, or remodeling or redecorating of an existing one; having a relative move in with you; getting a new roommate.

- Personal changes: health; sleeping patterns; diet; appearance; lifestyle.

- Financial changes: increase or decrease in income; a recent loan or mortgage; failed investments; new financial obligations; a new budget.

- Inner changes: spiritual awakening; religious conversion; psychological insight gained in therapy; new values; changed self-image.

If you are dealing with any of these events while also trying to make transitions in your career, you might feel overwhelmed and unable to approach your career decisions with a clear head and good judgment. In that case, the best plan may be to delay making any major decisions about your career until the other matters are settled. Of course, if unemployment or underemployment—or being unhappily employed—is the cause of one of the other problems (such as those in the financial or health areas), then you must take care of the job problem before the others can be resolved.

> **"**
> Few people stop to reflect on the radiating waves of change in their lives ...The big events—divorce, death, losing a job, and other obviously painful changes—are easy to spot. But others, like marriage, sudden success, and moving to your dream house, are forgotten because they are good events and therefore not supposed to lead to difficulty.
> —William Bridges, in *Transitions* (Addison-Wesley, 1980)
> **"**

Making the Move

When you accept an offer on mutually satisfying terms, it might feel like it's all over but the celebrating. While savoring the victory of a successful job hunt is something you certainly deserve to do, don't be too quick to relax just yet. You need to take care of a few other things to ensure a smooth transition.

Confirming the Offer

To avoid any potential disputes, it is important that you confirm the offer in writing. In many cases—particularly at organizations with well-organized human resources functions—you'll receive a confirmation letter or letter of agreement to approve and sign. A sample of such a document is provided in Appendix D, "Important Documents." This letter should state your position title, start date, and salary. It may also outline the terms of your probationary period and benefits package, and remind you that your offer is contingent upon satisfactory results of reference and background checks, if they weren't done already. No details of the document should come as a surprise to you, as the letter should reflect the results of your offer negotiations. Nevertheless, you must read the letter carefully and not feel shy about asking for clarification of any part of it.

    If your new employer does not have a policy of issuing written confirmations, you need to initiate the process yourself. Compose a letter including the same information but using phrases such as, "It is my understanding that..." or "As we agreed, I will..." The letter should be businesslike and to the point, but you can convey your enthusiasm for the position and express your appreciation for the offer.

Unofficially...
Don't assume you'll be signing an employment contract before starting a new job. The employment laws of some states, as well as the nature of many positions, dictate that you be hired at-will, meaning that you or the employer can terminate the arrangement at any time and are not bound by a contract.

Bright Idea
It is not essential, but it is a nice gesture, to send thank-you notes to everyone at the organization with whom you interviewed or interacted in some way (such as the hiring manager's assistant or the receptionist who took all your phone messages). It's nice to acknowledge their efforts and helps you start off on good terms in case you start working with them.

If multiple people were involved in the hiring decision, you should send copies of the letter to each person. The letter is typically addressed to the human resources representative who extended the formal offer and who handles the administrative aspects of your hiring and orientation. You then CC the hiring manager of the department in which you will work. (This is often your new boss.)

Managing How You Leave Your Job

If you'll be resigning from a current job to go to the new one, you shouldn't neglect the strategy needed to leave your job. When thinking about how they will leave a job, most people focus on how much notice to give and what to say in a resignation letter. There's more to it than that, however. You need to leave with an eye toward three matters:

- Leave your department and the organization as a whole in good shape. Don't leave projects and files in a mess. Don't have the attitude that it won't be your problem anymore so you don't have to worry about how you leave things. Try to tie up loose ends, and offer to come in during your off-hours or to be available by phone to your successor.

- Leave with your relationships intact and positive. Don't boast about the great salary or impressive title you're getting with the new job. Don't flaunt the fact that you're moving on or up. Be sensitive to the feelings of colleagues who might also want to leave but who aren't having any success with their searches. You should not leave people feeling like they are breathing your dust. Thank them for being good colleagues, and tell them what you've learned from them. Also be sure to write a cordial resignation letter. Leaving gracefully is not merely a nice thing to do—it's also smart. Your former co-workers and bosses might be valuable members of your network in the future.

- Leave with your future career development in mind. Go through your files and collect anything you can put in your portfolio (being careful not to take confidential, proprietary information with you). Also, while the job is still fresh in your mind, and while you have access to files or reports that you won't be taking with you, update your accomplishments log. Also ask for letters of recommendation from bosses, clients, or coworkers even though you presumably won't need them for a long time to come.

Getting Off to the Right Start

You'll recall from Chapter 1, "How Hiring Decisions are Made," and from the discussion of image in Chapter 6, "Presenting the Right Image," that having your act together is an important element of getting hired. It is also an important element of staying employed. Even the most seasoned professionals have a trial period when they begin a new job. In that trial period, they are being judged by people at the new place of work—and they, in turn, are judging the new job and organization. To make that honeymoon period go smoothly, take care of the following:

- Put some thought into the start date of your new position. If you have any say in the matter, and if you are not in an urgent need for money, try to wait a week or two before starting the new job. This period of time will give you a chance to decompress from your old job, or from your

Watch Out!
Be careful of promises you might make to recruit your old coworkers once you get to your new employer. While you might be able to have your friends follow you, don't make promises you can't keep.

job search, and will enable you to take care of the tasks suggested in the points that follow.

- Tie up all loose ends in your life. You don't need any distractions during the first several weeks on a new job. Your sole focus should be on the job, not the renovations in progress in your kitchen.

- Adjust your life accordingly. Make any necessary changes to your daily routine, and anticipate any bumps in the road. Plot out the route for a new commute, get used to a new sleep schedule, make sure your child care is reliable, or assemble an appropriate wardrobe to fit the new position or environment.

- Update members of your network. Call or write anyone who should be apprised of—or would find it interesting to know—where you have ended up. It is particularly important that you notify those who helped with your search. This includes personal contacts, such as the friends, family, and acquaintances who granted you job interviews, exploratory interviews, or who put you in touch with other people. Also include recruiters at employment agencies or search firms who helped you and any career counselors, or job search coaches you worked with. Most people are genuinely interested in knowing where you end up. And, you might need their help in the future, so it is important to maintain the relationships.

- Keep your expectations realistic, and be patient. Be aware that there will be a learning curve on your new job. You might be overwhelmed at first, or even bored. You may not receive enough training, or you might be smothered by too much supervision. It is normal to have mixed feelings about a new job until you have a chance to settle in. Don't make any final judgments until at least a few months have gone by.

Just the Facts

- The key to evaluating a job offer is to identify your priorities so that you know how the job can satisfy your interests and help you reach your goals.

- To make a good decision about a job, you need have a clear picture of what it would entail, and you should look for red flags indicating potential problem areas.

- Good decisions are based on a combination of objective and subjective analysis.

- To be sure you're getting a fair deal when it comes to salary and other compensation, conduct thorough research.

- Always confirm a job offer in writing before starting.

- Manage how you leave your old job as strategically as you managed how you got the new one.

Glossary

Aptitude An ability to acquire a particular proficiency or to develop a particular skill; implies an innate talent or strength as opposed to a tangible skill learned through training or experience.

Avocational Adjective describing all activities, interests, responsibilities, or roles not related to one's job or career; personal, as opposed to professional or vocational in nature.

Boolean logic A system that narrows a keyword search conducted on the Internet. Boolean logic involves connecting words with "and" or "or" to specify more narrowly the information one is seeking. For example, "Microsoft and litigation" pulls up all references that include both those subjects, while keyword "Microsoft" brings up *all* references to that company, whether related to lawsuits or not.

Cognitive psychologist A psychologist concerned with thought processes, such as attitude and opinion formation, learning, information processing, and memory.

Employment agency A business that fills job vacancies for employers by recruiting and screening applicants. Employment agencies typically place applicants for clerical, administrative, entry-level, and lower- to mid-level management; executive search firms place higher-level employees at higher salaries. (See *executive recruiter.*) Some employment agencies specialize in particular industries, while others handle jobs in a variety of industries.

Executive recruiter An executive recruiter works in an executive search firm, identifying and screening candidates for mid-level to high-level positions with employers, who are the search firm's clients. Some executive search firms have minimum cut-offs for the salaries that candidates must be, or have been, earning. For example, they might work only with candidates earning $50,000 per year or higher, or $100,000 or higher. Executive recruiters typically place managers or candidates with highly specialized skills and expertise.

Exempt An employment classification used in determining salary, benefits, and rules and policies applicable to an employee. Exempt employees are generally at the management or non-clerical level, while non-exempt are clerical and administrative staff.

Group interview An interview in which one or more representatives of the prospective employer interviews more than one candidate simultaneously.

Headhunter Slang for an executive recruiter or employment agent.

Hiring authority For the purposes of this book, this is a catch-all term for any person or persons within an organization involved in the decision-making process related to hiring employees for that organization.

Hiring manager This is a term commonly used among human resources professionals and employment specialists to signify the person in a given department or area of an organization who is involved with interviewing and hiring people for that area. The term usually refers to someone not in the human resources department. For example, if there is a job vacancy in a company's marketing department, the hiring manager might be the vice president of marketing, while the recruiter (see *recruiter*) would refer to the human resources representative also involved in recruiting and interviewing applicants for that position.

In-house   Within an organization or corporation, as in, "We administer our payroll in-house rather than having an outside bookkeeping firm handle it."

Not-for-profit   An alternative to "non-profit"; a term coined in the 1990s to more accurately reflect the status of non-private, non-governmental organizations that may show a profit in their earnings but are not in business for the purpose of making a profit.

Outsource   The practice of contracting with outside organizations to provide services, products, or personnel rather than handling those matters in-house.

Panel interview   An interview in which one or more candidates is interviewed by more than one representative of the prospective employer.

Prospective employer   For the purposes of this book, this refers in most cases to the overall organization in which someone is seeking employment. In some contexts, it may refer to the individual person responsible for interviewing and hiring.

Recruiter   For the purposes of this book, this refers to anyone in the human resources department of an organization who is responsible for identifying, interviewing, and hiring new employees. In some contexts, *recruiter* may refer to someone in an employment agency or search firm.

Sector   The labor market in the United States is typically divided into three major sectors: private, which includes corporations and all for-profit businesses; not-for-profit, which includes charitable, educational, and other non-corporate organizations; and government, which includes all local, state, and federal governmental offices and agencies.

Social psychologist   Specialists who study human interaction, whether in pairs, groups, or with society-at-large.

Trait   A personality characteristic evident in everyday behavior.

Transferable skills   Skills that are not specific to any one type of job, organization, or industry but that may be of value to a variety of prospective employers; skills that enable individuals to transfer between jobs, departments, organizations, or career fields.

Vendor   A business or individual that supplies products or services to another business.

World view   A person's assumptions, opinions, attitudes, and understanding of the world based on his or her culture, including race, ethnicity, geographic upbringing or location, work experiences, educational background, gender, sexual orientation, and more.

Resource Directory

Useful Organizations

American Management Association
135 West 50th Street
New York, NY 10020
212-586-8100
www.ama.org

American Society for Training and Development
1640 King Street, Box 1443
Alexandria, VA 22313
703-683-8100
www.astd.org

Association of Image Consultants International
1000 Connecticut Avenue NW, Suite 9
Washington, D.C. 20036
800-383-8831

Association of Professional Writing Consultants
3924 South Troost
Tulsa, OK 74105
918-743-4793

377

Bureau of Labor Statistics
Division of Information Services
2 Massachusetts Avenue, N.E., Room 2860
Washington, D.C. 20212
202-606-5886
http://stats.bls.gov

Career Planning and Adult Development Network
4965 Sierra Road
San Jose, CA 95132
408-559-4946
www.careertrainer.com
(A network representative can refer you to a career
counselor or a job search coach in your geographic
area.)

Employment Management Association
4101 Lake Boone Trail, Suite 201
Raleigh, NC 27607
919-787-6010

Five O'Clock Club
300 East 40th Street, #6L
New York, NY 10016
212-286-4500
(A nationwide job search coaching and networking
group)

Forty Plus Club
15 Park Row
New York, NY 10038
212-233-6086

International Association of Career Management
Professionals
P.O. Box 1484
Pacifica, CA 94044
650-359-6911
www.iacmp.org

International Personnel Management Association
1617 Duke Street
Alexandria, VA 22314
703-549-7100
www.ipma-hr.org

Job Accommodation Network
P.O. Box 6123
809 Allen Hall
Morgantown, WV 26505
800-526-7234
(A resource for job seekers with disabilities)

National Association for Female Executives
135 West 50th Street
New York, NY 10019
212-445-6235
www.nafe.com

President's Committee on Employment of People
with Disabilities
1331 F Street NW
Washington, D.C. 20004
202-376-6200

Society for Human Resource Management
606 North Washington Street
Alexandria, VA 22314
703-548-3440
www.shrm.org

Relevant Web Sites

The following Web sites are valuable sources of information on career planning and employment. Some are full-service sites that offer such resources as: advice on career decisions and job hunting; networking opportunities through message boards and chat sessions; research aids such as company profiles and links to other sites; job listings; and resume

posting services. Other sites focus solely on employment, listing job openings, or posting your resume
for prospective employers to browse. The final category of Web sites listed here includes those that
human resources professionals frequent. Visiting
these sites can help you get the inside scoop on hiring practices.

Comprehensive Career Sites

About Work
www.aboutwork.com

Career Action Center
www.careeraction.org

Career Center for Workforce Diversity
www.eop.com
(for minorities, women, and people with
disabilities)

Career Crafting
www.careercraft.com
(for people making career transitions)

Career **Magazine**
www.careermag.com

Career Paradise—Colossal List of Career Links
www.service.emory.edu./CAREER/Main/
Links.html

Career Toolbox
www.careertoolbox.com

CareerWeb
www.cweb.com

The Monster Board
www.monster.com

National Association of Colleges and Employers
www.jobweb.org

O*Net: The Occupational Information Network
www.doleta.gov/programs/onet

Riley Guide
www.dbm.com/jobguide/

Student Center
www.studentcenter.com

Sites Where You Can Post Your Resume and/or Access Job Listings

Be aware that some of these sites overlap with the previous category in that they provide job search or career management advice and networking opportunities along with employment services. Their emphasis, however, is on the latter.

America's Employers Resume Bank
www.americasemployers.com//resume.html

America's Job Bank
www.ajb.dni.us

Career Mosaic
www.careermosaic.com

CareerPath
www.careerpath.com

E-Span
www.joboptions.com

Exec.U.Net
www.execunet.com

HeadHunter.Net
www.headhunter.net/

Internet Career Connection
iccweb.com/employ.html

JobBank USA
www.jobbankusa.com/

JOBTRAK
www.jobtrak.com
(Accessible only to students and alumni of select colleges and universities)

The Monster Board
www.monster.com

Online Career Center
www.occ.com

Shawn's Internet Resume Center
www.inpursuit.com/sirc

Yahoo Classifieds
http://classifieds.yahoo.com/employment.html

Human Resources Sites

Brian Weis Recruiter's Network—Resources for Internet Recruiting
www.recruitersnetwork.com

HR **Magazine**
www.shrm.org/hrmagazine

HR Management Resources on the Internet
www.nbs.ntu.ac.uk/staff/lyerj/hrm.link.htm

HR Professionals Gateway to the Internet
www.telport.com/~erwilson

HRWorld
www.hrworld.com

Workforce Online
www.workforceonline.com

Recommended Reading

The process of interviewing takes place within the broader context of your overall career planning and job search, so included in this appendix are books that I highly recommend on such topics as: assessing your skills, personality, interests, and values; choosing a career direction; changing career fields; writing resumes and cover letters; assembling a portfolio; and networking.

In addition, interviewing requires that you be effective in many areas tangentially related to career planning and job search, such as business etiquette, image, and communication. I have only touched on such subjects in this book because a full treatment of them is beyond the scope of this work, and, frankly, beyond the scope of my expertise. You should read more about how to dress for an interview from the image and fashion experts, how to mind your manners from such etiquette notables as Letitia Baldrige, and how to speak effectively from communication gurus.

You will also find here books and directories that can help you research organizations, industries, and occupations—as well as learn about trends in the world of work to understand the employer's perspectives. The titles in the section entitled "Biographies and Corporate Profiles" will give you insight into a sampling of professions and industries, as these books are about leaders or leading organizations in various fields. I've also included books that human resources and recruiting professionals read to give you a glimpse into how they learn to conduct interviews and make hiring decisions.

Most publications in this reading list can easily be found in bookstores and libraries. I have also included selected newsletters, magazines, and other useful periodicals. Please note that many of the business directories listed in the section on researching organizations and industries are not publications you would normally buy (unless you run a library!). They are expensive reference materials that are most easily used in a library or online.

The categories of publications provided in this appendix, and the order in which you'll find them, are as follows:

- Career planning
- World of work trends
- Researching occupations
- Networking
- Biographies and corporate profiles
- Researching organizations and industries
- Professional associations
- Job search
- Negotiation
- Internet

- Image and attire
- Business etiquette
- Personality
- Oral communication
- Cross-cultural communication
- Written communication
- Books recruiters read
- Employment-related periodicals

Career Planning

Boldt, Laurence. *Zen and the Art of Making a Living.* New York: Penguin USA, 1993.

Eikleberry, Carol, and Richard Nelson Bolles. *The Career Guide for Creative and Unconventional People.* Berkeley, CA: Ten Speed Press, 1995.

Kanchier, Carole. *Dare to Change Your Job and Your Life.* Indianapolis, IN: JIST, 1995.

Kissane, Sharon F. *Career Success for People with Physical Disabilities.* Lincolnwood, IL: VGM Career Horizons, 1996.

Krannich, Ronald L., and Caryl Rae Krannich. *Discover the Best Jobs for You.* Manassas, VA: Impact Publications, 1997.

Reinhold, Barbara. *Toxic Work: How to Overcome Stress, Overload, and Burnout and Revitalize Your Career.* New York: Plume, 1997.

Sher, Barbara. *I Could Do Anything If I Only Knew What it Was.* New York: Bantam Doubleday Dell, 1994.

———. *Wishcraft: How to Get What You Really Want.* New York: Ballantine Books, 1986.

Tieger, Paul, and Barbara Barron-Tieger. *Do What You Are.* New York: Little, Brown, 1995.

World of Work Trends

Abrahamson, Vickie, Mary Meehan, and Larry
    Samuel. *The Future Ain't What it Used to Be: The
    40 Cultural Trends Transforming Your Job, Your
    Life, Your World.* New York: Riverhead Books,
    1998.

Bridges, William. *Job Shift: How to Prosper in a
    Workplace Without Jobs.* New York: Addison-
    Wesley, 1994.

Lareau, William. *Dancing with the Dinosaur: Learning
    to Live in the Corporate Jungle.* Winchester, NH:
    Winchester Press, 1997.

Hakim, Cliff. *We Are All Self-Employed.* San Francisco:
    Berret-Koehler, 1995.

Hall, Douglas T. and Associates. *The Career is Dead:
    Long Live the Career.* San Francisco: Jossey-Bass,
    1996.

Hesselbein, Frances, Marshall Goldsmith, and
    Richard Beckhard (Eds.). *The Organization of
    the Future* (Drucker Foundation Future
    Series). San Francisco: Jossey-Bass, 1997.

Howard, Ann. *The Changing Nature of Work.* San
    Francisco: Jossey-Bass, 1995.

Kotter, John, and James Heskett. *Corporate Culture
    and Performance.* New York: Free Press, 1992.

Kotter, John. *Leading Change.* Boston: Harvard
    Business School Press, 1996.

Kurtzman, Joel. *Thought Leaders: Insights on the
    Future of Business.* San Francisco: Jossey-Bass,
    1998.

Labovitz, George, and Victor Rosansky. *The Power of
    Alignment: How Great Companies Stay Centered
    and Accomplish Extraordinary Things.* New York:
    John Wiley & Sons, 1997.

Rifkin, Jeremy. *The End of Work*. New York: Tarcher/Putnam, 1995.

Rosenbluth, Hal. *Good Company: Caring as Fiercely as You Compete*. New York: Addison-Wesley, 1998.

Researching Occupations

Colvin, Donna, and Ralph Nader. *Good Works: A Guide to Careers in Social Change*. New York: Barricade Books, 1994.

Farr, J. Michael, and LaVerne Ludden. *Best Jobs for the 21st Century*. Indianapolis, IN: JIST, 1999.

Field, Shelly. *100 Best Careers for the 21st Century*. New York: Arco, 1996.

Kleiman, Carol. *100 Best Jobs for the 1990s & Beyond*. Chicago: Dearborn Trade, 1992.

Krannich, Ronald and Caryl Krannich. *Best Jobs for the 1990s and into the 21st Century*. Manassas Park, VA: Impact Publications, 1993.

Petras, Kathryn. *Jobs '98*. New York: Fireside/Simon & Schuster, 1997.

U.S. Department of Labor. *Occupational Outlook Handbook 1998-99*. Lincolnwood, IL: VGM Career Horizons, 1998.

Wright, John W. *The American Almanac of Jobs and Salaries 1997-98*. New York: Avon Books, 1996.

Yate, Martin. *Career Smarts: Jobs with a Future*. New York: Ballantine Books, 1997.

The Top 100: The Fastest Growing Careers for the 21st Century. Chicago: Ferguson Publishing, 1997.

VGM's Career Encyclopedia (4th edition). Lincolnwood, IL: VGM Career Horizons, 1997.

Biographies and Corporate Profiles

Bradlee, Benjamin C. *A Good Life: Newspapering and Other Adventures.* New York: Simon & Schuster, 1995.

Chernow, Ron. *The House of Morgan: An American Dynasty and the Rise of Modern Finance.* New York: Simon & Schuster, 1990.

Cohen, Ben, and Jerry Greenfield. *Ben & Jerry's Double Dip: How to Run a Values-Led Business and Make Money Too.* New York: Fireside/Simon & Schuster, 1998.

Cronkite, Walter. *A Reporter's Life.* New York: Ballantine Books, 1997.

DeGeorge, Gail. *The Making of a Blockbuster: How Wayne Huizenga Built a Sports and Entertainment Empire From Trash, Grit, and Videotape.* New York: John Wiley & Sons, 1996.

Drucker, Peter. *Peter F. Drucker: Adventures of a Bystander.* New York: John Wiley & Sons, 1978.

Graves, Earl. *How to Succeed in Business Without Being White.* New York: Harper Business, 1998.

Heilbrun, Carolyn. *The Education of a Woman: The Life of Gloria Steinem.* Ballantine Books, 1996.

Lowenstein, Roger. *Buffett: The Making of an American Capitalist.* New York: Doubleday, 1995.

Ogilvy, David. *Ogilvy on Advertising.* New York: Random House, 1987.

Slater, Robert. *Ovitz: The Inside Story of Hollywood's Most Controversial Power Broker.* New York: McGraw-Hill, 1997.

Tye, Larry. *The Father of Spin: Edward L. Bernays and the Birth of Public Relations.* New York: Crown Publishers, 1998.

Wallace, James. *Overdrive: Bill Gates and the Race to Control Cyberspace.* New York: John Wiley & Sons, 1998.

Walton, Sam, with John Huey. *Sam Walton, Made in America: My Story.* New York: Bantam Books, 1993.

Researching Organizations and Industries

Corptech (Eds.). *Hidden Job Market: A Guide to America's 2000 Little-Known Fastest Growing High-Tech Companies.* Princeton, NJ: Petersons, 1997.

Farr, J. Michael. *Career Guide to America's Top Industries.* Indianapolis, IN: JIST, 1995.

Hamilton, Leslie. *100 Best Nonprofits to Work For.* New York: Arco, 1998.

Hoover's Directory of Human Resources Executives 1996. Austin, TX: Hoover's Inc., 1995.

Hoover's Guide to Computer Companies (2nd ed.). Austin, TX: Hoover's Inc., 1997.

Hoover's Handbook of American Businesses. Austin, TX: Hoover's Inc., 1997.

Hoover's Handbook of Emerging Companies. Austin, TX: Hoover's Inc., 1998.

Hoover's Handbooks (Ed.). *Fortune Guide to the 500 Largest U.S. Corporations.* New York: Warner Books, 1996.

Hoover's Masterlist of Major U.S. Companies 1997-98. Austin, TX: Hoover's Inc., 1997.

Jankowski, Katherine. *The Job Seeker's Guide to Socially Responsible Companies.* Detroit: Gale Research, 1994.

Levering, Robert, and Milton Moskowitz. *The 100 Best Companies to Work for in America.* New York: Penguin Books, 1994.

Mickens, Ed. *The 100 Best Companies for Gay Men and Lesbians.* New York: Pocket Books Simon & Schuster, 1994.

National Directory of Minority-Owned Business Firms (9th ed.). Business Research Services, 1998.

National Directory of Women-Owned Business Firms (8th ed.). Business Research Services, 1996.

Owners and Officers of Private Companies. Detroit: Gale Research, 1995.

Plunkett, Jack W. *The Almanac of American Employers 1998-99.* Galveston, TX: Plunkett Research, Ltd., 1998.

The Directory of Management Consultants 1997-98 (8th ed.). Fitzwilliam, NH: Kennedy Information, 1997.

The Job Bank Series (titles for most major U.S. cities). Holbrook, MA: Adams Media (annual).

Thomas Register of American Manufacturers. New York: Thomas Register, (annual).

Standard & Poor's Register of Corporations, Directors, and Executives. New York: Standard & Poor's, 1998.

Ward's Business Directory of U.S. Private and Public Companies. Detroit: Gale Research, 1998.

Networking

Backus, K., and Furtaw, J.C. (Eds.). *Asian American Information Directory* (annual). Detroit: Gale Research.

Big Book of Minority Opportunities. Chicago: Ferguson, 1997.

Big Book of Opportunities for Women. Chicago: Ferguson, 1997.

Bunkley, Crawford. *The African-American Network: Get Connected to More than 5,000 Prominent People and Organizations in the African-American Community.* New York: Plume, 1996.

Burg, Bob. *Endless Referrals: Network Your Everyday Contacts into Sales.* New York: McGraw-Hill, 1993.

Fraser, George. *Success Runs in Our Race: The Complete Guide to Effective Networking in the African-American Community.* New York: William Morrow & Co., 1994.

Tullier, Michelle. *Networking for Everyone: Connecting with People for Career and Job Success.* Indianapolis, IN: JIST, 1998.

Professional Associations

Encyclopedia of Associations (annual). Detroit, MI: Gale Research.

NTPA: National Trade and Professional Association of the United States (annual). Washington, D.C.: Columbia Books.

SRA: State and Regional Associations (annual). Washington, D.C.: Columbia Books.

Job Search

Betrus, Michael. *Guide to Executive Recruiters.* New York: McGraw-Hill, 1997.

Bolles, Richard. *What Color is Your Parachute?* Berkeley, CA: Ten Speed Press, (annual).

Dorio, Marc. *The Complete Idiot's Guide to Getting the Job You Want.* New York, NY: Alpha/ Macmillan, 1995.

Elkort, Martin. *Getting from Fired to Hired: Bounce Back from Losing Your Job and Get Your Career Back on Track.* New York: Arco, 1997.

Garrison-Jenn, Nancy. *The Global 200 Executive Recruiters.* San Francisco: Jossey-Bass, 1998.

Haft, Timothy. *Trashproof Resumes.* New York: The Princeton Review/Random House, 1995.

Kennedy, James. *Directory of Executive Recruiters* (27th ed.). Fitzwilliam, NH: Kennedy Information, 1997.

Kimeldorf, Martin. *Portfolio Power.* Princeton, NJ: Peterson's, 1997.

Krannich, Ronald. *Change Your Job, Change Your Life.* Manassas, VA: Impact Publications, 1995.

Lauber, Daniel. *Government Job Finder 1997-2000.* River Forest, IL: Planning/Communications, 1997.

Lauber, Daniel. *Professional's Job Finder 1997-2000.* River Forest, IL: Planning/Communications, 1997.

Noble, David. *Gallery of Best Resumes.* Indianapolis, IN: JIST, 1994.

Snell, Alice. *The Directory of Executive Temporary Placement Firms* (8th ed.). Fitzwilliam, NH: Kennedy Information, 1995.

Tullier, Michelle, Tim Haft, Margaret Heenehan, and Marci Taub. *Job Smart.* New York: The Princeton Review/Random House, 1997.

Wendleton, Kate. *Targeting the Job You Want.* New York: Five O'Clock Books, 1997.

Yate, Martin. *Cover Letters that Knock 'em Dead* (3rd ed.). Holbrook, MA: Adams Media, 1997.

Yate, Martin. *Knock 'em Dead: The Ultimate Job-Seeker's Handbook*. Holbrook, MA: Adams Media, 1998.

Yate, Martin. *Resumes that Knock 'em Dead* (3rd ed.). Holbrook, MA: Adams Media, 1997.

Negotiation

Krannich, Ronald, and Caryl Rae Krannich. *Dynamite Salary Negotiations*. Manassas Park, VA: Impact Publications, 1997.

Miller, Lee. *Get More Money On Your Next Job*. New York: McGraw-Hill, 1997.

Fisher, Roger, and William Ury. *Getting to Yes: Negotiating Agreement Without Giving In*. New York: Houghton-Mifflin, 1992.

Mira, Thomas K. *Negotiate Smart*. New York: Princeton Review, 1995.

Farr, Michael. *The Quick Interview & Salary Negotiation Book*. Indianapolis, IN: JIST, 1995.

Internet

Battle, Stafford, and Rey Harris. *The African-American Resource Guide to the Internet & Online Services*. New York: Computing McGraw-Hill, 1996.

Butler, John A. *Cybersearch: Research Techniques in the Electronic Age*. New York: Penguin, 1998.

Crispin, Gerry, and Mark Mehler. *CAREERXROADS*. Kendall Park, NJ: MMC Group, 1997.

Dixon, Pam and Sylvia Tierston. *Be Your Own Headhunter Online*. New York: Random House, 1995.

Gagnon, Eric. *What's on the Internet: The Definitive Guide to the Internet User Newsgroups* (published twice yearly). Berkeley, CA: Peachpit Press/Internet Media.

Gagnon, Eric. *What's on the Web?* (published twice yearly). Berkeley, CA: Peachpit Press/Internet Media.

Internet and World Wide Web Simplified (2nd ed.). Foster City, CA: IDG Books, 1997.

Jandt, Fred, and Mary Nemnich. *Using the Internet and the World Wide Web in Your Job Search.* 1996.

Kennedy, Angus J. *The Internet and the World Wide Web: The Rough Guide.* New York: Rough Guides, 1998.

Kent, Peter. *The Complete Idiot's Guide to the Internet* (5th ed.). New York: Alpha/Macmillan, 1998.

Kiesler, Sara. *Culture of the Internet.* Mahwah, NJ: Lawrence Erlbaum Associates, 1997.

McGuire, Mary, Linda Stilborne, Melinda McAdams, and Laurel Hyatt. *The Internet Handbook for Writers, Researchers, and Journalists.* New York: The Guilford Press, 1997.

Pack, Ellen. *Women's Wire Web Directory.* Indianapolis, IN: Lycos Press/Que Corp., 1997.

Riley, Margaret. *Guide to Internet Job Searching: 1998-99.* Lincolnwood, IL: VGM Career Horizons, 1998.

Wolff, Michael. *netjobs.* New York: Michael Wolff & Co., 1997.

World Wide Web Yellow Pages (annual). Indianapolis, IN: New Riders Publishing/Que Corp.

Image & Attire

Ailes, Roger. *Getting What You Want by Being Who You Are: You Are the Message.* New York: Doubleday, 1995.

Begoun, Paula. *Blue Eyeshadow Should Absolutely Be Illegal.* Seattle, WA: Beginning Press, 1994.

Begoun, Paula. *The Beauty Bible.* Seattle, WA: Beginning Press, 1997.

Bixler, Susan, and Nancy Nix-Ric. *The New Professional Image: From Corporate Casual to the Ultimate Power Look.* Holbrook, MA: Adams Media, 1997.

Crawford, Cindy. *Cindy Crawford's Basic Face: A Makeup Workbook.* New York: Broadway Books, 1996.

Grow, Kim Johnson. *Work Clothes: Casual Dress for Serious Work.* New York: Knopf, 1996.

Hartman, Tori. *Fabulous You: Unlock Your Perfect Personal Style.* New York: Berkley Books, 1995.

Irons, Diane. *The World's Best Kept Beauty Secrets.* Naperville, IL: Sourcebooks, 1997.

Jackson, Carole. *Color for Men.* New York: Ballantine, 1984.

Karpinski, Kenneth. *Mistakes Men Make that Women Hate: 101 Image Tips for Men.* Manassas Park, VA: Impact Publications, 1994.

Lavington, Camille. *You've Only Got Three Seconds: How to Make the Right Impression in Your Business and Social Life.* New York: Doubleday, 1997.

Molloy, John T. *John T. Molloy's New Dress for Success.* New York: Warner Books, 1995.

Molloy, John T. *The New Women's Dress for Success.* New York: Warner Books, 1997.

Nicholson, Joanna. *110 Mistakes Working Women Make and How to Avoid Them: Dressing Smart in the 90s.* Manassas Park, VA: Impact Publications, 1994.

Spillane, Mary, and Christine Sherlock. *Color Me Beautiful's Looking Your Best: Color, Makeup and Style.* Lanham, MD: Madison Books, 1995.

Walker, Morton. *The Power of Color.* Garden City Park, NY: Avery Publishing Group, 1991.

Weber, Mark. *Dress Casually for Success … For Men.* New York: McGraw-Hill, 1997.

Business Etiquette

Baldrige, Letitia. *Letitia Baldrige's New Complete Guide to Executive Manners.* New York: Scribner, 1993.

Craig, Elizabeth, and Betty Craig. *Don't Slurp Your Soup: A Basic Guide to Business Etiquette.* St. Paul, MN: Brighton Publications, 1996.

Fountain, Elizabeth Haas. *The Polished Professional.* Hawthorne, NJ: Career Press, 1994.

Klinkenberg, Hilka. *At Ease Professionally: An Etiquette Guide for the Business Arena.* Chicago: Bonus Books, 1992.

Pachter, Barbara, Marjorie Broody, and Betsy Anderson. *Complete Business Etiquette Handbook.* Englewood Cliffs, NJ: Prentice Hall, 1994.

Sabath, Anne Marie. *Business Etiquette: 101 Ways to Conduct Business with Charm and Savvy.* Holbrook, MA: Adams Media, 1993.

Stewart, Marjabelle Young, and Marian Faux. *Executive Etiquette in the Workplace.* New York: St. Martin's Press, 1994.

Personality

Berent, Jonathan, and Amy Lemley. *Beyond Shyness: How to Conquer Social Anxieties.* New York: Fireside/Simon & Schuster, 1994.

Kroeger, Otto, and Janet Thuesen. *Type Talk at Work.* New York: Dell Publishing, 1993.

Myers, Isabel Briggs, and Peter Myers. *Gifts Differing.* Palo Alto, CA: Consulting Psychologists Press, 1995.

Schneier, Franklin, and Lawrence Welkowitz. *The Hidden Face of Shyness: Understanding and Overcoming Social Anxiety.* New York: Avon Books, 1996.

Tieger, Paul, and Barbara Barron-Tieger. *Do What You Are.* New York: Little, Brown, 1995.

Oral Communication

Alessandra, Anthony, and Phillip Hunsaker. *Communicating at Work.* New York: Fireside/Simon & Schuster, 1993.

Axtell, Roger, and Mike Fornwald. *Do's and Taboos of Public Speaking: How to Get Those Butterflies Flying in Formation.* New York: John Wiley & Sons, 1992.

Bodin, Madeline. *Using the Telephone More Effectively* (Barrons Business Success Series). Hauppage, NY: Barrons Educational Series, 1997.

Booher, Dianna. *How to Say It Right the First Time.* New York: McGraw-Hill, 1994.

Friedman, Nancy. *Telephone Skills from A to Z.* Menlo Park, CA: Crisp Publications, 1995.

Fulfer, Mac. *Amazing Face Reading: an Illustrated Encyclopedia for Reading Faces.* Ft. Worth, TX: Creative Alternatives 1997

Genua, Robert. *Managing Your Mouth: An Owner's Manual for Your Most Important Business Asset.* New York: AMACOM, 1993.

Griffin, Jack. *How to Say it at Work: Putting Yourself Across with Power Words, Phrases, Body Language and Communication Secrets.* Englewood Cliffs, NJ: Prentice Hall, 1998.

Griffin, Jack. *How to Say it Best: Choice Words, Phrases, and Model Speeches for Every Occasion.* Englewood Cliffs, NJ: Prentice Hall, 1994.

Heyman, Richard. *Why Didn't You Say That in the First Place? How to Be Understood at Work.* San Francisco: Jossey-Bass, 1994.

Kalish, Karen. *How to Give a Terrific Presentation.* New York: AMACOM, 1997.

McCallister, Linda. *I Wish I'd Said That! How to Talk Your Way Out of Trouble and into Success.* New York: John Wiley & Sons, 1994.

Mira, Thomas K. *Speak Smart: The Art of Public Speaking* (Smart Series). New York: Princeton Review, 1997.

O'Connor, Regis. *High Impact Public Speaking for Business and the Professions.* Lincolnwood, IL: NTC Publishing Group, 1997.

Qubein, Nido. *How to Be a Great Communicator.* New York: John Wiley & Sons, 1997.

Roane, Susan. *What Do I Say Next? Talking Your Way to Business and Social Success.* New York: Warner Books, 1997.

Tannen, Deborah. *That's Not What I Meant! How Conversational Style Makes or Breaks Your Relations with Others.* New York: Ballantine Books, 1992.

Toogood, Granville N. *The Articulate Executive: Learn to Look, Act and Sound Like a Leader.* New York: McGraw-Hill, 1997.

Weiss, Donald. *Why Didn't I Say That?!: What to Say and How to Say it in Tough Situations on the Job.* New York: AMACOM, 1996.

Young, Lailan, and Waters, Rod. *The Naked Face: The Essential Guide to Reading Faces.* New York: St. Martin's Press, 1994.

Zebrowitz, Leslie. *Reading Faces: Window to the Soul?* New York: Harper Collins, 1997.

Cross-Cultural Communication

Axtell, Roger. *Do's and Taboos Around the World.* New York: John Wiley & Sons, 1993.

Axtell, Roger. *Do's and Taboos Around the World for Women in Business.* New York: John Wiley & Sons, 1997.

Axtell, Roger. *Gestures: The Do's and Taboos of Body Language Around the World.* New York: John Wiley & Sons, 1998.

Kenna, Peggy, and Sondra Lacy. *Lincolnwood International Business Culture Series.* Lincolnwood, IL: NTC Publishing Group, 1994. (A series with titles such as *Business France: A Practical Guide to Understanding Business Culture, Business Mexico ..., Business Taiwan ...,* and many others)

Lewis, Richard. *When Cultures Collide: Managing Successfully Across Cultures.* Nicholas Brealey Publishing, 1996.

Morrison, Terri. *Kiss, Bow, or Shake Hands: How to Do Business in Sixty Countries.* Holbrook, MA: Bob Adams, 1994.

Passport to the World Series. World Trade Press, 1997.
(A series with titles such as *Passport China:
Your Pocket Guide to Chinese Business Customs
and Etiquette* [1996], *Passport India* ...[1996],
Passport Japan ...[1996], and many more)

Yamada, Haru. *Different Games, Different Rules: Why
Americans and Japanese Misunderstand Each
Other.* New York: Oxford University Press,
1997.

Written Communication

Bailey, Edward P. *The Plain English Approach to
Business Writing.* New York: Oxford University
Press, 1997.

Benjamin, Susan. *Words at Work: Business Writing in
Half the Time with Twice the Power.* Reading,
MA: Addison-Wesley, 1997.

Bozek, Phillip. *50 One-Minute Tips to Better
Communication: A Wealth of Business
Communication Ideas.* Menlo Park, CA: Crisp
Publications, 1997.

Brock, Susan. *Better Business Writing: Techniques for
Improving Correspondence.* Menlo Park, CA:
Crisp Publications, 1997.

Dumaine, Deborah. *Vest Pocket Guide to Business
Writing.* Englewood Cliffs, NJ: Prentice Hall,
1998.

Geffner, Andrea. *Business English: A Complete Guide
to Developing an Effective Business Writing Style.*
Hauppage, NY: Barrons Educational Series,
1998.

Books Recruiters Read

Adams, Bob, and Peter Veruki. *Adam's Streetwise Hiring Top Performers.* Holbrook, MA: Adams Publishing, 1997.

Byars, Lloyd, and Leslie Rue. *Human Resource Management* (5th edition). Chicago: McGraw Hill, 1997.

Falcone, Paul. *96 Great Interview Questions to Ask Before You Hire.* New York: AMACOM, 1996.

Gellermann, William, Mark Frankel, and Rover Ladenson. *Values and Ethics in Organization and Human Systems Development.* San Francisco: Jossey-Bass, 1990.

Harris, Jim. *Getting Employees to Fall in Love with Your Company.* New York: AMACOM, 1996

Jeanneret, Richard, and Robert Silzer (Eds.). *Individual Psychological Assessment: Predicting Behavior in Organizational Settings.* San Francisco: Jossey-Bass, 1998.

Kaye, Beverly. *Up Is Not the Only Way: A Guide to Developing Workforce Talent.* Palo Alto, CA: Consulting Psychologists Press, 1997.

Messmer, Max. *The Fast Forward MBA in Hiring* (The Portable MBA Series). New York: John Wiley & Sons, 1998.

Pinchot, Gifford, and Elizabeth Pinchot. *The Intelligent Organization: Engaging the Talent and Initiative of Everyone in the Workplace.* New York: Berret-Koehler, 1996.

Reichheld, Frederick. *The Loyalty Effect: The Hidden Force Behind Growth, Profits, and Lasting Value.* Boston: Harvard Business School Press, 1996.

Rosen, Robert, and Lisa Berger. *The Healthy
    Company: Eight Strategies to Develop People,
    Productivity, and Profits.* New York: G.P.
    Putnam's Sons, 1992.

Rosse, Joseph, and Robert Levin. *High Impact
    Hiring: A Comprehensive Guide to Performance-
    Based Hiring.* San Francisco: Jossey-Bass, 1997.

Ulrich, Peter. *Human Resource Champion: The Next
    Agenda for Adding Value and Delivering Results.*
    Boston: Harvard Business School Press, 1997.

Wendover, Robert. *Smart Hiring: The Complete Guide
    to Finding and Hiring the Best Employees.*
    Naperville, IL: Sourcebooks Trade, 1998.

Employment-related Periodicals

Career Opportunities News
Ferguson Publishing
200 W. Madison, Suite 300
Chicago, IL 60606
Tel: 312-580-5480
email: connews@aol.com

Harvard Business Review
Tel: 800-274-3214
www.hbsp.harvard.edu

HR Magazine
606 North Washington Street
Alexandria, VA 22314
Tel: 703-548-3440

Fast Company
Tel: 800-688-1545
www.fastcompany.com

National Employment Business Weekly
Tel: 800-JOB-HUNT
www.nbew.com

Important Statistics

THE 10 OCCUPATIONS WITH THE FASTEST PROJECTED EMPLOYMENT GROWTH, 1996–2006

(Numbers in thousands of jobs)

Occupation	Employment		Change, 1996–2006	
	1996	2006	Number	Present
Database administrators, computer support specialists, and all other computer scientists	212	461	249	118
Computer engineers	216	451	235	109
Systems analysts	506	1,025	520	103
Personal and home care aides	202	374	171	85
Physical and corrective therapy assistants and aides	84	151	66	79
Home health aides	495	873	378	76
Medical assistants	225	391	166	74
Desktop-publishing assistants	30	53	22	74
Physical therapists	115	196	81	71
Occupational therapy assistants and aides	16	26	11	69

Source: Bureau of Labor Statistics

THE 10 INDUSTRIES WITH THE FASTEST PROJECTED EMPLOYMENT GROWTH, 1996–2006

(Numbers in thousands of jobs)

Industry description	Employment		Change, 1996–2006	
	1996	**2006**	**Number**	**Present**
Computer and data-processing services	1208	2509	1301	108
Health services, nec.	1172	1968	796	68
Management and public relations	873	1400	527	60
Miscellaneous transportation services	204	327	123	60
Residential care	672	1070	398	59
Personnel supply services	2646	4039	1393	53
Water and sanitation	231	349	118	51
Individual and miscellaneous social services	846	1266	420	50
Offices of health practitioners	2751	4046	1295	47
Amusement and recreation services, nec.	1109	1565	457	41

Source: Bureau of Labor Statistics

EXPECTED GROWTH IN SELECTED OCCUPATIONS, 1996–2006

Occupation	Total employment (thousands)		1996–2006 change in total employment (percent)	1996–2006 average annual job openings (thousands) due to growth and total replacement needs	Hourly earnings quartile*
	1996	2006			
Database administrators, computer support specialists, and all other computer scientists	212	461	117.8	60	VH
Computer engineers	216	451	109.1	59	VH
Desktop-publishing specialists	30	53	73.5	9	H
Dental hygienists	133	197	48.2	16	VH
Artists and commercial artists	276	354	28.3	54	H
All other physical scientists	43	55	27.5	4	VH
Designers (except interior designers)	279	351	25.7	48	H
All other health professionals and paraprofessionals	430	531	23.5	59	H
Computer programmers	568	697	22.8	60	VH
Architects (except landscape and marine)	94	113	19.6	7	VH

Note: VH = Very High; H = High; L = Low; VL = Very Low; n.a. = not available

continues

Occupation	Total employment (thousands)		1996–2006 change in total employment (percent)	1996–2006 average annual job openings (thousands) due to growth and total replacement needs	Hourly earnings quartile*
	1996	2006			
College and university faculty	864	1026	18.8	134	VH
Dietitians and nutritionists	58	69	18.2	9	VH
Construction managers	249	294	18.0	32	VH
Credit analysts	40	46	15.8	7	VH
All other teachers and instructors	671	770	14.8	158	VH
Curators, archivists, museum technicians, and restorers	20	23	14.7	4	H
All other engineers	326	373	14.4	36	VH
Brokers, real estate	78	89	14.1	11	–
Accountants and auditors	1002	1127	12.4	122	VH
All other legal assistants, including law clerks	82	92	12.1	9	H
Dentists	162	175	8.1	3	VH
All other social scientists	41	43	5.1	5	VH
Actuaries	16	16	1.9	2	VH
All other life scientists	1	1	-3.0	0	VH
Computer operators (except peripheral equipment)	258	181	-29.8	32	H

Human service workers	178	276	55.4	62	L
Engineering, science, and computer systems managers	343	498	45.2	58	VH
Emergency medical technicians	150	217	45.1	26	L
Flight attendants	132	178	35.1	8	VH
Marketing, advertising, and public relations managers	482	620	28.5	93	VH
Electrical and electronics engineers	367	472	28.5	32	VH
Loan officers and counselors	209	268	28.1	39	VH
Interior designers	63	80	27.5	11	H
Insurance adjusters, examiners, and investigators	165	203	23.1	15	VH
Licensed practical nurses	699	848	21.2	45	H
Landscape architects	17	20	20.7	1	VH
Lawyers	622	740	19.0	36	VH
Financial managers	800	946	18.3	95	VH
General managers and top executives	3210	3677	14.6	393	VH
Electrical and electronic technicians and technologists	297	341	14.5	37	VH
Legal secretaries	284	319	12.5	44	H
Hairdressers, hairstylists, and cosmetologists	586	644	9.9	71	VL

Occupation	Total employment (thousands)		1996–2006 change in total employment (percent)	1996–2006 average annual job openings (thousands) due to growth and total replacement needs	Hourly earnings quartile
	1996	2006			
Electricians	575	627	9.1	80	VH
Librarians, professional	154	162	4.8	25	VH
Insurance sales workers	409	426	4.3	43	VH
Physical corrective therapy assistants and aides	84	151	78.6	25	L
Medical assistants	225	391	74.0	49	L
Physical therapists	115	196	70.8	15	VH
Occupational therapy aides and assistants	16	26	68.7	4	H
Paralegals	113	189	67.7	29	H
Occupational therapists	57	95	66.1	7	VH
Physician assistants	64	93	46.6	6	VH
Musicians	274	366	33.4	54	H
Nursing aides, orderlies, and attendants	1312	1645	25.4	340	VL
Physicians	560	678	21.0	32	VH
Personnel, training, and labor relations specialists	328	387	17.9	74	VH

Occupation				
Personnel, training, and labor relations managers	216	254	17.8	30	VH
Pharmacists	172	194	12.6	7	VH
Optometrists	41	46	11.7	2	VH
Pharmacy assistants	47	52	10.7	7	L
Mathematicians and all other mathematical scientists	16	17	9.1	2	VH
Police detectives and investigators	70	75	7.8	6	VH
Plumbers, pipefitters, and steamfitters	389	406	4.5	53	VH
Proofreaders and copy markers	26	16	-38.5	5	L
Recreational therapists	38	46	26.2	3	H
Registered nurses	1971	2382	.7	183	VH
Teachers, preschool and kindergarten	499	596	1.1	56	L
Property and real estate managers	271	315	41.7	42	H
Teachers, elementary	1491	1644	0.0	170	VH
Salespersons, retail	4072	4481	4.5	1272	VL
Psychologists	143	154	41.0	18	VH

Occupation	Total employment (thousands)		1996–2006 change in total employment (percent)	1996–2006 average annual job openings (thousands) due to growth and total replacement needs	Hourly earnings quartile
	1996	2006			
Purchasing managers	232	251	0.0	33	VH
Stenographers and/or court reporters	98	101	27.2	13	H
Statisticians	14	14	0.0	1	VH
Radio and TV announcers and newscasters	52	52	0.0	11	L
Secretaries (except legal and medical)	2881	2794	1.9	378	H
Reporters and correspondents	60	58	8.6	6	H
Systems analysts	506	1025	102.8	133	VH
Teachers, special education	407	648	59.1	49	VH
Speech-language pathologists and audiologists	87	131	50.6	10	VH
Respiratory therapists	82	119	45.8	8	VH
Securities and financial services sales workers	263	363	37.8	52	VH
Teacher aides and educational assistants	981	1352	37.7	296	VL
Social workers	585	772	32.1	96	H

Radiology technologists and technicians	174	224	28.9	14	H
Public relations specialists and publicity writers	110	140	27.2	23	H
Teachers, secondary school	1406	1718	22.2	131	VH
Veterinary assistants	33	42	28.0	11	VL
Travel agents	142	176	24.0	19	L
Veterinarians and veterinary inspectors	58	71	22.7	3	VH
Writers and editors, including technical writers	286	347	21.2	43	VH
Telephone and cable TV line installers and repairers	201	242	20.5	18	H
Waiters and waitresses	1957	2163	10.5	711	VL
Welders and cutters	352	384	9.0	37	H
Underwriters	95	100	6.1	4	VH
Urban and regional planners	29	31	4.7	4	VH
Total, all occupations	132353	150927	14.0	26666	-

A

abilities, 5
  content knowledge, 6
  personal qualities, 7–8
  questions about, 229–235
  skills, 6–7
academic interviews, 180
  career goals and, 195
  graduate school, 194–196
accepting the offer, 368
  confirmation letter, 367
  decision making, 360–366
  during interview, 45–46
  negotiating, 337, 353–360
accessibility information
    from interviewer, 315
accessories (attire), 132–133
accomplishments, questions
    about, 236–237
advancement possibilities,
    247
The Age Discrimination in
    Employment Act (1978),
    300
age-related questions, 301
alcohol at mealtime inter-
    views, 189
annual reports in research,
    60
anxiety, 106–107
  combating, 109–115
  group interviews,
    108–109
appearance-related ques-
    tions, 302
applications, 146

aptitude tests, 272–274, 373
arrest record, 303
assessment
  observation, 260–266
  see also testing
asset statements, 85
  behavior-based interviews
    and, 172
  common concerns, 91–93
  comparing and contrast-
    ing assets, 89–91
  development form, 93–94
  employer's needs and,
    86–87
  examples' age, 92
  past accomplishments,
    88–89
  qualifications questions,
    233
  questions and, 228
  reviewing, 202
assets, examples, 92–93
attentiveness, 43
attire, 11
  accessories, 132–133
  appropriateness, 41
  color consultants, 129
  grooming, 133–135
  publications, 395–396
  see also image
attitude, 99–116
  confidence, 44–45, 103
  follow-up interview,
    183–184
authority, bowing to mis-
    take, 31–32
avocational (adj.), 373

The *Unofficial Guide*™ Reader Questionnaire

If you would like to express your opinion about aceing the interview or this guide, please complete this questionnaire and mail it to:

The *Unofficial Guide*™ Reader Questionnaire
Macmillan Lifestyle Group
1633 Broadway, floor 7
New York, NY 10019-6785

Gender: ___ M   ___ F

Age: ___ Under 30   ___ 31–40   ___ 41–50
___ Over 50

Education: ___ High school   ___ College
___ Graduate/Professional

What is your occupation?

_____

How did you hear about this guide?
___ Friend or relative
___ Newspaper, magazine, or Internet
___ Radio or TV
___ Recommended at bookstore
___ Recommended by librarian
___ Picked it up on my own
___ Familiar with the *Unofficial Guide*™ travel series

Did you go to the bookstore specifically for a book on aceing the interview?   Yes ___   No ___

Have you used any other *Unofficial Guides*™ ?
Yes ___   No ___

If Yes, which ones?

_____
_____
_____

What other book(s) on job interviewing have you purchased?

_____

_____

_____

Was this book:
___ more helpful than other(s)
___ less helpful than other(s)

Do you think this book was worth its price?
Yes ___   No ___

Did this book cover all topics related to job interviewing adequately?   Yes ___   No ___

Please explain your answer:

_____

_____

_____

Were there any specific sections in this book that were of particular help to you?   Yes ___   No ___

Please explain your answer:

_____

_____

_____

On a scale of 1 to 10, with 10 being the best rating, how would you rate this guide? ___

What other titles would you like to see published in the _Unofficial Guide_™ series?

_____

_____

Are _Unofficial Guides_™ readily available in your area?   Yes ___   No ___

Other comments:

_____

_____

_____

_____

Get the inside scoop...with the *Unofficial Guides*™!

The Unofficial Guide to Alternative Medicine
ISBN: 0-02-862526-9   Price: $15.95

The Unofficial Guide to Buying a Home
ISBN: 0-02-862461-0   Price: $15.95

The Unofficial Guide to Buying or Leasing a Car
ISBN: 0-02-862524-2   Price: $15.95

The Unofficial Guide to Childcare
ISBN: 0-02-862457-2   Price: $15.95

The Unofficial Guide to Cosmetic Surgery
ISBN: 0-02-862522-6   Price: $15.95

The Unofficial Guide to Dieting Safely
ISBN: 0-02-862521-8   Price: $15.95

The Unofficial Guide to Eldercare
ISBN: 0-02-862456-4   Price: $15.95

The Unofficial Guide to Hiring Contractors
ISBN: 0-02-862460-2   Price: $15.95

The Unofficial Guide to Investing
ISBN: 0-02-862458-0   Price: $15.95

The Unofficial Guide to Planning Your Wedding
ISBN: 0-02-862459-9   Price: $15.95

All books in the *Unofficial Guide*™ series are available at your local bookseller, or by calling 1-800-428-5331.

About the Author

Michelle Tullier is an experienced career counselor who has helped thousands of people find satisfying employment. She has been a career counselor with Barnard College of Columbia University and with New York University, and runs a private practice which attracts clients from across the U.S. and abroad. She is a consultant to outplacement firms, counseling senior executives in transition, and conducts seminars for Fortune 500 corporations and not-for-profit organizations.

She is the resident career planning expert for the Web site StudentCenter and has been quoted in *Fortune,* the *Washington Post, New York Newsday, Chicago Tribune, Los Angeles Times, National Business Employment Weekly, Cosmopolitan,* and *Glamour.*

Michelle is also an adjunct faculty member of New York University's School of Continuing and Professional Studies where she teaches the methods of career advising and testing to beginning and experienced career consultants and human resource professionals.

Michelle is the author of four other career and job hunting guidebooks including: *Networking for Everyone: Connecting with People for Career and Job Success* (JIST Works, Inc.)and *Work Smart* (The Princeton Review/Random House). She holds Ph.D. and master's degrees in counseling psychology from UCLA and is a graduate of Wellesley College.